Hive Management History Series: No. 60

Library of Congress Cataloging in Publication Data

Spooner, Henry John, 1856–
    Wealth from waste.

    (Hive management history series, no. 60)
    Reprint of the 1918 ed. published by G. Routledge,
London, in series: Efficiency books.
    1. Waste (Economics) 2. Natural resources.
I. Title. II. Title: Elimination of waste a world
problem. III. Series: Efficiency books.
HC53.2.S7 1973   333.7'2   73-8599
ISBN 0-87960-063-2

WEALTH FROM WASTE

ELIMINATION OF WASTE
A WORLD PROBLEM

By

HENRY J. SPOONER, C.E., F.G.S.

M.I.MECH.E., M.INST.A.E., A.M.INST.C.E., F.R.MET.S., HON.M.J.INST.E.,
MEMBER OF THE AMERICAN SOCIETY FOR THE PROMOTION OF ENGINEERING EDUCATION, ETC.,
MEMBRE DE LA SOCIÉTÉ ASTRONOMIQUE DE FRANCE,
DIRECTOR AND PROFESSOR OF MECHANICAL AND CIVIL ENGINEERING IN THE POLYTECHNIC
SCHOOL OF ENGINEERING, REGENT STREET, LONDON,
LECTURER ON POWER PLANT DESIGN, AND INDUSTRIAL EFFICIENCY, ETC.

Author of
Machine Design and Construction, Motors and Motoring,
Industrial Fatigue in its Relation to Maximum Output, etc., etc.

With a Foreword

BY

The Rt. Hon. LORD LEVERHULME

EASTON
HIVE PUBLISHING COMPANY
1974

DEDICATED

TO

MY GOOD FRIENDS,

MAJOR FRANK B. GILBRETH, M.AMER.S.M.E.,

AND

MRS. LILIAN M. GILBRETH, PH.D., M.L.,

OF PROVIDENCE, RHODE ISLAND, U.S.A.

In grateful appreciation of their kindness in keeping me in touch with their remarkable work in the cause of waste reduction, and of industrial efficiency, over a period of many years ; and of much inspiring encouragement received. Also in token of admiration, esteem and attachment.

FOREWORD

By Lord Leverhulme

My good friend Professor Spooner has asked me to write a Foreword to his book on " Waste," and it seems to me that, whatever else may be said of this request, it certainly will open the book with an apt illustration of that kind of " waste " which is the saddest type of all wastes—a wasted opportunity. Here was an opportunity for Professor Spooner to have secured someone profoundly skilled in putting into language of clear and concise words and sentences occupying one page that would say all that could be required. But, as for myself, I can only waste printers' ink and paper and the reader's time and patience—and one of the greatest wastes of all is waste of time.

It is said—and articles by Professor Spooner in this book go to prove its truth—that owing to our waste of labour through bad organisation and our bad use of the forces that Nature has placed within our reach, we can to-day by overwork and overstrain in workshop and factory for forty-eight or more hours per week barely produce sufficient for our needs, whilst we might with the means science has already placed at our disposal, and which are all within our knowledge, provide for all the wants of each of us in food, shelter, and clothing by one hour's work per week for each of us from school-age to dotage, thus clearly showing what can yet be accomplished simply by avoidance of waste.

Nature knows no waste. The dust blown from the high-road settles in the nooks and crannies of walls and rocks, and is there capable of nourishing growing plants which in turn yield fruit or herbs for the use of man or creatures. The surplus yield of seeds not required for new repetitions of plants, trees, or vegetables is not wasted ; it is food for man or creatures. Mankind are the only wasters, and our greatest wastes are those of time, opportunity, health, and life. In many countries we find the proverb " Paint costs nothing," and this is merely another way of saying that by painting we avoid decay and consequent waste. Science and the teaching of science equally costs nothing. We can make a calculation as to the wealth certain scientists have earned for the nation whilst at college, apparently earning nothing, and, in fact, paying out for their expenses of living and learning, whilst preparing themselves for wealth-earning beyond the dreams of avarice. In such a calculation the total earnings due to the scientist's discoveries and their yield of wealth to the nation and world can be very roughly estimated, and the total divided equally over the working years of the scientist's life from school-age to dotage. Then another total can be made of the earnings of the ordinary youth who went straight from school to earning salary at fifteen years of age, and his earnings from school-age to dotage can also be averaged equally over that period, and the final results when compared will show that the time the former spent at school and college, although apparently wasted so far as the then earnings were concerned, was the most fruitful period of the whole life viewed by the results of the rich harvest that followed.

But the greatest wasters are those who concentrate

their whole time on mere efforts for immediate and direct money-making; and the greatest economists are those who, like the successful farmer with his land, cultivate and prepare themselves for more efficient service for their fellow-man. Time spent on preparation for efficient service and on unselfish service for mankind is never wasted, whilst time spent with selfish aims and objects exclusively in view is often wasted, because such efforts most often fail to realise their own selfish aims and objects.

As civilisation progresses this waste will cease, for we shall have learnt we must be unselfish for self's sake, and enlightened self-interest will end all waste of this kind. We welcome Professor Spooner's clear statement of our present-day wastes, and accept this book as a stimulus to careful thought and study of this great question.

LEVERHULME.

April 12th, 1918.

PREFACE

THE world's interest in its problem of waste-prevention is, we may hope, not represented by the fact that apparently no book in any language exists dealing with this encyclopedic subject. As to ourselves, we are a strange people, and, as is well known, it is a failing of our race that we never do anything that represents a departure from routine activities until we are compelled to do so. Hence it was not until the exigencies of the war constrained us to begin to become economical in the use of means and of materials, etc., that we felt obliged to energise in all directions to conserve, to preserve, and to utilise. How extensive the field is in which such activities can be exercised is known only to those who have attempted to explore it. As to my own investigations and researches, which have been carried out over a number of years, perhaps I may be permitted to say that the labour involved in attempting to put their results into readable form has been gladly undertaken, in the hope that they may be found useful and helpful to my fellow-countrymen at this critical juncture in the history of our beloved country. The limitations of space precluded me from touching on some important aspects of the subject that have more or less academic interest only at the present time, such as the waste due to the depredations of animals, waste of animal life by human agency, waste of human life due to pestilence, and to the destruction of oboriginal races, the waste due to the destruction of cities, works of art, libraries, and of literature, etc., etc.

If we agree with Lavater, that " there are but three classes of men, the retrograde, the stationary, and the progressive," the grave times we are living in call loudly

PREFACE

for our inclusion in the class of the resolutely progressive in all economical matters; particularly in the solution of those pressing problems relating to the conservation of human life, to increased output, and to the education and training of our young people.

For an outline of the field covered by this work the reader is referred to Chapter I. In dealing with such a wide range of matters, freedom from blemishes is hardly to be expected, therefore notification of any the reader may detect would be gratefully received and acknowledged.

In the dedication note I have referred to the help and encouragement I have received from two of my valued American friends, but I cannot refrain from expressing sincere appreciation of much kind help in the field of industrial economics that I have received from my friend Prof. William S. Ayars, M.E,. of Halifax Technical College, B.C.(formerly of Pennsylvania State College). Among other American friends who have been most kindly helpful in the past I may venture to mention Prof. Johnson of the Virginia Polytechnic Institute, Blackburgh, Prof. Magruder, M.E., of the Ohio State University, Prof. Marshall, M.E., C.E., of Yale University, and Prof. Frank E. Sanborn, S.B., of the Ohio State University.

My best thanks are due to my true friend, Lord Leverhulme, for his kindness in writing the Foreword. Having a profound respect for his sound judgment, and for his ripe experience as a great and humane captain of industry, I greatly appreciate his approval of my efforts, as expressed in his most generous and inspiring introduction.

HENRY J. SPOONER.

April 15th, 1918.

CONTENTS

PART I

CHAPTER I

CHAPTER II

MILLIONS FOR THE WAR IN HOUSEHOLD WASTE :
AN URGENT APPEAL FOR MUNICIPAL ORGANISATION

CHAPTER III

WASTE TIME

CHAPTER IV

WASTE DUE TO TRADITIONAL METHODS IN MANAGEMENT

Old Methods and the New. Increased Output by Less Work.

xi

CONTENTS

CHAPTER V

WASTE DUE TO HUMAN FATIGUE

FATIGUE IN ITS RELATION TO OUTPUT

CHAPTER VI

WASTAGE OF LIFE, LIMB, AND HEALTH, AND ITS ECONOMIC EFFECT

CHAPTER VII

THE FOOD QUESTION IN RELATION TO WASTE

PART II

GLOSSARY

INTRODUCTION

SECTION I

THE ROMANCE OF WASTE

CONTENTS

SECTION II

MISCELLANEOUS HOUSEHOLD WASTES AND ECONOMIES

INTRODUCTION

SECTION III
TRADE, INDUSTRIAL, AND OTHER WASTES
INTRODUCTION

PART I

WEALTH FROM WASTE
ELIMINATION OF WASTE A WORLD PROBLEM

CHAPTER I

Introduction and Outline

THE current of public opinion has been flowing strongly in the direction of economy and the elimination, or at least the reduction, of wastes since the War sounded a call upon every one to wake up ! And our national ills and weaknesses due to extravagance and inefficiency are daily receiving attention, whilst the need of organisation in every part of our working system, and in all our activities, is day by day becoming more pressing. Before the war everything was so different ; in the full enjoyment of unparalleled prosperity, extravagance and waste were rampant in the land; there was little or no thought of economy in any form ; indeed, there seemed to be a general adoption of the American child's maxim, " Pa's rich and Ma don't care." The War, with its colossal requirements in men, munitions, material, and money has changed much of that, and the era of retrenchment, frugality, economy, and thrift has dawned, whilst the gospel of the prevention of waste is being preached at every turn. We are beginning to realise that wicked waste is occurring everywhere,[1] far

---

[1] Archdeacon Potter said at an Economy Meeting at Mitford, near Godalming (Jan. 26, 1916) : " I have travelled all over the world and I have never known any nation or people so wilfully wasteful as the people of our own country. In no other country do people so absolutely fling away God's goods as they do in England."

and wide; waste of money, waste of food, waste of materials, labour, fuel, energy and time, waste of human strength and thought, waste of health, and waste of life itself.

Many forms of waste are obvious to the least careful and observant, but, unfortunately, it is too often the trifling wastes that are not easily detected, wastes that in their cumulative effect are most serious; indeed, as Beecher truly said, " Little wastes in a great establishment, constantly occurring, may defeat the energies of a mighty capital." In every household there are numberless little wastes occurring all day and every day. In almost every manufacturing process, in the various industries, mechanical and chemical, there is usually prodigal waste, and the elimination of these wastes and the utilisation of waste products offer the widest possible field for saving. Anyone taking the trouble to explore this field, and to look carefully into the vast economic possibilities there are, would soon become convinced that a vigorous campaign against every form of waste would lead to the nation quite easily saving at least a million sterling a day.[1] Indeed, in household waste alone if one-half of what is wasted could be saved the high cost of living would almost cease to be a problem.

The habits of a people are not easily changed, but it

[1] An additional million a day could easily be secured by our working harder and saving more. According to Mr. Lowther, the family drink-bill throughout our country in 1916 was 6s. 6d. a week, and this halved would save the State £80,000,000 a year. There are welcome signs that the drink evil is on the wane and that we may reasonably hope for a marked decrease in the shocking waste due to it. The following words of the great Tribune, uttered over forty-seven years ago, might well be recalled : " If we could subtract from the ignorance, the poverty, the suffering, the sickness and the crime which are now witnessed amongst us, the ignorance, the poverty, the suffering, the sickness and the crime which are caused by one single, but the most prevalent, habit or vice of drinking needlessly, which destroys the body, and mind, and home, and family, do we not feel that this country would be so changed, and so changed for the better, that it would be almost impossible for us to know it again ? "—Speech of the Right Hon. JOHN BRIGHT, at Birmingham, Jan., 1870.

has been said that " the greatest asset of this country is the common sense of the common people," and a strong appeal to that common sense in the cause of waste-prevention would, we might well hope, not be made in vain ; indeed, England ought at this time to be placarded with posters, " Stop the waste," and our young people should be consistently and perseveringly taught and encouraged to assist in the crusade. The detection of waste is an endless pursuit, its prevention a sacred duty to the State. For the good of the State the doctrine of waste-prevention should be handled in a broad spirit, for there are justifiable wastes and dangerous economies ; for example, we do not trouble about wasting water in putting out a conflagration ; but if after the embers have died out the water is left running, there is waste. A great statesman may engineer beneficent legislation, the effect of which may enrich the country by conserving the lives of its workers, and by increasing their well-being and working efficiency. This may mean money flowing out of the national coffers like water, in overcoming in a reasonable time the inertia of things and in mastering the stupendous difficulties in creating the necessary machinery to give effect to the reforms. In peaceful times, from the practical standpoint this would not be waste ; but if, after such schemes were properly launched and the machinery made to run smoothly, certain parts were found to be redundant, and other parts only working at a 50 or 60 per cent. efficiency, then there would be waste, and very serious waste at that.

Among other types of waste we have *absolute waste,* such as crockery and glassware broken beyond repair ; waste due to corrosion or to wear, such as occurs on railways and tramways, the steel rails and tyres of the rolling-stock wearing away to an extent of thousands of tons a year in this country alone. We also have what may be called *nominal waste ;* for example, nearly everything we use wears or gets unshapely ; clothes may become rags, but cotton rags of all kinds have for years been in demand for the manufacture of paper, and woollen rags for the manufacture of shoddy and mungo fabrics. Then we have *new waste*, such as the waste pieces that are invariably left when round lids are cut out of tin-plate, or garments out of a length of cloth. There would, of course, as a rule be more loss than gain in manufacturing such pieces into the forms required for specific articles, but if a hundred or two garments have to be cut out exactly the same pattern, it is worth while to spend great care on so planning the cutting out of the cloth that only a few small pieces are wasted ; [1] thus one planning is made to suffice for many tasks. In this we have an example in the economy of skill.

In our chemical industries, and in trades where the services of chemists are required, the possibilities of the elimination of waste, and in the utilisation of so-called waste products, are unlimited. For, as Dr. Johnson truly said, " there are qualities in the products of nature undiscovered, and combinations in the powers of art yet untried. It is the duty of every man to endeavour that something may be added, by his industry, to the hereditary aggregate of knowledge and happiness."

By creating entire new fields of industry, and multiplying the diffusion of useful commodities, the science of chemistry has for years been growing in importance. The extraordinary success of the German dye industry is based upon the utilisation of waste products, and on the comprehension of the value of chemical science in the manufacture of chemical products. In Germany, manufacturers use the services of industrial and research chemists to an extent undreamt of by many of our own captains of

[1] Of course there is a market for the waste scraps of material, such as cloth, tin-plate, etc.

industry. Mr. Pease in 1915 told us that four firms in Germany employ 1,000 chemists in connection with their dye-works, whilst in the whole of our own industries there are only 1,500 chemists employed ; and he explained that there were over 3,000 German students (even during the War), studying research work in connection with their university life, whilst in this country we had only about 350 engaged in such work.

In Germany there is practically no waste; should a refuse accumulate in a works, a few chemists, or it may be a little army of them, are set to work on it to see whether it can be utilised for some useful purpose ; then, possibly after a year or two of research and experiment, and the expenditure of many thousands of pounds, a valuable product is put upon the market, which at once becomes a monopoly, as the raw material of the product being a waste owned by them alone, for which they have practically nothing to pay, the manufacturers reap a rich reward for their wisdom, enterprise, perseverance, and patience. Among the hundreds of valuable by-products the Germans have recovered from coal-tar alone may be mentioned saccharin, salicyl, phenacetin,[1] antipyrin, artificial vanilla, fruit ether, picric acid, tar camphor, etc., etc. Many years must pass, unfortunately, before we have available a sufficient number of research chemists to staff our industries as they should be ; so if we are to tackle seriously the problem of industrial waste, the cry should be chemists, and still more chemists.

Unfortunately, the application of science to particular problems takes time, often a great deal of time before any

[1] The folly of allowing ourselves to be dependent upon Germany for this and other indispensable drugs is now realised. The price of phenacetin tabloids before the war was 1s. 2d. per hundred. It is now 8s. 9d. or more. In July, 1914, the wholesale price of aspirin was 2s. 10d. a pound ; in November, 1915, it was £3 8s. 0d. a pound ; and the tale of our folly could be continued by referring to other coal-tar products and by-products—the aniline dyes, for instance.

useful progress is made. On remarking to a great in-
dustrialist that the employment of a good scientific staff
was an excellent investment, the author was astonished to
hear him remark in rather an angry way, " I have over
forty research chemists in my works, and very little they
have done for me during the past two years." Thus it
will sometimes happen, as the history of industrial science
abundantly proves, that years may be spent by distinguished scientists working in a certain field before
something of commercial value is discovered ; before,
perhaps, some waste matter, or some refuse that is a
nuisance and encumbrance, is found to be a suitable raw
material for a new product. But when this is achieved
the reward is often so great that all the expenses due to the
researches and experiments are soon repaid many times
over.

Happily, for some years many of our foremost manufacturers have been wise enough to fully avail themselves
of the services that science can render, and they wisely
realise that the " goal of yesterday will be the starting-
point of to-morrow." They are well aware that the days
have passed when they could look to experience, accumulated slowly and at great cost, as the only basis to work
upon. Day by day, in increasing numbers, they are
showing their appreciation of the interdependence of
science and industry on one another, by utilising the
services of the consultant, the chemist, and the physicist,
as will be better understood when it is possible to discuss
all the industrial triumphs of the past three years : but the
remarkable achievements in almost every industry that
have characterised the past few decades, when reviewed,
go to show that we have used science more than is generally
realised, and that British men of science can bear comparison with those of any other country.

Endless industrial processes and operations have been

perfected with the aid of science and industry, and have been made to pay handsomely by the frugal use of time, energy, and materials ; for, as Franklin said, " the way to wealth is as plain as the way to market ; it depends chiefly on two words—industry and frugality." Science is of no nation ; often the development of a process or an industry is the outcome of the labours of scientists of different nations, and we know to our cost that many of the most important and valuable discoveries and inventions that have been developed abroad owed their origin to this country. We are a strange people, and are too apt to belittle and decry the achievements of our own country- men, and to over-esteem those of foreigners, particularly if they be Germans, who are the best advertised people in the world. But even so, we should be wise enough to look to our shortcomings, particularly those that have been revealed during the War, and profit by any new de- velopments of importance and value in science, education, and industry, whether they be made at home or abroad.

As to education in science, technology, and commerce, a new spirit is noticeable in all quarters, and the authorities are wisely doing a great deal to foster the latent genius of our race in these fields, so that in due course we may have an adequate supply of technologists to staff our industries and educational institutions, and of consummate men of business to conduct our commercial affairs ; for such men are as " rare almost as great poets, rarer perhaps than saints and martyrs." [1]

Energising in the new atmosphere, progress and reforms must be something more than mere slogans. We must live up to the standard that Lord Palmerston believed we had reached some sixty or seventy years ago, when he said, " There was a time when it was the fashion for public men to say, ' Show me a proved abuse, and I will do my best to

[1] Sir Arthur Helps.

correct it.' Times are changed ; men now say, ' Show me
a practical improvement, and that improvement I will do
my best to realise.' "

The War has changed everything, and we no longer
need the kingly clarion call to wake up ! It has caused a
searching light to be thrown upon our industrial deficiencies,
and praiseworthy attempts have been made to organise
our industries and factories and increase their efficiency.
It is true that some of our factories are so perfectly organised and managed that they are running with a very high
efficiency, and have little or nothing to learn from abroad ;
but this, unhappily, can only be said of a few, for in the
words of our great Prime Minister, Mr. Lloyd George, " We
have been employing too many of the haphazard, leisurely,
go-as-you-please methods," we have fought shy of the
wonderful system of " scientific management," the art
and science of industrial management that is doing so
much to increase the earnings of both workers and employers in many parts of America ; indeed, in the United
States " efficiency " is a living movement and not a mere
slogan, a movement that supports a flourishing efficiency
society. In such matters we must indeed wake up and see
that our engineering colleges and technical institutions
include in their curricula the subjects of industrial
efficiency, industrial organisation, and economics, so that
waste and ignorance in respect of our industries and
natural resources may largely give way to scientific control,
and traditional methods be improved or abandoned
(Chapter IV).

In matters relating to organisation Germany is hard
to beat, but even the German manufacturers are clever
enough to utilise the best American brains in organising
their factories ; but of course they would not admit it. As
to ourselves, we must organise from the bottom upwards
if we are to hold our own in the coming industrial war.

We must increase the rate of production to enable us to pay high wages, to enhance the economic power of the nation, and to amortise the national debt. And one of the problems requiring for its solution the highest statesmanship and patriotism will be the one relating to labour unrest. It will be necessary for far-seeing and humane men to devote themselves to the institution of beneficent reforms for improving the conditions under which our workers live and labour. Great efforts will have to be made to secure and maintain industrial peace between employers and workers, as labour unrest represents a menace to the State in war time and progressive economic ruin in the time of peace.

The author has dealt with the waste due to the fatigue of workers and to inefficient lighting, etc., also with the question of working hours, more fully elsewhere,[1] and therefore has not attempted to deal with them at length in these pages (Chapter V). The wicked waste due to adulteration should be arrested, so the question is examined in Chapter VIII, as the adulteration of our foodstuffs and materials, which is apparently on the increase, calls for serious attention ; and much more drastic action on the part of the authorities is needed to prevent the people being defrauded, and injured in health.

Government and municipal waste is fortunately receiving a large amount of official and public attention, and we may reasonably hope that valuable and much needed economies will materialise, giving the country a serviceable lead and anxiously-waited-for examples.

When many millions are being spent weekly on manufactures, transport and supply in connection with the war, the factor of urgency, in the nature of things, must lead to a large amount of waste; but the appalling examples of colossal waste that have come to light from time to time

---

[1] " Industrial Fatigue in its Relation to Maximum Output." Published by Co-Partnership, 6, Bloomsbury Square. Price 6d.

since the commencement of hostilities must be due in a large measure to an unpardonable degree of incompetency and muddling on the part of some of the countless officials, and these matters we may hope will not escape the serious attention of the Government.

The waste of health and life that is daily occurring is so appalling, and the economic loss due to this wastage so great, that a chapter (number VI) is devoted to it in the hope that, attention being called to the causes, action may be taken to greatly reduce what in a large proportion of cases are quite avoidable accidents.

The food question has been so much before the public during the past two or three years that it might appear unnecessary to touch upon it, but there are some aspects of the great question in relation to waste that should again and again be discussed in the best interests of all, particularly at the present time, so some pages have been devoted to it in Chapter VII.

No attempt to deal with the subject of waste could be seriously made without giving a good deal of attention to the coal question.   Mr. Lloyd George in glowing words uttered a timely warning that " coal is the life-blood of the nation in peace, and in the time of war is paramount.' Everyone should know that coal is the foundation of our national wealth, and that our very civilisation is built upon it.   This fossil-fuel we have in abundance ; it supplies us with warmth in the winter, it is our fuel directly or indirectly for all our cooking purposes : it supplies our industries with heat, light, and motive-power, and our railroads and steamships are also dependent upon coal for their motive-power.   Further, it is an ideal material for exportation, as it is of sufficient weight and volume for use as outgoing cargoes in place of ballast, to assist in balancing the cumbersome cargoes imported ; and it renders a priceless service in helping to pay for our imports.   Now, although we have enormous stores of this miraculous and indispensable mineral yet to be mined, there is only a certain amount available at workable depths ; and as the home consumption and the amount exported year by year increase, the final exhaustion of our coal-fields, and therefore of our main wealth, is only a matter of time. Unfortunately for posterity, this length of time has been materially shortened owing to the wasteful way in which our coal has been, and is being, used. There is no kind of waste that is so economically harmful to the vital interests of the State and of the Empire than this extravagant use of an asset that can never be replaced. Chapter IX deals with some aspects of this important question.

The submarine menace, grave as it is, has compelled us to make a supreme effort to resuscitate our oldest and principal industry. Before the war our agriculture had been gradually languishing and our imports of foodstuffs were ever increasing ; hundreds of millions were yearly spent by us in purchasing eatables from abroad, much of which could quite well have been grown in this country, if we had had the wisdom and enterprise that have so much enriched some of the small countries of Europe. Our past insane folly is alarmingly apparent, now that we are seeing what our fair land is capable of producing, for we have already worked wonders under extremely adverse conditions, demonstrating what is possible if we make full use of the human material available, the land available, and of the most advanced agricultural and engineering science. Unfortunately, few people realise what a highly technical industry farming is, if the soil is to be used to produce its richest yield ; but a glance through Chapter X, in which an attempt has been made to deal with some of the problems we are confronted with in facing the coming agricultural revolution, will satisfy the reader that the country needs its best brains and sinews to develop the latent wealth in the land, and to protect us from the peril of starvation in war and economic loss in peace.

The grave problem of maintaining our food supply brings to the front questions relating to the utilisation of our waste lands, which amount in the aggregate to millions of acres up and down the country ; so in Chapter XI some attention is given to what appears might be done to bring under economic cultivation or to improve the productive capacity of vast tracts of land now of little use to man or beast. It is commonly known that an enormous amount of land that at present is absolutely useless, owing to its being waterlogged or subject to flooding, could be made valuable for the production of foodstuffs by suitable embanking and drainage to bring it into a state fit for cultivation, so some important points relating to the reclamation of waste land are discussed in Chapter XII.

The interruption of our supply of timber from abroad, and the enormous amount of home-grown timber now being used, has focussed attention on our folly in neglecting matters relating to afforestation. Having the smallest amount of land under tree plantation in the whole of Europe, we have never given serious attention to the science of forestry. Now although it is not possible for us to become self-supporting in the matter of timber, a great deal can be done that would have a lasting effect on our production of it in the future. In Chapter XIII an attempt has been made to deal with some of the more important aspects of the problem that should be generally understood if we are to do our share in delaying the coming timber famine, as most countries of the world are using timber at a faster rate than they are producing it.

But to-day waste of every kind must be avoided, for, in the great world-struggle of nations, the nation that can organise and use all the resources at its disposal is going to be the winning nation. We must change entirely our mental attitude in relation to waste and thrift. We have been too apt to laugh at the so-called petty economies of the Germans, at their sale of kitchen refuse at a halfpenny the pailful, of sawdust at a penny the bucketful, of wood ashes at sixpence the sack, of old rags, clothes, boots, bottles, and metal; but we ourselves might well humble our lofty pride and advance a little in the same direction with beneficial results. In every home there should be an atmosphere of thrift, and children should be taught to remember that economy is the very antithesis of waste, as it avoids all waste and extravagance and applies money, labour, materials, energy, and time, etc., to the best advantage. That it means simplicity, and extricating ourselves from the complexities of artificial existence that have grown up out of unthinking prosperity ; that " abundance, like want, ruins many," and that it is possible to observe the most exact economy without either meanness, discomfort or loss of efficiency ; indeed, that it is the character of true economy to be as comfortable with a little as others who are wasteful can be with much : and that to achieve a purpose with a small outlay, as others who are extravagant do with a large one, is a worthy act, as economy practised in the right spirit is a virtue to be proud of.

As to the grown-ups, it is to be feared from what is to be seen at every turn in our spending departments, and among the well-to-do, that there is still a dangerous amount of unjustifiable extravagance rampant. When millions are being circulated day by day, and successful manufacturers are picking up money like dirt (as one was heard to remark), the temptation to save is not very great. That all this wasteful expenditure is the worst possible example for the people goes without saying ; their conscience is not controlled by human laws, although they are very human ; and it is quite understandable that they are influenced far more by example than by precept ; in fact, they badly need object lessons from those who have it in their power to set the fashion, as, unfortunately, any form of thrift is unpopular with a large proportion of our workers at the present time—a time when so many of them are earning higher wages than they have ever received at any other period. The pity of it is that there are certain classes of workers who only degenerate when their wages are increased suddenly and out of proportion to their accustomed standard of living. How happy they would be if they could take to heart the wise words once addressed to the working-men of Huddersfield by Cobden :

" The world," he said, " has always been divided into two classes—those who have saved and those who have spent—the thrifty and the extravagant. The building of all the houses, the mills, the bridges, and the ships, and the accomplishment of all other great works which have rendered man civilised and happy, has been done by the savers, the thrifty ; and those who have wasted their resources have always been their slaves. It has been the law of nature and of Providence that this should be so ; and I were an impostor if I promised any class that they would advance themselves if they were improvident, thoughtless and idle."

We are a very conservative and imitative people where our habits and customs are concerned ; and it is to be feared that we sadly lack the moral courage to break away from any custom that has grown with our national life, the abandonment of which might suggest a want of friendly feeling or some form of meanness. Present-giving, particularly at Christmas, may be taken as an instance of how this conservatism and unthinking want of patriotism operates against the best interests of the State. Here we are, well into the fourth year of the great War, when every penny that can be spared is needed to carry it through to a successful issue, and stirring appeals at every turn are being made by the Government for money ; and what have we seen during the two or three weeks preceding Christmas ? Why, tens of thousands of people crowding the shops, lavishly spending money on what is to a large extent the merest trash ! Shops that were elaborately dressed with things artistically displayed to catch the eye, ranging from ermine coats at a thousand guineas, to the most tawdry articles of no intrinsic value, resulting in a perfect orgy of money-waste, time-waste, mental-waste, and waste of human energy. Surely the time has arrived when this insane folly should cease, and the lavish display of luxury articles in shop-windows be forbidden. A strong lead is needed from those in Society who set the fashion in these matters and things, for if the word went forth that it is bad form to indulge in such extravagances, and people were freed from the temptation of the shop-windows, it is safe to say many millions a year would be available for investment in War Stock, people would be relieved from the worries attending the selection, purchase, and dispatch of such things, and others engaged in their manufacture would be available to do work of national importance.

The vast possibilities in the utilisation of almost every kind of waste matter and refuse can perhaps be best understood by reviewing some of the triumphs of past workers in this rich field ; so an attempt has been made to bring together in Part II (the Glossary) a large number of more or less typical examples ; and, as some of these are so wonderful, the section dealing with them (Section I) is entitled " The Romance of Waste."

In Section II, " Miscellaneous Household Wastes and Economies," a wide range of household wastes is conveniently grouped, and suggestions are made as to how many things that are usually regarded as wastes can be economically utilised. Some paragraphs are also devoted

c

to several matters of a domestic character that appear to demand attention.

Section III, " Trade, Industrial, and other Wastes," is devoted to a fairly wide range of wastes that occur in our trades, industries, and activities other than purely domestic ones. In some cases attention is called to what has been done, more or less efficiently here and there, in eliminating or reducing waste, that is worthy of further research or of general adoption.

Many items in both sections might appear at first sight to be undeserving of attention, but if we are to abolish waste, or at least to greatly minimise it, and if civilisation is to be at war with waste, nothing should be too trifling for consideration. Doubtless human progress will show that what is now the veriest waste may, in the course of time, assume a condition of value. Thus will science and art be made to approximate to nature, in that it will know no waste, as " nature is avariciously frugal ; in matter it allows no atom to elude its grasp ; in mind no thought or feeling to perish. It gathers up the fragments that nothing be lost." [1]

So, if we are to make war on waste in real earnest, it would be well to commit the following most apt lines to memory :

> " Oh ! waste not thou the smallest thing
>   Created by Divinity ;
> For grains of sand the mountains make
>   And atomies infinity ;
> Waste thou not, then, the smallest time,
>   'Tis imbecile infirmity ;
> For well thou know'st, if aught thou know'st,
>   That seconds form eternity."
>   —EDWARD KNIGHT.

[1] David Thomas.

CHAPTER II

Millions for the War in Household Waste

AN URGENT APPEAL FOR MUNICIPAL ORGANISATION

THE submarine menace is so serious, the loss of tonnage so great, that it is a patriotic duty of all to do everything possible to increase the home supply of materials by saving every useful scrap which from the household point of view is mere refuse, but from the economic point of view is raw material for the manufacture of many materials that are ordinarily imported, and in which there is at present a great shortage. By increasing the home supply of these we set free cargo space in merchant vessels for the importation of food and other necessaries which must come from abroad, and for the transport of the gallant American troops to the seat of war.

In April, 1917, the author was interviewed by a representative of the *Daily Graphic* on the subject of waste, and in the issue of April 27th of that journal his views were given on the large number of trifling things that are ordinarily wasted or thrown away. Attention was called to what Wimbledon and Merton had done by organising the regular collection of waste things in every part of the district, the proceeds going to the local War Funds. The kinds of things that can be utilised are waste-paper and cardboard of all kinds, and all other kinds of valuable refuse, such as leather, twine and cord, every scrap of woollen and cotton material, rags, bones, bottles of all kinds and broken glass, jars, empty tins, old pots and pans, disused electric-light bulbs, iron, brass, zinc, copper, lead and other metals, fats and grease, also any spare articles, old clothes, old boots and shoes, and furniture, should be included ; but of course no article should be diverted from any useful purpose to which it is now applied, and wearable clothes and boots should be given to the poor. Other districts and towns have happily energised in this patriotic movement ; for example, in Islington over 100,000 empty bottles were collected, realising £460, which purchased a motor-ambulance for the front; and Gipsy Hill and Wandsworth followed, each realising about £100. Holborn is specialising in old pots and pans, Edinburgh and Preston in waste-paper, whilst the Birmingham Corporation, with the aid of the dustman and baling presses, has increased the amount of waste-paper and cardboard recovered from 400 to about 1,000 tons per annum, the average value being about £5 per ton. Indeed, it is estimated that with proper organisation over £1,000,000 a year could be easily saved from this source only. We might well ponder over the fact that in Paris alone the rag-pickers collect refuse whose annual value is £500,000, not reckoning the £120,000 worth of fatty products used for making manure.

SOME USES TO WHICH WASTE MATERIALS ARE APPLIED

In the following pages much information as to how a wide range of waste trifles and materials is utilised is given, but we are in urgent need of :

Fat, grease, and bones, as a source of glycerine for the preparation of explosives by the Munitions Department.

Woollen scraps, as raw material for clothing, and blankets for the Army and Navy.

Cardboard for making *papier maché* splints for our wounded soldiers.

Cotton scraps to be made into paper.

Broken white flint glass, now so valuable for its potash and lead contents.

Horse-chestnuts for the Director of Propellant Supplies.

Sunflower seeds and fruit-stones for the production of oils.

Acorns for the local piggeries, and

Food scraps to be converted into feeding-stuff for pigs and poultry.

URGENT CALL FOR ORGANISED COLLECTION

The marked success attending the spasmodic and sporadic attempts that have been and are being made to collect waste articles is a sure indication of the enormous amount of wealth awaiting organised collection and treatment. The municipalities have it in their power to render great services to the State by organising a complete system, including house-to-house calls by voluntary women helpers. But nothing of real importance is likely to be done on an extensive scale until such schemes are organised throughout the country from some State department, such as the Local Government Board. Our Municipal Councillors are remarkable for their public spirit and self-denial. They are proud to serve their fellow-citizens without fee or reward, and would cheerfully do all that is possible to adopt a well-thought-out scheme and adapt it to local conditions. Committees could be formed, including the scout-masters of the districts, chief officers of the Girl Guides, and some public-spirited residents. These committees would organise the collecting, sorting, compressing, and disposal of the waste things, or their transmission to the main depôts, and would engineer in each district a campaign. Once it became realised that the movement was a valuable contribution towards the furtherance of victory, the lumber-rooms, attics, outhouses, and odd corners all over the country would be cleared of their accumulated rubbish and unconsidered trifles, and each householder would enjoy the satisfaction of knowing that he had parted with something that was of little or no value to himself, but of immense value in the aggregate to the nation. At our best, we are unexcelled as organisers, but such a far-reaching, comprehensive movement needs someone to officially initiate it and to organise the organisers, who, in their turn, would appeal to the reason, conscience, and patriotism of individual citizens, and particularly to the borough and district engineers or surveyors, whose services would be of the greatest value in arranging schemes and organising depôts with their properly equipped departments for different materials, such as one for paper and cardboard, with inexpensive baling-press, another for empty tins with a press for flattening them out, and perhaps a furnace for de-tinning, a third for woollen and cotton rags, and so on. A properly organised national scheme would have its well-defined main depôts for the reception and sale of materials in districts where they would be utilised : and arrangements would be made with the railway and canal companies for the use of trucks and barges that are being returned empty, and for space in their yards for the dumping of waste materials ; and, in the country, waggons delivering manure, etc., might be utilised in carrying old tins and iron, etc. (which are usually got rid of by burying), to the railway-station on their way, instead of returning empty.

These are some of the obvious directions in which we should energise, if by co-ordinating our efforts we are to utilise the vast store of neglected trifles that have a real war value.

CHAPTER III

Waste Time

HOW TIME IS WASTED

" The hours perish and are laid to our charge."

" Time and tide wait for no man."

THERE is no form of waste more economically important than the waste of time ; and probably there is no waste that is so lightly regarded. How few realise that in a life-working period of forty years the precious productive hours rarely exceed 100,000 ! It is true that business men know the value of time, and are apt to quote the classic maxim that " time is money." It is such men more than any others who are shocked when they see the appalling amount of dawdling and slacking that go on around us on the part of those who are supposed to be at work. In pre-war times it was to be seen at every turn, and need not be further particularised, but we may express more than a pious hope that education will ere long do something to improve matters : the young should be taught that it is little short of a crime to waste time, and that an economical use of time is the true mode of securing leisure. There are wastes in time that are particularly galling to those who know how to value it, and among these should be mentioned the loss of time in travelling. It is true that travelling facilities have enormously increased in London during the past few years, and that the tube railways are a great convenience, but the valuable odd bits of time wasted in waiting for the lifts, and in walking along lengthy passages, make a short

journey by tube out of the question to any but people of
leisure, as, taking into account the delays, the average
speed of such journeys rarely exceeds some five miles an
hour. Some of our suburban train services are extremely
wasteful when the time factor is considered ; for example,
a journey between Charing Cross and Erith (a very busy
industrial place), a distance of some thirteen miles, may
take seventy-five minutes—indeed, often does. Then there
is the loss of time at railway junctions due to badly-timed
connections, or delays on the line, often causing groups of
busy men to cool their heels for long spells on end in
impotent rage and vexation of spirit. But we are a long-
suffering race, and have become so accustomed to these
forms of waste that we are apt to go on our way uncom-
plaining. Then, too, there is the vexatious loss of time
in telephoning, as things often are at present; but the
time must soon come when a demand will be made for
drastic reforms in these matters, to our great economic
advantage.

Waste of Time in Factories

*" Time is the deadliest of the neutral powers. We must see that we enlist
him among our allies, and the only way to win time is not to lose it."*

This is hardly the place to deal with the time that is so
much wasted in our factories in various ways (we have
touched on this matter in the next chapter) ; but too often,
even in factories that are supposed to be well managed,
the flow of work to important machines is so badly arranged
that an idle machine may be seen eating its head off at the
rate of anything up to eight or ten shillings an hour, to
say nothing of the loss due to the machinist being idle.
And we may see a heavy piece of work machined at a
rapid and efficient rate, only to find that the lifting tackle
to remove it is not in position, and a quarter of an hour or
more may be wasted in getting it rigged up. These are

examples that occur to the author at the moment, and they relate to one particular trade, but a careful observer in any factory would be astonished at the loss of time that occurs in one way and another through the lack of efficient organisation, preparation, and supervision. It is proverbial that the busiest people can generally find time to do odd jobs, it is they who know how to utilise the fragments of spare time which the idle or careless workers permit to run to waste. If the young were properly taught to consider the value of time, they would be astonished at what can be done by its economy, and it would also inspire habits of punctuality and enable them to understand the full meaning of the expression, " Time is the essence of the contract," and of Napoleon's remark, " Ask anything of me but time ; it is the one thing I cannot give you." (Las Cases, " Memorial de Sainte-Hélène.")

Time-Saving Mechanical Appliances, etc.

" *Lost somewhere between sunrise and sunset—*
A Golden Minute—set with sixty diamond seconds.
No reward is offered—for it is gone for ever."
—From an Old Sampler.

Much valuable time could be saved by the more general adoption of the card index system, card ledgers, vertical files, loose-leaf ledgers, invoicing and adding machines, dictaphone, rotary duplicator, and addressing and calculating machines, most of which have been much improved in recent years ; also, as an aid to calculation, the slide rule is a great time-saver, and it could with much advantage be more generally used in certain types of commercial work involving calculations.

Waste of Public Time

The delays which occur in the administration of the law are proverbial and innumerable, and are too well known to

justify an attempt to specify them. In the past they have
been accepted as in the ordinary nature of things, and it
is not comforting to contemplate the vast amount of
wicked waste that has occurred and is occurring in this
connection—a waste that would be impossible with an
efficient system of scientific administration, which we may
hope for when the new order of things comes into being.
However, as a sign of the times, it is refreshing to hear a
distinguished magistrate calling public attention to one
phase of this waste, as Mr. Mead did at Marlborough St.
on December 31, 1915, when he had before him a case in
which he could not give an adequate sentence by dealing
with it summarily. He remarked that in view of recent
legislation, passed apparently in consequence of ignorance
of what occurred at that court, he was obliged to commit
for trial. In some cases, without rhyme or reason, the
magistrates at that court could give twelve months; in
other cases their power was limited to six months. He
thought an apology was due to the witness; *his time was
squandered, the time of the public was squandered, and the
public were put to very large expense indeed* in consequence
of prisoner having to be tried at the Central Criminal
Court.

Waste due to Red Tape

The official formalities represented by the common
expression *red tape* are notoriously responsible for an
enormous amount of waste in this country. Government
departments (and many municipal ones) in particular are
extraordinarily wasteful in the matter of letter-writing and
stationery, and nothing beyond a little common sense is
required to effect a reform in this direction which would
add to the efficiency of the departments concerned, and
eliminate a great amount of totally unnecessary labour.

When it is possible to set the whole of the machinery of a great municipal authority to work to hand over to an heir two penny stamps left by a pauper lunatic, the time has surely arrived when a demand should be made for more sane and economical methods.

The following, reported in the Press on February 15, 1917, is another amazing example of such waste :

" An applicant before the Camberley Tribunal who had been directed to produce his birth certificate stated yesterday that he had applied to Somerset House and enclosed 3s. 6d. He had received a reply that the fee for the certificate was 3s. 7d. The certificate would be sent to him on the forwarding of another penny, which, it was intimated, should be sent by postal-order, payable to the Registrar-General."

It is well known that one of the most retarding and blighting factors in bureaucratic activities is *the docket,* a paper containing a summary of a writing, that wanders from department to department for their remarks ; often on its journey raising fresh points or side issues which call for further remarks from other departments. In due course it returns to the department originating the docket, where, on examination of the remarks and minutes, further questions may be raised that are only remotely related to the main issue. This may give it a new lease of life and a further tour of other departments before action is decided upon. There can be little doubt that the docket system is the primary cause of the rapid growth in the staffing of departments and of the endless delays in arriving at decisions that precede actions, even in the most unimportant matters. So it is good news that M. Clemenceau, a clear-headed, forceful man possessed of strong driving power and not afraid to use it, has by a stroke of the pen done away with the waste of time and labour involved in red-tape methods, as will be seen from the following, which appeared in the Press of December 18, 1917 :

" PARIS, MONDAY.

" M. Clemenceau, the Premier and Minister of War, has declared war on red-tape in all departments of the War Office and the army.

" In a circular he orders that in future all questions not requiring a long inquiry shall be dealt with within three days.

" The system of demanding written reports from subordinates in the same building is abolished, and officials who carry on long correspondence about matters which could be settled in two minutes' conversation are threatened with severe punishment.

" Minutes are not to be written until a definite decision has been reached.—EXCHANGE."

WASTE OF TIME AT ASSIZES

More than forty years ago the Judicature Commissioners, including some of the most distinguished judges of the day, declared that the assize system resulted in " a great waste of judicial strength and a great waste of time," and some twenty years later the Council of Judges prepared an elaborate scheme for reducing the number of assize towns from fifty-six to eighteen. Nothing effective, however, has yet been done to reform the wasteful system which compels High Court judges to visit periodically towns where only one or two cases are waiting for trial, and these, as a rule, not above a county court or police level.

A glaring case of such waste occurred on January 15, 1917, at the Cambridge Assizes, where about one hundred persons, including sixty jurymen, were present to dispose of one criminal and one civil case.

Sir Harry Poland has suggested that every county should have a court analogous to the Central Criminal

Court, where the minor cases are tried by minor judges. One effect of this change would be to remove a serious blot on our administration of justice, as it not infrequently happens, owing to the long and irregular intervals between the assizes, that an accused person is kept in prison three or four months before, on being tried, he is found to be innocent.

Thus we see how very much needed is a thorough reform of the circuit system, in the interests of efficiency as well as economy.

Waste of Time in Parliament

A better appreciation of the value of time will, we may hope, in the not distant future induce our legislators to conduct the affairs of the House in a more businesslike way. The House of Commons was once led by a very able business man, Mr. W. H. Smith, who knew the value of time, and expeditiously carried out the duties of his high office with a brevity that was rewarded by general approval.

Time wasted in Manipulative Work

" Be sure to make the most of time, for it flies away so fast. Yet method and care will teach you to make the most of time."—GOETHE.

It is common knowledge that the profits of many industrial undertakings very much depend upon the care that is taken of the odds and ends of time; for as the ocean is made up of drops of water, as the beach is composed of grains of sand, so the aggregation of small intervals of time economically utilised by the diligent workers of a factory means increased output, which benefits both the workers and employer. Now it will appear to many as a most strange thing that a skilful worker performing the simplest operation often moves his limbs in such a way that there are needless ill-directed and ineffective motions,

with their unnecessary fatigue. If there be a probability
of such waste occurring in a simple operation there is a
certainty of its occurrence when the operation is complicated ; and it is the business of the modern scientific
engineer to eliminate, or at least to greatly reduce, all such
waste. Unfortunately, we have not yet made use of the
beautiful and effective micro-motion study expedients used
in the United States and in Germany, which have been
developed in a remarkable way by Major Frank B.
Gilbreth.[1]

Although a full description of motion-study work
cannot be attempted in these pages, it may be explained
that the object of a motion study is to determine the proper
elementary motions necessary to accomplish a certain act.
Such a study enables us to eliminate all unnecessary
motions, so that the arrangement of the work may be
determined to enable the operator to execute the sequence
of motions with the least expenditure of time and effort—
in short, to build methods of least waste.

A SIMPLE MOTION STUDY

In making a simple motion study, a motion-picture
camera and a speed clock or microchronometer with a
rapidly revolving second hand, and other accessories for
assisting in measuring the relative efficiency and usefulness
of motions, are used as a device for recording elements of
motion and their corresponding times simultaneously.
The microchronometer is placed in the photographic field
near the worker whose motions are to be studied, with
his equipment, and against a cross-sectioned background
or in a cross-sectioned field and at a cross-sectioned bench

---

[1] Applied in several industries by him with extraordinary increases of
output. See " Applied Motion Study." The Efficiency Method applied to
Industrial Preparedness. Published by George Routledge & Sons, Ltd.
Also " Motion Study," by Frank B. Gilbreth (Constable & Co., Ltd.).

or table; the worker then performs the operation according
to the usual methods, while the picture-camera records the
various stages of the operation, and the position of the
pointer or hand of the microchronometer simultaneously.
Thus on the motion-film intermittent records of the paths,
the lengths, the directions and the speeds of the motion, or
times accompanying the motions, are obtained simultaneously; and the details of the surroundings that are
visible to the eye are recorded without the failings of
memory. The film being completed, the picture is thrown
on a screen and the film moved so slowly that every
movement of the worker can be examined and analysed,
so that his purposeless motions may be cut out and
awkward ones corrected. In a word, from the data on the
film and the observations of the observer, an improved
method can be formulated.

Use of Time Studies in Increasing Output [1]

Time studies, which are complementary to motion
studies, are required in establishing standards which must
be lived up to by the worker. They also enable us to
measure the relative efficiency of old and new methods.
In making time studies the " decimal " stop-watch is
used, the minute or outer circle being divided into a
hundred parts; a small dial registers minutes, and the
watch is arranged to be stopped and started with the
thumb of the left hand. If an observation has been taken
and the watch stopped, say at 1·32 minutes, it can be
started again on a second observation which adds to the
first ; or if it is desired to throw back the hands to zero
before taking the second observation, so that it only will
be registered, a pressure of the forefinger on the stem is
necessary.

[1] From the Author's articles on " Fatigue," etc.

The time-study man must be skilled in the trade under investigation, with sound judgment, patience, and an open mind ; his powers of obseivation must be well developed and he must be exact, tactful, and diplomatic. He should also be well trained in silent rhythmic counting, as often useful observations can be taken in this way, where the production of a stop-watch would alarm the worker or make him nervous.

IRON PLATE PUNCHING TIMED

The art of making ordinary time studies cannot be explained in a few words, but sometimes the output can be increased by a very elementary application of the art. A case in point may be cited, in which the study was made not primarily to demonstrate to the satisfaction of the management that the time used to perform a certain job could be shortened, but rather to give information to the workman himself. The component operations in iron plate punching were timed. It was found that the workman took four times as many seconds for a certain operation in the case of one plate as for the same operation on a preceding plate, or, say, twenty seconds as against five seconds. Other variations were noticed in the analysis of the job, the observation extending over several hours. Then the minimum times were added, this total representing the time in which a plate could be punched in the various places called for if the workman performed each fractional operation in the best time he had made, working in his accustomed way.

It was a surprise to the workman to be told that such inequalities existed in the time he took for the simple operations. The proposal was made that if he finished within an hour a certain indicated number of plates—a number which the analysis of his own motions had shown he could finish, with a margin of time left—he would be given a considerable advance over the rate he was receiving. There was no unwillingness to make the attempt, and the increased output that resulted was continuously profitable both to the management and the man. Time saving of this sort, resulting from a close study of manual operations, is typical of a great deal that could be done in an enormous number of works in which no attempts have been made to organise them to be run on modern lines. Such saving is not due to the application of the spur or to the driving of an unwilling worker ; it is rather the bringing out of information not available before and making it serviceable to the worker and his employer. Viewed in that light and carried out with tact, such methods of checking waste, increasing output and reducing fatigue, ought to win their way without forcing or friction.

CHAPTER IV

Waste due to Traditional Methods in Management

OLD METHODS AND THE NEW.—INCREASED OUTPUT BY LESS WORK

THE science of good management, as represented by good dividends, is a very complicated and difficult one, embracing in most cases every element in industry; but we are only concerned here with some aspects of it that must receive attention if we are to continue to hold our own in the industrial world. It will be freely admitted that some of our factories are so perfectly managed that we may well suppose there is little or no room for improvement; but, having regard to the wonderful developments that have taken place, particularly in America, during the past twenty years or more, in what is termed " scientific management " or " industrial management by scientific methods," we must freely admit that much remains to be done in the direction of securing higher wages for the workers and lower labour costs for the employer by the saving of human energy, time, and materials, and by diagnosis for the detection of leaks in producing a particular thing in the quickest and most efficient and economical way. In short, by securing the highest productive efficiency in labour and the highest degree of productivity for a given expenditure of materials, labour, and the mechanical appliances utilised by labour.

Those who are familiar with our typical factories know

how much room there is for all-round improvement when
the traditional methods in use are compared with the
carefully worked out ones that are employed where scientific management [1] prevails ; and it is to be hoped that
under *post-bellum* conditions it will be possible to induce
our workers and employers to adopt all the methods in
scientific management that appear to be best for us in our
various industries ; for, alas ! there will be fewer of the old
well-trained workers to take part in the industrial war to
come, and our economic position will be such that every
form of waste should be eliminated or reduced, and everyone should be called upon to work at his highest efficiency
to make good the ravages of war, to increase our exports
and reduce our imports, and to amortise our gigantic
national debt.

CONSERVATISM OF OUR CAPTAINS OF INDUSTRY

It is true that we have raised our industries to an
extraordinary degree of prosperity, and that our workers at
their best are unsurpassed in energy, intelligence, and
inventive ability ; but we are a very conservative people
when the question of change in habits and methods is
concerned, particularly when any proposed innovation is
based upon science. It must not be overlooked that
employers are not in business for the good of their health ;
indeed, their first concern is rightly to produce at a profit ;
as a rule they fight shy of any expedients, methods, processes and inventions that may be more or less untried.
The temptation to let other firms do the pioneer work and
prove its worth so that they may come in and reap the
benefit of such enterprise is understandable, but in the
industrial war to come this attitude in relation to progress
will probably spell ruin to not a few.

[1] The author dealt with some aspects of this movement in an article
on " National and Industrial Efficiency," published in the *Journal of the
Junior Institution of Engineers*, Aug. and Sept., 1914.

Of course our captains of industry are well aware that English trade unions are much stronger than those of America, and in the past have been much less disposed to tolerate any departure from their traditional methods of working ; and this has often been put forward as an excuse for not attempting to profit by the progress that has been made in workshop economy and science. Employers are also apt to suggest the impossibility of applying an ideal system in a factory where a wide range of work that is continually changing in character is turned out ; and they will not willingly admit that, even in such cases, a great deal can be done to increase the all-round efficiency. But unfortunately the same mistaken attitude is met with in cases where the factory is turning out more or less standardised articles or pieces of machinery, and in which all the conditions are favourable for the adoption of more scientific methods, and of perfect organisation.

If we are ever to successfully cope with foreign competition in the open markets of the world after the war, we must be as ready as our competitors are to profit by the progress of other countries ; for, in spite of their fiendish barbarism and treachery, the Germans have learnt to become great organisers, as we know to our cost. Further, Germans freely make use of the best American brains and the best American science, and adapt themselves to the most up-to-date conditions of production in the twinkling of an eye. Indeed, the German worker is a very apt pupil, and if there is little evidence amongst the Germans now either of genius or of the very highest types of talent, they probably produce the best trained average of any nation. So it behoves us to put our house in order, and to engineer a crusade with the object of raising the efficiency of every worker for the economic good of the State.

Reluctance of Workers to do their Best

Unfortunately, one of the most serious difficulties arising in the employment of labour in pre-war times was the reluctance of the majority of employees to work to the best of their ability. They felt, in the first place, that if they worked hard they might be keeping another man out of a job—a widespread fallacy, as even from the purely personal view of the wage-earner this policy was short-sighted; the production of wealth is itself the only means of creating employment, for in the long run a workman can only be paid out of the product of his own labour, and if that product is restricted the wage will be restricted also. Employees also felt that by turning out their work in a shorter space of time they might be establishing a basis for a lower rate of pay. There is, it is true, some foundation for this fear, as undoubtedly there are many foremen and employers who will take advantage of a man's exceptional efforts and reduce the scale of payment. The knowledge that this does happen explains to a large extent the reluctance of workmen to work at their highest efficiency, and to some extent the adoption of the in-famous " soldiering " or " ca'-canny " methods, now happily abandoned for the higher standard.

The false economic and false moral theories upon which the policy of restricting output are based have done in the past incalculable and apparently irreparable harm. Now, under scientific management great care is taken to fairly fix the rate of pay in the first instance, and when once the rate is fixed the employer is pledged to make no alteration in it so long as the operation remains unaltered.

There is, however, a third cause of inefficient labour which has in this country received nothing like the attention it deserves, namely, the fact that the actual method of working is usually left entirely to the worker himself, on the " go-as-you-please " day's work plan, and he is often so poorly equipped on the technical side that he cannot plan out the most efficient way of doing his own work. This is where scientific management comes in, as a feature of this system is the planning department, in which the brain-work is done by men especially fitted for their tasks, and trained in their especial lines, instead of leaving it to be done by the skilled mechanics, who are well qualified to work at their trades, but poorly trained for work of a more or less clerical type. Indeed, practical experience has proved that work done in accordance with the principles of scientific management results in an enormous increase of output with reduction of waste, and with less fatigue to the workman.

HUMAN MECHANICS

One of the most fundamental things about scientific management is that the worker should be taught to do the greatest amount of useful work with the least amount of fatigue. Now, many highly skilful fitters have used their chipping-hammers day by day for years without discovering the least wasteful way of working ; they lift the whole arm in raising the hammer to the end of its sweep, instead of swinging the hammer about the wrist and elbow. Badly taught pianists do a large amount of unnecessary work in raising their hands and arms in striking the notes, instead of keeping their forearms at practically the same level and using their wrists and knuckle-joints as fulcra ; and the strange thing is that such workers and musicians will continue these wasteful movements until someone comes along who understands animal mechanics, but who may lack the skill of the fitter or pianist, and explains how fatigue may be avoided by the elimination of needless movements.

TRADITIONAL METHODS IN MANAGEMENT 39

Needless and Ineffective Motions

Major Frank B. Gilbreth,[1] as we have seen, has shown us how we can obtain methods of least waste, and take in hand the worker in any industry, examine and analyse the movements of his limbs in performing any operation, no matter how complicated it may be, and cut out all needless, ill-directed, and ineffective motions, and their unnecessary fatigue; for, as he truly remarks, " there is no industrial opportunity that offers a richer return than the elimination of needless motions, and the transformation of ill-directed and ineffective motions into efficient activity."

It is common knowledge that the profits of any industrial undertaking very much depend upon the care that is taken of the odds and ends. Often for want of a little scheming and skill a great deal of valuable material is wasted, and the dividend will vanish if there is much waste. If this be true of material, it is equally true of time, as the aggregation of small intervals of time economically utilised by the diligent workers of a factory means wealth both for the workers and the employer. So economists of the new school rightly consider no pains too great when there is a possibility of saving time by cutting out unnecessary motions.

Economies Resulting from Standardising Machine Details

No firms manufacturing machines can claim to be up to date unless they have adopted a system of standardising details or single parts of their machines, so that the same units can be used on a number or perhaps all of

[1] " Applied Motion Study." The Efficiency Method applied to Industrial Preparedness. Published by George Routledge & Sons, Ltd.
Major Gilbreth is now—since the lamented death of Dr. Taylor, the great Pioneer of Scientific Management—the most distinguished exponent and practitioner of the new science.

their machines. The practical and economic advantages of such a system are so important and so obvious, that it should be hardly necessary to call attention to them. But the fact remains that in this country there are still too many machine-makers, many of them doing a very considerable business, who, for one reason or another, have made no attempt to simplify, increase the efficiency, and reduce the cost of work in the drawing-office and shops by extending the principle of interchangeability of parts, and in so doing to incidentally improve the standard of accuracy in machine work and fitting. For standardising in most cases means an extended use of gauges. Further, there is the all-important advantage due to manufacturing units in large quantities and storing them, thereby considerably reducing the cost of manufacture and increasing the adaptability of workshop arrangements, often making it possible to run expensive tools continuously, even in slack times. Doubtless the excellent work already done by the Engineering Standards Committee in standardising systems of limit gauges, and such articles as bolts and nuts, spanners, pipe flanges, screw-threads, etc., etc., will give a great impetus to the general use of standard parts.

When standards are introduced by a firm the work of designing and drawing is greatly simplified, as it is no longer necessary to set out in detail from general and auxiliary drawings separate parts which have been standardised ; it is sufficient to state the number of the standard part on the drawing and in the list of parts. This greatly facilitates the getting out of new designs and of making suitable drawings.

The system of supplying each workman with a small dimensioned sketch showing the parts, and those parts only, which he has to work on, and giving particulars of the kind of fits that may be required, is one of great value, as it prevents, or at any rate very much reduces, the many costly mistakes occurring which every works manager is familiar with.   It also often makes it possible to get work done by men who are not necessarily technically trained to read complicated drawings, but who are intelligent enough to follow the instructions on a simple sketch.

AMERICAN ENTERPRISE IN MOTOR-CAR CONSTRUCTION

Some of our motor-car manufacturers have little to learn in this direction, but by neglecting to cater for the man of modest means they have allowed our American friends to flood our markets with cheap cars, machines which they turn out with the facility of shelling peas ; indeed, in one factory, at the rate of a car every two or three minutes.   A car is carefully designed, constructed, tested, improved, and standardised.   Then a plant is put down capable of turning out tens of thousands a year ; and many of these cars, after being shipped thousands of miles, are marketed here at a price we cannot at present compete with.

In America they know all about the economic advantages due to manufacturing on a very large scale, and to disposing of their surplus stock in a free foreign market, whilst we have no such foreign market and are still waiting for the appearance of the light home-made car that can hold its own in price against the foreign-made ones that are flooding our markets.

The Ford Motor Car Factory in the United States employs 17,000 men, and Messrs. Dodge Brothers are claimed to have produced 25,000 machines in the first five months of their existence; whilst another huge development is announced in connection with the Briscoe car, Mr. Benjamin Briscoe having completed plans for an output of 50,000 machines a year.   The eight-cylinder car has also received a deal of attention in America, and it is reported that the Hallyei Company have made arrangements to turn out 10,000 of these as a first instalment.

MOTOR-CARS FROM AMERICA

The increase in the importation of motoi-cars from America to the United Kingdom reached alarming figures up to 1915, as the following particulars from the Board of Trade returns will show :

May, 1915.	Number of complete cars,			4,036	valued at		£1,179,171
June, 1915.	,,	,,	,, ,,	2,486	,,	,,	468,127
July, 1915.	,,	,,	,, ,,	1,559	,,	,,	287,412
Aug., 1915.	,,	,,	,, ,,	1,496	,,	,,	262,393
June to August (3 months), chassis,				538	,,	,,	213,830
Total number imported in four months				10,115	Total		£2,410,933

The parts of motor-cars imported were :

	TYRES, TUBES, ETC.	OTHER PARTS.
June, 1915	value £45,270	£50,532
July, 1915	£85,416	£100,509
August, 1915	£121,194	£195,858
	Total £251,880	Total £346,899

In May, 1914, we imported from America 663 cars, valued at £111,356, and for eleven months, ending May, 1915, the figures were 11,688 cars, valued at £3,347,233, as compared with 6,982 cars, valued at £1,122,770, for the corresponding period ending May, 1914, and 3,503 cars, valued at £547,487, for 1913.

TRADE LITERATURE, ETC., FOR FOREIGN MARKETS

Not a little of the extraordinary success of the Germans in capturing foreign trade is due to the careful way in which they get up their trade catalogues. These are published in the language of the country in which they are circulated ; the weights, measures, and prices, etc., are given in accordance with the system in use in that country, and just the kind of information that a potential purchaser is likely to require is fully supplied ; whilst too often little attention is given to these points by British manufacturers. Take, for example, the catalogues issued by some of the great steel-making firms of Germany ; they contain the fullest information, and are usually copiously illustrated. Official tests of the strengths of different qualities and sections are freely given ; whilst, on the other hand, British firms, as a rule, supply only the scantiest information, and that, too, in most cases in English only.

When it comes to the question of tenders for important work, the Germans easily score ; and even when their estimate is no lower than a British one they too often get the contract, as no pains are spared in setting out the most complete particulars, detailed in such a perfect way that everything they propose to supply is precisely described and sometimes illustrated : the whole document will be neatly type-written (or even perhaps printed) and bound, so that those who are about to place the order know exactly what they will be supplied with ; whilst often the British tender is so lacking in detailed information, and the time required to get this may be so long, that the order is lost to us. Furthermore, we are not so adaptable and accommodating as the German, who is, as a rule, ready to change his patterns, etc., to meet the requirements of his customers. Then, too, the push-and-go German agent or representative is a linguist : he is sure to speak fairly good English and French, and very often Spanish and Portuguese, an advantage he makes good use of, to our cost.

With our factories and workshops fully supplied with work, we have not perhaps in the past suffered so very much through the absence of these advantages, but in the time to come we must not continue to waste our opportunities, but must rather take a leaf or two out of the enemy's book if we are to hold our own. The nation is

badly in want of an adequate supply of young linguists
who have received a sound commercial training, and as
there will probably be great developments in the commercial relations of this country and Russia [1] after the
War, there should be some good openings for our young
commercial men who specialise in the Russian and Polish
languages.

ENGLAND, AND GERMAN COMPETITION

The extraordinary industrial developments, particularly in the engineering trades, that have been made
during the past decade or two in Germany, have threatened
British and American supremacy to such an extent that
there has been much seeking for the reasons and the
underlying factors, quite apart from the fiscal ones. A
careful examination of opinions formed by experienced
engineers who have visited Germany from time to time,
with the object of studying her manufactures and methods,
leads to the belief that the basis of her wonderful prosperity
is education, with the advantages due to natural ability,
a remarkable capacity for work, accommodating industrial
banks, and a paternal government where industrial
expansion is concerned.

The highly skilled German mechanical engineer is now
about the equal of anyone working in the same field, for
although we practically taught mechanical engineering to

[1] On Aug. 30, 1915, the *Daily Chronicle* Special Correspondent at
Petrograd reported that Prince Vsevolod Shahovskoi, the Russian Minister
of Commerce and Industry, had granted him an interview, at which the
Prince presented a picture of a new industrial Russia after the war. The
removal of mills and factories from what is now a German sphere of
influence to the interior is referred to by the statesman as a permanent
work ; lands, plant, and workmen are being established in the new centres.
The co-operation of British business men is invited, not only in the setting
up of their own factories in Russia, away from the German zone, but also
in the further opening up of sea routes, which will help to found a new
and greater commercial Russia ; in the south and south-west, with its
outlet too, to the north ; the development of Muscovy's eastern wealth,
and the fullest use of trade routes of Archangel and the Dardanelles may
be looked for.

the whole world, our willingness to make the science of intensive production a live subject, as it is in America and Germany, has not kept pace with our prosperity, so therefore we have lost ground, although fully employed, whilst our rivals have gone ahead. The German manufacturer goes for the thing that is best and he studies the best and cheapest way to produce it; being a student of detail he takes nothing for granted, but finds out what has been done elsewhere and how far it goes; then he studiously, and on practical lines, seeks ways and means by which to go one better.

It has been said that the Germans are natural mechanics, intelligent and resourceful; although they are not inventive to the extent of originating things, they have the greater facility, from the commercial standpoint, of taking advantage of things which may have originated elsewhere, improving them, perfecting them, and making the best possible use of them. But perhaps their greatest cleverness is displayed in their readiness to profit by utilising the best organising brains of America at almost any cost, and by adroitly trading upon our folly in belauding and overrating their achievements, knowing how ready we have been to take them at their own valuation.

Before the War, German labour was cheaper than it was in this country, but it apparently was going up faster than with us; on the other hand, German efficiency grows as the cost increases. The War will undoubtedly have a disastrous effect upon German industries for a long period, and it will fortunately give us breathing time; but the industrial struggle for supremacy in neutral and competitive markets will sooner or later be renewed with added intensity, as German manufacturers are located under favourable conditions for materials and markets; they have plenty of coal, iron, and limestone at their doors, and, if they succeed in retaining the greater part of these and of their large mercantile fleet, will again become one of our most formidable competitors.

Probably the War will solve for us some of our most difficult labour problems, and bring together master and man with a clearer vision of their mutual and interdependent interests. Should this happily come about, something in the nature of a fresh start, with the adoption of less wasteful and more economic methods—those that have been well tried—and the performance of a fair day's work for a fair day's pay, would lead to an industrial renaissance undreamt of three or four years ago.

CHAPTER V

Waste due to Human Fatigue

FATIGUE IN ITS RELATION TO OUTPUT

AT a time when the Empire's needs are such that we are all rightly called upon to exert ourselves to the utmost, we must be careful not to overstrain ourselves or work beyond the limits of endurance and in so doing reduce our capacity for work. We must do all that is possible to keep ourselves fit, to develop our vital power, and to preserve our health, so that our output, whatever form it may have, may reach the maximum possible without injury to the human machine ; as maximum output may be said to depend upon the physical condition of the worker, the conditions under which the work is done, and the number of hours worked per week.

Now, if any one of these factors be unsatisfactory, the worker will more or less suffer from fatigue, and his output will fall below the maximum. This being so, it will be convenient to deal with the subject by first giving some attention to the fatigue problem, in the light of the investigations which have been officially made on war workers ; following this by dealing with some of the minor causes of fatigue that have hitherto received little attention, but are known to greatly affect the comfort and labouring condition of the workers, and therefore of their output.

The human machine may be in good working condition,

and may be well stoked with suitable food, but, if it is to
work at its highest efficiency, proper attention must be
paid to everything needful in building up and maintaining
vital power; therefore it will not be out of place to include
in this chapter a few remarks on what has been found by
experience to be pertinent in this connection.

THE RELATION OF OUTPUT TO HOURS OF WORK

Fatigue problems have received a great deal of attention
during the past thirty years, but since the outbreak of
war, and the nation's call upon the industrial army to
work the longest hours possible—a call that was nobly and
patriotically responded to—the wastefulness of excessive
work soon called for official attention, owing to the number
of workers who fell out of the ranks due to fatigue and
breakdown.   And it was soon seen that when the hours
and the conditions of labour were such as to cause great
wear and tear of body or mind, or of both, and where there
had been a marked want of that leisure, rest, and repose,
which is one of the necessaries of efficiency, then the labour
had been extravagant from every point of view that
matters.

Indeed, observations and experience have shown that
when the working hours have been too long, fatigue toxins
develop inevitably after a certain period of action, and
that the weariness due to this reduces the exhilaration of
effort, increases the nerve strain, and tends towards a
breakdown.

Some important investigations carried out by Dr. H. M.
Vernon for the Health of Munition Workers Committee,
and published in their Memorandum, No. 18 (Cd. 8628),
1917, give the relations of output to hours of work in four
different operations, carried out by women, men, and

youths. These are briefly shown in the following table :

TABLE GIVING COMPARISON OF RESULTS

Operation.	Reduction in weekly hours of actual work.	Alteration of total output effected.
Men sizing	58·2 to 51·2 = 7·0	+ 22 per cent.
Women turning fuse bodies	66·2 to 45·6 = 20·6	+ 9 per cent.
Women milling a screw-thread ..	64·9 to 48·1 = 16·8	— 1 per cent.
Youths boring top caps	72·5 to 54·5 = 18·0	— 3 per cent.

And an examination of the above table of comparison will show :

(1) That when the hours of the men sizing were decreased from 58·2 to 51·2 = 7, the total output was increased by 22 per cent.

(2) That there was an increase of 9 per cent. total output when the hours of work of women turning fuse bodies were reduced from 66·2 to 45·6 = 20·6, and that there was only a reduction of 1 per cent. in the total output when the hours of work of women milling a screw-thread were reduced from 64·9 to 48·1 = 16·8.

Thus we see by these investigations how the gross output is increased when long hours of labour are reduced, and the problem to be solved is what length of working day on the whole is the most economical, best for the worker that he may not suffer through loss of vitality, best from the point of view of maximum production.

Our investigations tend to prove that with the abolition of ordinary Sunday work and the shortening of working hours, the more general adoption of short intervals of rest, varying in length and frequency with the nature of the work done, would still further appreciably increase output, the other conditions remaining the same ; but there are

E

obvious difficulties in arranging these in practice. Fortunately, it was discovered in time that in the absence of
Sunday rest the fatigued worker had no opportunity for
complete recuperation, and therefore his output, though
more uniform, remained permanently at a lower level
than shown on Monday by a worker who had rested on
Sunday.

Effects of Holidays and of Incentive

The near approach of a holiday seems to act as an
incentive to increase the efforts of the workers. Thus in
the case of one hundred women turning fuse bodies, it was
found that there was a typical rise in their hourly output
of about 6 to 10 per cent. before the Christmas holidays, but,
on the other hand, on returning to work after the holidays
there was an immediate fall of about 16 per cent. in hourly
output, with a subsequent considerable increase, whilst the
total output rose to a maximum of 12 per cent. greater
than that of the pre-Christmas period. Thus *holiday fatigue*
first leads to a falling off in production, but the recuperative
effects of the holiday are soon operative, with consequent
increase in production.

Fatigue and the Eye

Anything that is fatiguing to the eye soon causes
fatigue of the nervous system, as most workers are aware.
Those in particular who are engaged upon fine work know
how the sight becomes enfeebled by fatigue towards the
end of the day. Of course, this fatigue is more pronounced
if the lighting is not efficient. Flickering rays of light
reflected from bright parts of machinery, etc., flaring lights
striking the eyes, in fact, anything that is worrying the
eyes, tends to cause fatigue of the nervous system, so that
everything practicable should be done, in arranging

operations and surroundings of workers, to make them as restful as possible to avoid eyestrain and fatigue.

FATIGUE AND THE EAR

The ear is also a very complex and highly developed organ, through which the nervous system is easily affected and fatigued, and most industrial workers know by experience that a period spent in the midst of working machines and mechanical operations, causing deafening and strident sounds of a wide range, and shocks to the auditory nerves, produces a feeling of sensory fatigue. Now although this fatigue attacks primarily a single organ, it little by little extends to the whole of the nervous system, leading in some cases to such a feeling of weariness that it may impair the capacity for work in a greater degree than severe muscular fatigue.

Nothing is more fatiguing to some workers, particularly if they be highly strung, than a noisy, unrestful, fussy atmosphere. There is far too much avoidable noise in many industrial works, and when it is realised that the human ear can be affected by vibrations of the air ranging from 16 to 40,000 in the second, it can be well understood how injurious noises may be to the nervous system.

FATIGUE AND THE FEET

As most workers are on their feet—upon which the whole weight of the body is supported—the best part of the day, any discomfort due to badly fitting or wrongly shaped boots, or to the condition of the feet, tends to cause fatigue ; and often fatigue of a very distressing kind. In fact, enduring comfort can only be secured by using boots or shoes that properly fit the feet. Unfortunately, boots as ordinarily made are rarely shaped so that there is room enough when the front pillar or ball of the foot widens as the weight of the body comes upon it. Often boots are made too narrow at the toes and too high at the heels.[1] Both these faults lead to fatiguing discomfort.

The high heel causes the foot to rest upon a somewhat steep inclined plane, and the foot in trying to slide down this plane becomes wedged in the narrow part of the boot near the toes, deforming the bones and muscles of the foot, and causing the greatest discomfort. High heels also alter the form of the human figure, causing an unnatural bend in the ankles, knees, and spinal column, which in turn affects the circulation and injures health. Compare the easy, restful figure and poise of anyone wearing properly shaped boots with rational heels, with the crooked figure and awkward, uneasy poise of another wearing fashionable boots, and the folly of such vanity is apparent.

Minor Causes of Discomfort and Fatigue

There are many minor causes of discomfort and fatigue that rarely receive attention but may seriously affect a worker's efficiency. Thus we have *corns*, arising from boots either too tight and causing pressure (which, if long applied, causes a hypertrophied condition of cuticle), or too loose and causing rubbing ; and soft corns caused by

[1] On Nov. 23, 1917, the author, in delivering a Chadwick public lecture on " Fatigue and the Worker " at H.M. Munition Works, Gretna, dealt with this matter and showed by lantern slides various workers wearing high and low heels, also drawings of distorted feet due to wrongly shaped and badly fitted boots, and he explained the ill effects of these. A week or two later he was interested to see, from the following paragraph in the *Daily Mail*, that our French friends are also gravely concerned at the evil effects of the injurious fashion :

" *Paris, December* 5, 1917.

" The French Academy of Science has solemnly anathematised the wearing of high heels by women at a meeting at which the latest scientific apparatus was employed to demonstrate their evil effects. The attack was led by Professor Quenu, who by a combination of X-rays and kinema films showed that the fashionable heel deforms the bones and muscles of the foot, affects the spinal column, and interferes with the circulation. ' This fashion,' declared the Professor, ' defies common sense and the rules of health, and is particularly pernicious at a moment when the future of the race is at stake.' "

pressure between the toes, or by overlapping toes, often most painful : also *bunions*, arising from ill-shaped boots, are most distressing. Then there may be pain due to ingrowing toe-nails, caused by cutting away the corners of the nails, instead of cutting them straight across. How extensively the human feet suffer from constrained treatment to which they are subjected is sufficiently known to artists, as a living model, perfect in the foot, as Nature made it, cannot be found in the fair sex after the age of childhood. *Chilblains* in various parts are often a source of irritation and pain. They are caused by the little vessels of the skin becoming distended with blood. This is due to weak circulation of the blood, and to especial weakening of the feet or hands, often caused by their alternation of exposure to cold and toasting at the fire.

FATIGUE DUE TO STOOPING

Often the exercise of a little common sense in supporting the work to be done in such a way that stooping on the part of the worker is not necessary, is a means of avoiding a good deal of fatigue. One sees at every turn work being done that involves a good deal of back-bending.

A striking example of stooping work occurs in fish-curing operations in Scotland. The bottoms of the " farlanes " or troughs containing the fish are commonly on or near the level of the ground, so that women while employed in gutting are compelled to bend their backs in a most uncomfortable way, the upper portion of the body forming nearly a right-angle with the legs, a back-breaking position from which they can only assume a vertical form at the cost of considerable pain.

GILBRETH'S FATIGUE-ELIMINATING CHAIRS

In industrial works where the science of management has received the most attention it is regarded as good

practice to arrange for any work to be done sitting that can
be done equally well in that position as when standing ;
but of course this means that chairs have to be made
specially arranged as to height and form for different kinds
of work. Major Frank Gilbreth, the great American
industrial efficiency engineer, has given much attention to
this somewhat modern departure from traditional practice,
and he has ingeniously devised a number of simple yet
effective fatigue-eliminating chairs, suitable for a wide
range of working conditions, and some devised for work
that has always been considered standing work. These are
raised so that the workers' arms are at the same height as
when standing, a foot-rest being used, either projecting
from the chair or the bench, chairs that are likely to be
often moved away from the bench being mounted on dome
castors.

Definitions and Maxims relating to Fatigue

As it is not possible to attempt to discuss the wide
range of matters that are represented by fatigue problems
in these pages,[1] the author has arranged the following
definitions and maxims, that are more or less well established, and believes that they will give in a condensed form
the accepted results of investigations and researches.

Fatigue is the sum of the results of activity which show
themselves in diminished capacity for work. From which
it follows that output in work will give the most direct test
of fatigue, other things being the same.

Fatigue does not increase proportionately with work,
but at a much faster rate than work. Work effected with
fatigued muscles is much more exhausting than work
effected with rested muscles.

---

[1] The author has dealt somewhat fully with the subject of fatigue in
his booklet, " Industrial Fatigue and its Relation to Maximum Output,"
and in an Article on " Some Aspects of Industrial Fatigue," in *Cassier's
Engineering Monthly*, October, 1917.

In **Muscular fatigue**, if the work is light, we feel a little weariness, if the fatigue is excessive we experience an uncomfortable and painful sensation which lasts several days.

Overstrain, or chronic fatigue, exists when the signs of fatigue noted in the evening after a complete day's work still persist after a night spent in repose.

The problems of industrial fatigue are primarily and almost wholly problems of fatigue in the nervous system and of its direct and indirect effects.

Nervous fatigue does not affect everyone in the same way.

Worry is insidious and it spreads over the brain like a leaven. The constant dwelling upon an idea which becomes an obsession tends to destroy mental balance.

Nerve and **tone** largely depend upon the mental attitude. Whatever causes mental depression or discord exhausts the nervous system generally. The same cause may give rise to pain or pleasure according to the individual temperament. As long as we are in good health we are little aware of intellectual fatigue, but as soon as ill health comes upon us we find how exhausting brain-work is. Extreme fatigue, whether muscular or intellectual, produces a change in our temper, causing it to become more irritable.

Attention is a limited quantity ; it requires time. If, then, attention be distributed over too wide a field, there is a corresponding loss of intensity and of distinctness.

We could lengthen our lives if we took *needed rest* habitually, for it is habit that kills or cures.

The problem of *scientific industrial management*, dealing, as it must, with the human machine, is fundamentally a problem in industrial fatigue. There are considerations so inexplicable at present in terms of physiology as to be called *psychological*.

These maxims will enable us to keep in view the general

problem of fatigue in all its complexities. We should not forget that the greatest enemy of fatigue is vital power, and that there is little vital power unless the general health be good and unless we pay uniform attention to the great essentials of health. To preserve good health we must obey the laws of hygiene; and, fortunately, it is becoming more generally understood that it pays employers to keep their workers healthy, and the workers on their part have no reason to regard medical care in industry as a charity.

But whatever the condition of health the worker's may be, a certain amount of exercise is necessary to keep him fit; indeed, we should be much happier in doing our daily work if we realised that honest labour is a blessing in disguise, and that congenial work is one of the chief pleasures of life. The body must undergo a certain amount of fatigue to preserve its natural strength and maintain all its muscles in proper vigour; such activity equalises the circulation and distributes the blood more effectively through every part. With hard work or violent exercise the muscles quickly tire, because of the inability of the functional processes to supply them rapidly enough with those elements that are used up by long-continued violent effort. But the full exercise of our muscular functions in bodily labour helps the lungs to do their work, helps the heart to do its work, and the stomach to do its work.

Walking is the most perfect form of exercise, as practically all the muscles of the body are brought into action. Athletes everywhere always make it a part of their training. It builds vital power and increases the vigour of the muscles they expect to use in their contests. Muscular work is not only a necessity for health of body, but for mind also; indeed, the diminution in the size of the body from deficient muscular work appears to lead in two or three generations to degenerate mental condition. In point of fact, there is no better cure for a good many

burdensome mental troubles and worrying feelings than
such bodily action as will hasten the removal of waste and
worn-out tissue and particles, and awaken the appetite for
wholesome food, in which we find new stores of freshness
and vigour.

ADJUSTMENT OF THE ORGANISM TO THE MEDIUM

The air we breathe cannot be too pure if we are to
keep fit. In breathing foul air our organism is injuriously
affected. The following interesting experiment was made
on sparrows to show the power of adaptation to an external
medium possessed by the organism. In an air-tight
glass bell-jar a sparrow was placed. After he had remained
there two hours another sparrow was introduced, and was
instantly suffocated by the foul air; nevertheless the
original occupant remained another hour in the glass, after
which he was withdrawn, nearly dead. The fresh air and
warmth revived him. In a little while he had recovered
sufficiently to fly. When he had recovered all his vigour,
he was again placed in the atmosphere from which he had
been withdrawn, and immediately died.

Experiments cannot be tried on human beings as on
animals, but disease and accident frequently furnish us
with experiments ready made. For example, two young
Frenchwomen were in a room heated by a coke stove.
One of them was suffocated and fell senseless on the
ground. The other, who was in bed, suffering from
typhoid fever, resisted the poisonous influence of the
atmosphere so as to be able to scream till assistance
came. They were both rescued, but the healthy girl, who
had succumbed to the noxious air, was found to have
paralysis of the left arm, which lasted for more than six
months.

Here, as in the case of the sparrows, we find the para-
doxical result to be, that the poisonous action of a vitiated

air is better resisted by the feeble, sickly organism than by the vigorous, healthy organism. Thus on entering a room filled with vitiated air we find those who have had time to adjust themselves to it breathing without apparent inconvenience, and because they have become accustomed to it they naturally suppose that no injurious effect can follow. On entering such a room the breathing becomes laborious ; the consequence of this is a depression of all the organic functions, and then the breathing is easy again, because we no longer require so much oxygen, and we no longer produce so much carbonic acid. Were it not for this gradual adjustment of the organism to the medium by a gradual depression of the functions, continued existence in a vitiated atmosphere would be impossible. Hence the great importance of perfect ventilation.

Vital Air

Just as any heat engine requires a proper amount of air to support the combustion of the fuel in producing mechanical energy, so in the human machine the production of muscular energy is dependent upon a proper supply of air to the lungs, and in both cases the available power rapidly falls off when the supply of air is not adequate. Of course it is the oxygen in the air that supports combustion ; nothing exhilarates like oxygen—indeed, it may be called the air of life.

Over one-fifth of the air we breathe is oxygen, and, therefore, the act of breathing purifies the blood, invigorates the body, and assists in removing the waste materials from it. The air enters the passages of the lungs and meets there with that wonderful surface, covered with the most delicate tufts of blood-vessels which stand upon the surface of 5,000,000 or 6,000,000 air-cells, with an area of about twenty square feet, and through which the blood flows with great velocity. Hence a feeling of slight fatigue usually passes away after a brisk walk in a clear atmosphere, as such exercise enables us to breathe more air, and with more air passing through the lungs the blood becomes purer, the heart is benefited, and our vitality is increased. Indeed, vitality is largely a matter of correct breathing ; with correct deep-breathing practice in the open air our lungs become larger, with a greater air-capacity, and more space in which to move and expand, and our blood becomes purer. By inflating our lungs as much as possible we can draw in some four times the normal quantity of air, the exhilarating effect of which can soon be felt, as nothing refreshes and recreates both body and mind like oxygen.

Correct Breathing

The art of breathing is easily explained. Exhale all the breath you can, drawing in the abdomen and forcing out as much air as possible, make two or three attempts to force out still more, and then begin to inhale ; draw in all the air you possibly can, expanding first in the region of the abdomen, drawing back the shoulders.

The use of tight clothes or corsets means compressing and displacing important parts of the body contained within the ribs, and finally displacing the ribs themselves. Such interference with the natural movements of the body due to respiration deprives the lungs of the full quantity of air needed, and leads to a dangerous lowering of vital power, and to an anæmic and weary condition. Fortunately, the trend of fashion has been in the direction of more rational garments, and a closer approach on the part of the fair sex to the twenty-eight-inch waist of the Milo Venus ; but it should be generally known that if all movement of the ribs and abdomen be stopped then death ensues. Such a case occurred some years ago, when a young miner was buried under a fallen roof in a pit-working. His head was quite uninjured and free to move, but his body was imprisoned and so surrounded that expansion became impossible, and so he died.

The Quantity of Air we Breathe

The air inhaled during ordinary respiration, called tidal air, amounts to about 20 to 30 cubic inches, and the amount left in the lungs after expiration, known as residual air, is from 75 to 100 cubic inches. There is also another 75 to 100 cubic inches (called supplemental air) in the chest after expiration. So it follows that after an inspiration there may be about $30 + 100 + 100 = 230$ cubic inches in the lungs and chest. Thus, in breathing, only some one-seventh or one-eighth of the contents of the lungs and chest are breathed out and taken in. The air in passing in loses about 4 to 6 per cent. of its oxygen, and in passing through the lungs gains 4 to 5 per cent. of carbonic acid.

The deepest possible inspiration may add a further 100 cubic inches (called complemental air) to the contents of the lungs.

In a state of quietude we breathe about 13 to 17 times a minute ; therefore the air taken in ordinarily per minute equals, say, $16 \times 30 = 480$ cubic inches. But in walking about four miles an hour some five times this quantity of air is breathed, say $5 \times 480 = 2,400$ cubic inches, whilst in running or walking at about 6 miles an hour, some $6\frac{1}{2}$ times the normal quantity of air is breathed, say $6\frac{1}{2} \times 480 = 3,120$ cubic inches. Thus we see how much more oxygen is passing through the lungs, invigorating the whole system, whilst we engage in active exercise.

And even whilst we are asleep Roscoe's experiments have shown us that the lungs, especially of working men, absorb more oxygen by night, the blood storing it up for the following day. But to keep pure air in a room, from 2,000 to 3,000 cubic feet should be allowed to pass through it every hour for each person sleeping or living in it. Vitiated air in our dwellings and surroundings is the most fruitful source of a depressed feeling and of disease.

THE QUALITY OF THE AIR WE BREATHE

Although the amount of air required by an individual for respiration is comparatively small, yet he fouls so much air, both by carbonic acid and organic exhalation, that a large quantity of air must pass through an apartment to keep it sweet. If the air contain even one cubic foot of carbonic acid to 1,000 cubic feet of air it is far from pure; indeed, it is vitiated air.

All external air contains a quite small proportion of carbonic acid, ranging from $\frac{3}{10,000}$ to $\frac{6}{10,000}$, but apparently this has no effect on animal life; but when air contains $2\frac{1}{2}$ per cent. of carbonic acid, through any cause, it ceases to support combustion, and with 3 per cent. it ceases to support life.

The amount of carbonic acid given off by a man in 24 hours is about 16 cubic feet, and this is contained in about 400 cubic feet of air exhaled. Stuffiness in a room or shop, due to vitiated air, produces langour, headache, and lassitude, and people who live more or less constantly in impure air become pale, partially lose their appetite, and sooner or later decline in muscular strength and spirits.

Carbonic oxide, a gas formed when the supply of air is inadequate to support complete combustion, is a deadly poison. Hence the danger of using closed stoves in rooms. It burns with a blue flame. All air, even the purest, contains dust particles; that at Colmonell, in Ayrshire, was found to contain 8,000 per cubic inch, whilst in the immediate vicinity of a Bunsen flame the gigantic number of 489,000,000 was found.

The dust from all grinding operations is most destructive to human life, and in the days before such precautions as masks and exhaust dust-extractors and the like were used to protect the worker, he rarely died of old age. Indeed, decades ago to find a needle-grinder older than forty was rare ; to discover one as old as forty-five was a prodigy. It was found that the steel dust from the needle points being inhaled along with the air into the lungs gave rise to a kind of consumption, which speedily terminated in death.

THE WATER OF LIFE

It is a common saying that water is more necessary to our existence than even solid food. Why this is so is easily explained. Every muscular effort is accompanied by movement and heat. The heat developed in the muscles is carried by the blood-stream to the surface of the body, where it passes off in three ways :

1. By the evaporation of the moisture of the breath.
2. By direct radiation and convection from the skin.
3. By evaporation of the moisture of perspiration.

The last is the most important, as more heat is got rid of by that means than by any other ; and should the body be too thickly clad to allow of the moisture evaporating rapidly, the temperature of the body will rise, possibly to an injurious extent.

In addition to the water thus lost through the action of the lungs and skin, there is the water thrown off by the kidneys. These losses of water tend to thicken the blood, and create the *thirst of necessity*, which is the cry of the thickened blood for water, the sensation of thirst in the mouth being the outward expression of the actual deficiency of water in the blood.

The generation of heat due to muscular contraction, and the cooling effect of the blood-stream, is, in point of fact, exactly similar in principle to what occurs in the petrol engine. In the case of the muscles we have, as the result of a nervous impulse which corresponds to the ignition spark of the engine, the combustion of constituents of the muscle (consisting essentially of carbon and hydrogen), and the consequent contraction of the muscle with the production of heat. In the case of the engine, we have the explosion of the compressed hydro-carbon gas mixture with the production of heat, and the temperature of the cylinder walls is kept down (to make lubrication possible) by the flow of water through the cylinder jacket and the radiator. The heat carried from the cylinder in this way passes away from the radiator by radiation and convection, and the heat from the human skin largely by evaporation.

Now in both cases the heat is removed from the place of its production, in the one case the muscles, in the other the cylinders, by a circulatory fluid ; and should this flow of heat be not rapid enough, the temperature of the circulating water in the one case, and of the blood in the other, will rise, and produce an over-heated condition, which in man we call " fever " or heat-stroke, and in the engine over-heating, with possible seizure of the piston.

Thus we see what an important part water plays in the working of the human engine ; but we must not overlook the fact that it is the best diluent and eliminator, promoting a free and equable circulation of the blood and humours through all the vessels of the body, upon which the due performance of every animal function depends ; indeed, water should be regarded as a necessary article of food, which undergoes no change in the body, and therefore requires no digestion. If taken hot, it supplies force-giving heat to the body, and may be considered as the only *real* stimulant.

That many people owe their freedom from illness and disease to the quart or two of water they daily take, there cannot be a doubt. In October, 1917, a Mr. Thomas Medlake died, at the ripe age of eighty-eight, at Hornchurch, and he attributed his long life, health, and energy to cold water, of which he drank a quart a day.

FATIGUE AND ALCOHOL

No factor in the fatigue problem is of greater importance than the one relating to alcoholic beverages. The author has dealt with this matter at some length elsewhere,[1] but would like to say that, although he is not an abstainer, he honestly believes, from observations on himself and on others, that alcohol does not increase the strength of man ; it may stimulate him for a short time to expend more energy, but even for this period there must be some store of energy capable of being called out at the moment, and also sufficient to carry on the necessary actions of the system afterwards : but as the effect of the stimulant is only transient, after it has worn off the worker's diminished strength will call for another dose of the stimulant, and this in its turn will enable him to make a still further call upon any reserve of energy he may have. In point of fact, if this demand on the potential strength of the victim is called for by repeated doses of the stimulant, the ultimate effect must be exhaustion. The conclusion, then, is a strange one : that when stimulants are taken to support the system, or keep up the strength, the potential energy must be there already or the stimulant can have no action whatever.

[1] " Some Aspects of Industrial Fatigue," *Cassier's Engineering Monthly,* Oct., 1917.

ALCOHOL AS AN ARTICLE OF DIET

No authority has tackled this vexed question in a fairer or more unbiassed way than Dr. Edmund A. Parkes, F.R.S., and therefore the following conclusion which he arrived at,[1] as to the use of alcohol, carries great weight :

" It is difficult to avoid the conclusion that the dietetic value of alcohol has been much over-rated. It does not appear possible at present to condemn alcohol as an article of diet in health, or to prove that it is invariably hurtful, as some have attempted to do. It produces effects which are often useful in disease and sometimes desirable in health, but in health it is certainly not a necessity, and many persons are much better without it. As now used by mankind (at least in our own and many other countries), it is infinitely more powerful for evil than for good ; and though it can hardly be imagined that its dietetic use will cease in our time, yet a clearer view of its effects must surely lead to a lessening of the excessive use which now prevails. As a matter of public health, it is most important that the medical profession should throw its great influence into the scale of moderation ; should explain the limit of the useful power, and show how easily the line is passed which carries us from the region of safety into danger, when alcohol is taken as a common article of food."

A FEW HINTS ON HOW TO MINIMISE FATIGUE

Much can be done to minimise fatigue by exercising common sense and intelligence in the arrangement of things. The following examples of how fatigue may be reduced by a little clear thinking in the light of present knowledge may be regarded as typical and suggestive. Many others will occur to the reader.

1.—*Work tables and benches*, etc., should be arranged in height to avoid unnecessary stooping.

[1] Parkes' " Practical Hygiene," p. 336.

F

2.—*Workers* should be *allowed to sit* when their work can be done equally well in that position. Inexpensive, adjustable seats that can be swung under the table when not in use are now available, and Gilbreth chairs are easily made.

3.—*The height and tilt of the seat* should be carefully arranged to suit the poise of the body, and high seats should be provided with foot-rests.

4.—*The raw material*, etc., for the job should not be placed on the floor, but at the most convenient level for handling.

5.—*High heels* and uncomfortable or tight-fitting clothing should be avoided.

6.—The *controlling handles* of machines, etc., should be arranged in height so that little or no stooping occurs in working them.

7.—Seek the most direct and efficient way of performing *manipulative operations*.

8.—The *lighting arrangements* should be the most efficient possible. Good lighting is a good investment.

9.—Provide *efficient heating and perfect ventilation*.

10.—Eliminate, or reduce as much as possible, every kind of *noise*.

11.—*Staircases* should be arranged so that the proportion of the tread to the riser may minimise the fatigue of ascent.

12.—Anything that adds to the *comfort of the worker* in the factory or the home tends to lessen the effect of fatigue.

13.—It has been truly said that to keep fit we must be well clothed, well fed, well housed, well aired, and well watered. And we should remember the doctor's advice to the medical student : "Treat your patient as you treat soiled linen ; wash it, dry it, and iron it "—alluding in this way to baths, to fresh air and sunshine.

14.—When we are out of sorts, and things get on our nerves, it is a sure sign that we need rest and fresh air.

15.—Those who think most, who do most brain-work, require most sleep. It is the simplest means to aid Nature in her work of reparation ; for we must agree with Ovid, that " alternate rest and labour long endure." As to how much sleep is needed, each must be a rule for himself, but we should remember Paul's apt and terse statement, " They that strive for the mastery are temperate in all things."

FATIGUE-ELIMINATION DAY

Our American friends are being urged by some of their wisest and most gifted countrymen to devote a day or part of a day yearly, the first Monday in December, to consider the fatigue problem seriously, and to do something towards reducing or eliminating avoidable and unnecessary fatigue in all their activities. Our friends, who are an efficiency-loving people, realised years before we did that one of the greatest sources of waste is the dissipation of human energy, due to a wide range of recognised causes, such as useless and ill-directed manipulative movements, unscientific methods of doing work, unskilful arrangements of work, the placing of individuals at work for which they are unfitted, the absence of suitable rest periods (about which there is little or no scientific data available), the condition of the work-place itself as to noise, lighting, ventilation, heating, etc., and the absence of suitable chairs and stools and other fatigue-reducing devices.

Human energy is also wasted when the working hours are too long and when alcoholic beverages are immoderately used ; and these are perhaps the more important factors that should receive attention. But quite apart from anything the management of a works may do in such matters, every worker, by self-examination, by observations, and by exercising his intelligence, is capable of making some little improvement in his methods, leading to an increase in his output with less effort and therefore with less fatigue; and however slight this gain may be, it becomes important in its cumulative effect. Now we must admit that much can be done in this direction if the worker, whatever his (or her) work may be, commences the day's work with the thought of fatigue-elimination in his mind on a day in the year especially set aside for the study of this problem—during and after working hours—and this is what " fatigue-elimination day " means.

This promising movement, initiated in the United States of America by Major Frank Gilbreth, and his distinguished wife, Lillian M. Gilbreth, Ph.D., author of the " Psychology of Management," will, I feel sure, be widely adopted, as it has much to recommend it on the grounds of humanity, of efficiency, and of national economy.

The New Movement launched in this Country

A most favourable opportunity occurred to launch this most happily conceived movement in our own country, when on November 23, 1917, the author delivered a Chadwick Public Lecture at H.M. Munition Works at Gretna, on " Fatigue and the Worker." He proposed to a representative audience that on December 3 (the first Monday in the month) they should fall into line with our American friends, and during that day should give deep thought to the question of fatigue-elimination and endeavour to improve their methods in some way, with the object of conserving human energy, by the elimination or reduction of waste. The suggestion received a most warm welcome and it was cheerfully adopted.

On returning to town, it was an easy matter to get some hundreds of engineering students, disabled soldiers, and munitionettes, who are being trained at the Polytechnic, to enthusiastically promise to keep the day in the spirit of the movement, and to write if they could a short account of anything they could think of that would enable them to do their work more efficiently, with less effort, or that would represent a saving of any kind, particularly of human energy. Now although the author was not particularly hopeful as to immediate results, he was astonished and delighted to find how the idea had appealed to the imagination of the young and had taken root, as the number and quality of the essays were sure indications that we have in this movement an educational instrument of great potential value.

The essays of the engineering students were, of course, the most praiseworthy ; they embodied suggestions that ranged from improvements in heating and lighting arrangements to the design of a drilling machine mechanism for registering the depth of holes drilled, to reduce manipulative work. This arrangement was shown by a beautiful little sketch, and a concise specification, the work of a born inventor who is not yet seventeen years of age. That some of the ideas were not new goes without saying, but the general success of this year's efforts proves beyond a doubt that we have, in the capacity of our young people to use their eyes and minds in the cause of economy, when their interest is aroused in a subject, a store of potential wealth almost untouched.

There is an indirect advantage of great importance due to this movement, as all who first take part in it probably talk the matter over in the home and with friends, thus tending to popularise all activities and all tendencies towards the true conservation not alone of human energy, but the best use of the many good things and the many resources which Nature has given us ; for we must agree with Carlyle that " reform, like charity, must begin at home. Once well at home, how will it radiate outwards, irrepressible, into all that we touch and handle, speak and work ; kindling ever new light by incalculable contagion, spreading, in geometric ratio, far and wide, doing good only wherever it speads, and not evil."

By the institution of " Arbour Day," Mr. Roosevelt, when President of the United States, showed the world what can be done, when the services of the children and youth of a nation are enlisted, to prevent another generation suffering from a famine in timber, caused by the advance of industrialism, and the destruction of forests due to railway developments. So, by a campaign of education in the cause of conservation, year by year the important problems would receive more attention from ever increasing numbers; teachers throughout the country should be encouraged to give special addresses on saving and conservation on fatigue-elimination day ; they would explain the economic advantages due to saving, and the still greater ones that flow from the true conservation of our vital powers, and all the useful things that Nature has provided us with. For to save is merely to keep ; to conserve is quite different ; indeed, it involves the idea of use, but of use in such a way, and in such conjunction with other things, as to obtain the greatest good and the greatest happiness.

The Ideal Working Day

But we must be more than careful lest in our beneficent efforts to reduce fatigue we reduce generally the number of working hours below what long experience has proved to be reasonably workable and profitable to all concerned. There are good reasons for believing that, on the whole, an eight-hour working day is, under present conditions, little short of the ideal, if in work that is exceptionally strenuous,

or that is carried out under exceptionally fatiguing conditions, due to heat, noise, or fumes, etc., shorter hours be
arranged.

But we must be careful not to imperil the economic
position by allowing the pendulum of fatigue relief to
swing too far the other way. Rather should we supplement the shortening of hours by vigorously attacking the
problem of building up the physique and vital powers of
our workers, to enable them to bear the burden and face
the problems of the near future, as the nation's economic
recovery from the devastating effects of the war will
depend upon the fullest use being made of its human
resources.

It may be explained that the labouring power of man
is represented by three quantities—the effort, the velocity,
and the number of units of time during which the work is
performed ; and that the most satisfactory attempt to
represent by a formula the law governing variations in
these quantities was made by Maschek,[1] one consequence
of this formula being that the best time of working per
day is one-third part of a day, or eight hours.

This equi-trimetrical division of the day, giving eight
hours for work, eight hours for sleep, and eight hours for
recreation, etc., appears to be little short of an ideal
standard for the average worker under present economic
conditions; and it makes possible a three-shift or a two-
shift system of working, with the considerable economic
advantages due to them ; but we may well hope that with
a general adoption of shorter hours, with improved methods
of working, and with unrestricted output, the time will
not be far distant when still further reductions in the
working-hours will be possible, until the six-hour day is
reached—with all its beneficial advantages—that has been
so powerfully advocated by Lord Leverhulme as an ideal.

[1] See article on " Some Aspects of Industrial Fatigue," by the author,
in *Cassier's Engineering Monthly*, October, 1917.

CHAPTER VI

Wastage of Life, Limb, and Health, and its Economic Effect

INTRODUCTION

DAY by day a sad, serious wastage of life occurs due to accidents on our railways and trains, in our workshops and factories, on our roads and streets, and in our mines. And now we are daily unhappily suffering from a shocking wastage of the best manhood of the country through the terrible War ; as under the voluntary system (which prevailed during the first year or two of the War) war will always call to arms a very large proportion of the more courageous, the more patriotic, the more virile and the simply brave—men of mind and character equally strong and brave.

In dealing with the wastage of life, the large percentage of infants who do not survive their first year must impress everyone as being deplorable and a serious loss to the State. If we exclude the War casualties, an examination of the causes and details of the wastage of life creates a conviction that a large portion of it is not a little due to negligence and preventable causes, as we shall see. Account should also be taken of the nation's loss due to permanent disablement, and to health impaired due to accidents and unhealthy employment.

INFANT MORTALITY

The Registrar-General of Marriages, Births, and Deaths reported (April, 1915) that " the infant mortality, measured by the proportion of deaths under one year of age registered births, was equal to 128 per 1,000, being 6 per 1,000 above the average in the ten preceding first quarters." It is estimated that almost an equal number die before birth, and that 100,000 babies die every year in the United Kingdom.

Surely something can be done in the direction of educating young mothers to enable them to more successfully tide the weakly over the first year of life, and in so doing to keep down this alarming mortality. It would be a noble work, although from the standpoint of eugenics its value would be perhaps somewhat doubtful.

The possibility of a low mortality is established; indeed, according to the *Times* (Benjamin Broadbent), for ten years together the infantile mortality rate was zero in the small French commune of Villiers le Duc. Yet in Great Britain apparently 175,000 children die of weakness and disease every year.[1] Much of this shocking waste of child life could be prevented without a doubt, as the following table, which shows the death-rate of infants amongst different classes of parents, should go to prove :

INFANT DEATHS OF EVERY 1,000 BIRTHS

Children of Doctors	-	- 39	Children of Artisans	-	-	113
„ Solicitors	-	- 41	„ Labourers (a)		-	97
„ Army Officers		- 44	„ „ (b)		-	152
„ Middle Classes		- 61	„ Miners	-	-	160

The Report of the Medical Officer for Islington (October, 1915) brings out strongly the alarming want of necessary knowledge to enable mothers to rear their children : "About 20 per cent. of the babies who died were under a week old, and 33 per cent. had not attained their first month."

[1] The economic value of each baby to the State has been estimated by Dr. E. S. Chesson to be £100. So if this be a fair estimate the annual loss to the State due to the death of 175,000 young children would amount to over £17,500,000.

Surrey's Defective Children

(Dr. Brind, *Westminster Gazette, July*, 1917)

" The ' damaged ' rate among Surrey school-children, according to Dr. Brind (medical officer of health), is : 10 per cent. below standard of nutrition on entering schools ; 70 per cent. with defective teeth, 16 per cent. suffering from tonsilitis or similar disease ; 5 per cent. with defective lungs. There was scarcely one case in which some organ or other of the body was not ' damaged.' "

Looking to the future, we should see the need of young and vigorous men of our breed to make good the ravages of war and to sustain a great imperial destiny. The child is as valuable in peace as in war, and if he is to be vigorous he must be properly looked after in the earliest years.

Death-Dealing Clothing

There is yearly a lamentable loss of young life due to mothers clothing their little ones in such highly-ignitible material as *flannelette*. Recently, at an inquest on a child burnt to death through this dangerous fabric, a coroner remarked that " flannelette was clothing children in gunpowder, and should be prohibited."

Child-Labour Exploitation

There is good reason to believe that not a little injury is done to a great many of our young people by overworking them at an age when there is a large call upon their vital energy to support their growth and development. Some very bad cases have come to light lately. For instance, in July, 1915, the Chairman of the Kingston Borough Education Committee, in dealing with the report of the school medical officer, which stated that several children were suffering from having to work before going to school, mentioned two very bad cases at Bonner Hill Road School : one of a boy nine years of age, who worked from 6 to 7 a.m. on seven days each week, half an hour in the middle of six days, and from 8.30 a.m. till 1.30 p.m. on Sundays, or a total of fifteen hours each week, and received the princely sum of 2s. The other case, he said, was even worse. A little boy, aged seven and a half years, worked from 6 a.m. till 8 a.m. on six days, and from 9.30 a.m. till 11 a.m. on Sundays, or a total of thirteen and a half hours a week, and received sixpence. Surely such cases represent a very unpatriotic form of exploitation.

WASTE OF LIFE DUE TO CONTAMINATED MILK SPREADING DISEASE

There is good evidence that the average milk sold in London contains an alarming amount of bacteria, and that it is a means of spreading tuberculosis, scarlet fever diphtheria, and other diseases, and that the dirt which it contains causes diseases of the intestinal tracts of infants, and is largely responsible for the shocking amount of infant mortality.

According to an article which appeared in the *Observer* of October 24, 1915, an average sample of London milk contains about the same number of bacteria to the cubic centimetre (a teaspoonful) as the sewage as it is received at the City of Birmingham Corporation sewage farm. Sewage usually contains about 5,000,000 bacteria per cubic centimetre, whilst samples of milk recently purchased in the West End contained as many as 28,000,000, the dirtiest sample found on the same day in Bethnal Green containing 3,200,000 per cubic centimetre.

" In all the large cities in the United States clean milk can be obtained—containing less than 10,000 bacteria per cubic centimetre. In England milk of this quality is practically unobtainable, in spite of the assurances of dairymen that their product is *pure*. In the city of Richmond, Virginia, to take an actual example approximately 40 per cent. of the entire supply during 1912 and 1913 contained less than 10,000, and 76 per cent. contained less than 50,000 bacteria per cubic centimetre. One result of our dirty supply is death and disease that could be prevented.

" There is no care of milk ; it just takes care of itself from the time it leaves the manure-begrimed hands of the milker, on its way to the railway station, by the train, dragged through the Metropolitan streets to the milk depôts, then in the milk-carts to the large private houses and the smaller milk-shops, and finally to the consumer, who fetches it in person and who has as much knowledge of how to keep the filthy stuff as she has of taming a lion. The sanitary authorities do all they can to prevent adulteration, and for that they possess full powers, but they have no power to compel clean collection and clean transit."

Briefly, " The contamination of milk occurs in four places—

" 1. On the farms where it is produced.
" 2. In transit from these farms to the towns.
" 3. In the dairies of the towns to which it is transported, and during distribution.
" 4. In the houses of consumers."

Bearing in mind the above revelations, surely the time has arrived when the nation must be roused to the necessity of improving our milk.

" This can only be done by teaching the consumer, the producer, the distributor, the medical practitioner, and the sanitary authority the importance of more hygienic supply and the means of creating the necessary improvements."

Apparently the greatest amount of contamination occurs on the farms where milk is produced, but there is good evidence to show that clean milk can be produced in old cow-stables *provided the milking is done in covered milking-pails which have been sterilised and by men who are trained to milk in a clean manner.*

Fortunately, the National Clean Milk Society,[1] of 2, Soho Square, W. 1, is determined to improve the hygienic value of our milk supply, but it needs members who wish to bring about this reform. This admirable society is opening a Clean Milk Department for the North Islington Maternity Centre, and the *Observer* of October 31, 1915, gave an account of the simple but effective expedients that are being employed at the farm that is to supply the clean milk, the general adoption of which would place our milk supply beyond reproach, and greatly reduce the shocking wastage of infantile life.

In April, 1916, in a case at the Carnarvon Borough Court, a farmer was summoned for selling a quantity of milk which contained 21·3 grains of sediment per gallon, of which three-fourths was cow-dung.

MILK WASTAGE DUE TO SOURING

It is estimated by the Committee on the Production and Distribution of Milk, in their second interim Report, issued on December 28, 1917, that of the 90,000,000 gallons of milk supplied annually to London, 2 per cent. is lost in the summer through souring in transit and keeping, and 1 per cent. in winter. Assuming an average loss of 1½ per cent., this means that there is an annual loss of about 1,350,000 gallons, which at 2s. per gallon amounts to £135,000. The Committee recommend that the milk should be chilled soon after milking at depôts conveniently situated for the producers, with good railway communications to cities, and that the Government should establish as soon as possible such depôts, where milk could be collected, chilled, and despatched in such quantities and at such times as might be required ; and where the surplus could be made into cheese and butter.

[1] Annual subscription for membership, one guinea.

WASTE OF LIFE IN FACTORIES AND WORKSHOPS

The Annual Report [1] of the Chief Inspector of Factories and Workshops is a very human document. It shows that the State is doing a great work, through its highly efficient inspectorate, in endeavouring to protect its industrials from many of the dangers that surround them in their daily work ; dangers that may be due to unprotected machinery, the presence of dust (particularly of that due to the grinding of metals), faulty ventilation, extremes of temperature, excessive humidity, dirty and badly kept premises, faulty lighting, want of cleanliness in sanitary conveniences, gas explosions, the presence of fumes in brass foundries and lead-smelting shops, long hours of employment in unhealthy trades, and overcrowding of workrooms, etc.

The inspector's duties are extremely onerous, for, in addition to giving attention to these matters, he has to see that the Education Act is not evaded by young workers and employers, and also to see that proper messrooms and suitable wash-basins are provided where lead is used or polishing done, so that meals may be handled free from contact with poisonous matter. He (or she) has also sympathetically to lend an ear to complaints that may be made by workers, and to generally see that the Factory Act is obeyed in the proper spirit.

Strangely enough, he does not always in his paternal efforts get the assistance from the workers themselves that he has a right to expect. The psychology of these workers is not easily understood, and many of them are apt to resent anything that may appear to in any way interfere with the full liberty of the subject, or anything suggestive of coddling, and it is to be feared that not a little of the vast wastage of life and limb is due to this strange attitude.

[1] Cd. 7491, 1914 ; price 1s. 7d.

There are nearly 300,000 works under inspection, and some 425,000 effective visits of inspection were made in 1913, and nearly 200,000 cautionary notices were issued, prosecutions being instituted in 3,872 instances. The reported fatal accidents numbered 1,309, and the non-fatal 178,161. These numbers are large, in fact, much larger than they would be if individual workers were more careful, even when we consider the very large number employed in works, etc., which the latest completed returns (for 1907) give as 5,127,109.

KILLED AND INJURED BY TRAINS AND RAILWAY VEHICLES

In 1913 there were 1,090 persons killed by the movement of trains and railway vehicles (exclusive of train accidents), and 8,183 injured. In the general report to the Board of Trade these accidents are dealt with under three headings, as follows :

		Killed.	Injured.
(a)	Passengers.	110	2,224
(b)	Railway servants	414	5,608
(c)	Other persons	566	351
	Totals	1,090	8,183

(a) PASSENGERS.—Although the number of passengers killed and injured is large, when referred to the number of journeys the accidents are not so striking. Thus, in 1913 one passenger was killed in every 13,200,000 journeys, and one injured in every 653,000 journeys. The Report [1] says that many of these accidents are due to want of care on the part of the passengers themselves. The number of killed through any one cause was 29, due to falling out of carriages during the running of trains, and the largest number of injured was 840, due to falling on to the platform when alighting from trains. In *train* accidents in 1913, one passenger was killed in every 44,000,000 journeys,

[1] Cd. 7595, price 2½d.

and one injured in every 2,300,000, which shows how small is the risk run when travelling on our railways.

(b) RAILWAY SERVANTS.—An examination of the causes of accidents to *railway servants* brings out the fact that the largest number killed through any one cause is 71, while working on the permanent way, sidings, etc., the number of injured being 89. This work is proverbially most hazardous, the approach of a train often being unheard, due to the noise of a passing train on another line of rails, or some such cause. It is not easy to suggest a remedy for this serious waste of life, except increasing the number of look-outs, as in most cases the traffic cannot be stopped whilst the repairs are being executed.

Braking, spragging, and chocking wheels during shunting operations accounts for the largest number of non-fatal accidents, the number injured being 700, but the number killed only 16. One of the most dangerous operations is the coupling and uncoupling of vehicles during shunting operations, which accounted for 16 deaths, and 684 injured. A great deal of ingenuity has from time to time been displayed in inventing so-called safety coupling appliances, but the men do not readily take to the use of these, and often their familiarity with the danger leads them to become venturesome or even negligent, with pitiable results.

The following classification of these accidents is interesting, and will speak for itself :

ACCIDENTS IN COUPLING AND UNCOUPLING RAILWAY VEHICLES IN 1913

	Killed.	Injured.
Coupling or uncoupling with pole	3	345
,, ,, ,, without pole	5	71
,, ,, ,, screw-coupled vehicles	6	261
Adjusting the automatic coupling	—	1
Coupling or uncoupling with chopper couplings ..	2	3
,, ,, ,, with pin and link couplings	—	3
Total	16	684

(c) OTHER PERSONS.—The accidents that occurred to

persons under this heading in the United Kingdom in 1913 were as follows:

		Killed.	Injured.
1.	While passing over railways at level crossings ..	64	46
2.	While trespassing on line	250	111
3.	Suicides and attempted suicides	208	21
4.	Persons on business at stations and sidings and other persons not included above	44	173
	Total of other persons	566	351

It will be seen by the above that the dangerous level-crossings caused the death of 64 persons—a serious wastage of life, that could be much reduced by the construction of footbridges at all crossings where there is much traffic. Trespassing is not so easily dealt with, but the large number of 250 killed whilst breaking the bye-law of the companies against it should lead to a sharper look-out being made.

Train Accidents

The casualties due to these accidents were made up as follows:

	Killed.	Injured.
Passengers	33	723
Railway servants	8	145
Other persons	—	3
Total	41	871

Thus we see, as might be expected, that the passengers, owing to their larger numbers, suffered most; but even so the risk is very slight, for, as we have seen, in 1913 only one in every 44,000,000 journeys was killed, and one in every 2,300,000 injured. The risk is really less than these figures indicate, since they take no account of the journeys of season-ticket holders.

Accidents due to Long Hours and Fatigue

From time to time when a railway accident, a crane accident or the like occurs, it is frequently shown that the primary cause was injurious fatigue of a worker. Indeed, in order to be on the safe side, and to avoid as much as possible such accidents, public safety calls for careful and scientific regulation of working hours so that no worker is unduly fatigued.

An analysis of the dock accidents in East London revealed the fact that—

" considerably more than 25 per cent.[1] occurred between 11 a.m. and 12 noon, and 3 p.m. and 4 p.m. ; or between the fourth and fifth hour, and eighth and ninth hours of work. It is suggested that this indicates the need of extra vigilance during those periods, but these are the hours before dinner and before stopping work, and it is not unreasonable to draw the conclusion that the higher incidence of accidents may be the result of fatigue."

Mr. McNair (Liverpool) has also made some inquiries on the subject of fatigue, and deals with accidents due to excessive spells of work as follows :

" There are the usual number of accidents which are partly due to fatigue, the result of men working too many hours at a stretch. In one fatal case a ' fall-man ' who had been employed for 23½ hours accepted a signal intended for another man and worked his fall, with the result that the load attached pushed another man into the hatchway. If this ' fall-man ' had been wide awake he could hardly have made this mistake, as the load was in view. In 81 cases noted, this practice of working long hours has, no doubt, been a contributory cause."

That the safety of the travelling public is imperilled by the long hours worked by railway signalmen, and by engine-drivers and others, the inquiries made from time to time by the inspecting officers of railways appear to show ; for 24 of the 37 railway accidents causing fatalities during the year 1913 were due to so-called negligence,[2]

[1] " Report of the Chief Inspector of Factories," 1914, p. 44.
[2] " General Report to Board of Trade on Railway Accidents," 1914, p. 15.

want of care, or mistakes of officers or servants, and of these 12 signalmen and 12 drivers were found to be in fault.

WASTE DUE TO INJURIOUS FATIGUE

The economic waste due to injurious fatigue is probably much greater than the waste from serious illness, as the number of fatigued persons is great, although the amount of incapacitation from fatigue is relatively small ; but the slight impairment of efficiency due to over-fatigue may lead to serious illness and breakdown in some cases. The whole question of industrial fatigue has received a great deal of attention during the past few years, more particularly since the outbreak of war compelled us to increase the hours of labour of our workers with the object of securing maximum output. Many official Reports bearing upon the general subject of fatigue have been published, notably the " Second Interim Report on an Investigation of Industrial Fatigue by Physiological Methods," by Professor Stanley Kent.[1] Another important Report is the Memorandum (No. 7), issued by the " Health of Munition Workers Committee," entitled " Industrial Fatigue and its Causes " ;[2] and the second Interim Report on " The Question of Fatigue from the Economic Standpoint," published by the British Association, September, 1916, should also be studied by those interested in the subject.

The question of fatigue is also happily receiving earnest attention in America, where one hundred highly qualified men have been for some two or three years considering the matter of national and individual health.

The author has dealt with some aspects of the fatigue question in the previous chapter, and also elsewhere, from the standpoint of maximum output ;[3] but it may be

[1] Cd. 8335, price 1s. 6d. (Wyman & Sons.)
[2] Cd. 8213, price 1½d. (Wyman & Sons.)
[3] A series of articles on " Industrial Fatigue in its Relation to Maximum Output " which appeared in the journal *Co-Partnership*, and is now available in pamphlet form at 6, Bloomsbury Square, London, W.C. Price 6d.

suggested that further researches should be made with the object of determining the most economic intervals of daily rest in the various industries to secure the greatest output with the least fatigue. But of course, in a general way, the remedy for fatigue is rest. " So necessary is rest," says Dr. Winslow Hall, " that it always should out-dure our proper toil, and the best worker is commonly the man who can most thoroughly rest."

DEADLY GAS TRAIN-LIGHTING

Train accidents under the most favourable circumstances are terrible affairs, but the use of gas as an illuminant for railway carriages, even when automatic shut-off valves are used in connection with the gas-cylinders, represents an additional danger that the travelling public have a right to be free from. It is little short of a scandal that not much more than a fifth of the chief railway companies light their vehicles by electricity. Railway companies should also be compelled by law to construct their vehicles of non-inflammable materials.

ACCIDENTS CAUSED BY VEHICLES ON STREETS AND ROADS

In the year 1915 there were 3,014 persons killed by road vehicles in Great Britain and Ireland, and 60,189 injured. There can be little doubt that a large proportion of this waste of valuable life was due to reckless and careless driving. Vehicles are driven with little regard for the rights and safety of pedestrians, particularly by certain types of motorists, who expect people to hop out of their way, and who often recklessly turn off from a main street into a side street, regardless of people who may be walking across that street. On the other hand, pedestrians are apt to be too venturesome in crossing roads, particularly when they are in a greasy condition and crowded with traffic ; or they may lose their heads when crossing and step back into the path of a vehicle. Leaving a bus or tram on the offside to cross the road and being caught by a vehicle coming in the opposite direction is a fruitful cause of accidents. And then we have deafness and abstraction as contributory causes of street accidents.

INSANE RULE OF THE PAVEMENT. DANGER OF KEEPING TO THE RIGHT INSTEAD OF TO THE LEFT

In 1916 nearly three times the number of fatal accidents occurred to pedestrians who stepped off the footways from their near side, with their back to the oncoming traffic, as compared with those which resulted from leaving the offside facing the oncoming traffic. This shows the folly of the present rule of the pavement, and the wicked waste of life due to it. The rule should be reversed forthwith.

ACCIDENTS CAUSED BY VEHICLES ON STREETS AND ROADS IN 1914 AND 1915 COMPARED

	1914.		1915.	
	Fatal.	Non-Fatal.	Fatal.	Non-Fatal.
England and Wales	1,991	53,481	2,564	54,222
Scotland	229	4,145	285	4,235
Ireland	110	1,714	165	1,732
Totals	2,330	59,340	3,014	60,189

ACCIDENTS IN MINES

The loss of life and limb underground is very great; during the last fifteen years 20,000 men were killed in the mines of Great Britain, and 2,500,000 men seriously injured. It is to be feared that there will always be wastage of life in underground working, as not a little of it is due to negligence; but science and improved methods

should do much in the time to come to keep down the
appalling waste of valuable lives.

WASTE DUE TO DISEASES PRODUCED BY IMPURITIES IN AIR

The effect which is produced on the respiratory organs
by substances inhaled into the lungs has long been known
as a potent cause of respiratory diseases, and acute
pneumonia and especially chronic non-tubercular phthisis [1]
(consumption) are produced. The suspended matter in
the air which may produce these affections may be mineral,
vegetable, or animal, but it would seem that the severity of
the effects is chiefly dependent on the amount of dust, and
on the physical conditions, as roughness, angularity or
smoothness of the particles, and not so much on the nature
of the substances, except in some special cases. A large
number of trades are unhealthy chiefly from this cause.
This is the case, in fact, with miners of all kinds. So,
without attempting to give a complete list of unhealthy
trades, the following may be mentioned : Dustmen,
corn-millers, teamen, maltsters, coffee-roasters, paper-
makers, snuff-makers, flock-dressers, feather-dressers,
shoddy-grinders, dressers of hair, dressers of coloured
leather, dressers of hemp, workers in flax, masons, wire-
grinders, some workers in wood, colliers, grinders and
polishers of metals, file-cutters, makers of firearms,
button-makers, china-scourers, and wool and silk spinners.
The makers of grindstones, and the workers in some kinds
of glassware-making and sandpaper-making also suffer.

Also in some trades, or under special circumstances, the
fumes of metals or particles of metallic compounds pass

---

[1] This term, we are told, although applicable to several forms of
wasting disease, is commonly used to designate a malady having for its
chief manifestation progressive emaciation of the body and loss of strength,
occurring in connection with morbid changes in the lungs and in other
organs.

into the air of the shop. This is particularly the case in brass-founding and lead-smelting, and through such causes coppersmiths, plumbers, tin-plate workers, etc., are affected; workers in mercury are subject to mercurialismus, and house-painters swallow much lead from want of cleanliness of the hands in taking food.

Air is also injuriously vitiated by other trades; thus there is hydrochloric acid gas from alkali works, sulphur dioxide and sulphuric acid from copper works, carbon dioxide, carbon monoxide and hydrogen sulphide from brickfields and cement works, carbon monoxide from iron furnaces, hydrogen sulphide from several chemical works, especially ammonia, phosphoric fumes from the manufacture of matches, carbon disulphite from some india-rubber works, and organic vapours from glue-refiners, bone-burners, slaughter-houses, and knackeries.

Thus it will be seen in what a wide range of our industries conditions exist favourable to the destruction of life, for the effect of dust or fume-laden air in the causation of disease is known to represent an appalling amount of suffering and a lamentable waste of life. An example of this wastage came to light in the Press on January 14, 1916, when it was reported that a Mr. Smith, in giving evidence before the Miners Federation at White-hall, stated that " the average age to which men lived who worked in the ganister mines was about forty years, as phthisis was very prevalent among them." In all such cases " prevention is better than cure," and statistics prove that in mines that are well ventilated the workers do not appear to suffer from an excess of pulmonary disease, or do so in a slight degree only. In fact, the importance of perfect ventilation in all industrial operations should be insisted on by the authorities and by the workers themselves, and more general attention should be given by all concerned to the study of industrial science.

Every precaution practicable should be taken to prevent the dust from any operation mingling with the air ; wet grinding should always be adopted when practicable, and mechanically ventilated wheel-boxes and linen covers for the work should be used more generally. The wearing of masks and coverings for the mouth, and such simple contrivances, if more generally adopted would do much to conserve life and reduce human sufferings, but, most important of all expedients, there should be a more general adoption of *localised exhaust ventilation*.

Factory and mining inspectors have done and are doing a great work in seeing that the Government regulations relating to hygiene are efficiently carried out, but there is good reason to believe that they do not get the assistance they should from the workers themselves, who in too many cases are ignorant of the protection they can legally claim.

Loss of Sight through Dangerous Toys

Through the carelessness of parents and laxity of the law, serious accidents are constantly occurring due to children being allowed to play with pop-guns and air-guns. The author knows of a case in which a beautiful young girl lost the sight of an eye through a child firing at her with a pop-gun.

On January 11, 1916, two cases were reported in the Press of persons being shot in the eye by air-guns. Mr. Bros, the Clerkenwell magistrate, was told the requirement of the police permit was that the barrel should not be more than nine inches in length. Mr. Bros pertinertly remarked : " I should be very much obliged if you will report these cases to the Commissioner with a view to getting the Home Office to alter the requirements. You may make use of this gun (produced in the first case) for any purpose you like. Test the spring and see how far it will carry, and give the Commissioner some idea of the mischief of these guns."

The insersate folly of allowing such so-called toys to be used is beyond comprehension. A further case may be cited from the *Observer*, Februaiy 6, 1916 :

" A girl of thirteen, Violet Williams, Holyport Road, Fulham, has lost the sight of an eye as the result of a shot, such as is used with an air-gun, being discharged at her by some person unknown as she was playing in Lillie Road."

SUMMARY OF REPORTED ACCIDENTS (1913) IN THE UNITED KINGDOM

	Fatal.	Non-Fatal.
Accidents in factories and workshops	1,309	178,161
Accidents caused by vehicles on streets and roads	2,099	42,544
Accidents caused by the movement of trains and railway vehicles, exclusive of train accidents	1,090	8,183
Accidents on railway premises	7	694
Train accidents	41	871
Total, exclusive of war casualties and accidents in mines	4,546	230,453

THE NATION'S ECONOMIC LOSS DUE TO ACCIDENTS

It is not easy to arrive at even a iough estimate of the economic loss to the nation due to the above wastage of human life (as we have attempted to do in the following article in dealing with war casualties) without knowing the sex and full particulars of the ages of the killed and injured ; but obviously the wastage is very great indeed.

ECONOMIC WASTE DUE TO WAR CASUALTIES

The appalling loss of life that the great War is causing is a matter of grave concern to the nation. Apart from the consideration that we are losing the pick of our splendid young manhood, whose divine heroism is the glory of our Empire, the loss tells on the nation, from an economic point of view, in three different ways.

In the first place, there is the loss of each man valued,

as a machine. Now each one, from the time of his birth till the time he is able to earn his own livelihood, is a source of expense : he consumes food and clothing, has to be housed, educated, trained, and otherwise attended to; all this being so much expenditure of capital. His rearing must be viewed as an enterprise on the part of his parents ; and that there will be a return for the outlay when the youth is capable of exerting himself is a reasonable expectation. In estimating such outlay, we may confine ourselves merely to the subject of expense, leaving out of the question parental hopes and anxieties, and, therefore, viewing each human being as a machine which has been perfected at so much cost.

In the case of our officers, most of these could not have cost their parents less than £800 each to feed, clothe, and educate up to the productive age (there are few officers of our regular army who have not caused an outlay of three or four times this amount). So, assuming this sum to represent the average outlay, we have for each 10,000 who have perished a total outlay of £8,000,000. And if we assume that on an average each private soldier cost his parents first and last £400, we have for every 100,000 who may perish a total outlay of £40,000,000.

In the second place, there is the loss caused by the abstraction of these able-bodied men from pursuits profitable to the nation. And as every man in a healthy state earns more than he consumes, this abstraction is something more than temporary inconvenience. The overplus is more or less, according to circumstances ; sometimes the increase belongs to the employer, sometimes it remains the property of the worker ; but be it one or the other, this increase cumulatively forms the national wealth.[1] So that

---

[1] We were spending in normal times about £2,000,000,000 a year in the ordinary way, merely for our living, and as we earned some 10 to 15 per cent. more than we consumed, the annual surplus, representing our savings and investments, amounted to from £200,000,000 to £300,000,000.

each man who perishes, or is made incapable of doing useful work, represents an annual loss. Put in another way, he is valuable to the State as a machine to the extent, it has been estimated, of the capital sum of £1,200. So the loss to the State would amount to £120,000,000 for each 100,000 men killed or totally incapacitated. To which must be added the £40,000,000, giving a total loss of £160,000,000 [1] per 100,000 men.

In the third place, the nation sustains a constant loss by the limitation of workers in the labour market. The abstraction of, say, 100,000 men either causes much more work to remain undone that ought to have been done, or it throws an undue amount of work into the hands of those who remain, thereby increasing the wages of all kinds of ordinary labour. For it should be obvious that if three men are left to do the work which should properly be done by four, they will in one way or another secure the wages of four, while they do the work of three only.

But this advantage enjoyed by the workers who remain is unsound and transient, as in the commonwealth all help each other, and the united savings of the nation form a fund out of which each has a chance of getting his share ; and the wealth that has for centuries been accumulating in this country is a stock out of which wages are paid and competencies realised.

WASTAGE DUE TO INEFFICIENT LIGHTING
" Let there be Light."

There is accumulating evidence that inadequate lighting in and about our factories is a contributory cause of accidents ; and insufficient lighting is known to be a cause

---

[1] Thus, should the total fatalities and permanently incapacitated of all the forces engaged amount to 12,000,000 by the time the war is ended, the countries concerned will be poorer by the staggering sum of some £19,200,000,000, due to the loss of life and incapacitation alone.

of eye-strain and headache, and in various ways to be prejudicial to health. But to many, a more convincing argument in favour of efficient lighting is that it improves the quality and quantity of the work turned out, at the same time making it easier to supervise the work and to keep the premises in a hygienic condition.

Now, having regard to its importance, the question might well be asked, What is efficient lighting? It certainly does not necessarily mean the brightest lighting, for that may be a light almost as inefficient as the mean, dismal, wasteful systems that are to be found in many of our industrial works, and in the class-rooms of many schools; but a good starting-point is the axiom which guides the managers of our most scientifically organised works and establishments, and that is, *the best light is the cheapest*.

Briefly, lighting should either be uniformly diffused, or be focussed on the work. The former is usually required for large areas of work, the latter for small ones. A perfect example of the latter is to be seen in a ready-made clothing factory in Walsall, where the electric light is so arranged as to throw an inch square light on the needle of each machine. The eyesight of the worker is saved and the waste of light is avoided. The conviction is growing that good lighting pays the manufacturer. Indeed, two large ship-building firms in Glasgow have entirely remodelled their lighting at considerable cost both for inside and outside work.

The variables involved as to what lighting is most desirable are many, which in most cases make the solution of the problem not a little difficult. In these matters no one is better qualified to speak with authority than the author's friend, Major Frank B. Gilbreth, who may be briefly quoted.

The Essentials of Efficient Lighting

Major Gilbreth says :[1]

" The subject of lighting has, indirectly as well as directly, a great influence upon the output and motions, as upon the comfort of the eyes depends, to a large extent, the comfort of the whole body. The arrangement of lighting in the average office, factory, or house is generally determined by putting in the least light necessary in order that the one who determines the location of the light may be able to see perfectly. This is wrong. The best light is cheapest. By that is not meant that which gives the brightest light ; in fact, the light itself is but a small part of the question. Go into any factory and examine every light, and you will notice that as a rule they are obviously wrong. A light to be right must pass five tests—

" 1. It must furnish the user sufficient light so that he can see.

" 2. It must be so placed that it does not cause the user's eyes to change the size of the diaphragm when ordinarily using the light.

" 3. It must be steady.

" 4. There shall not be any polished surfaces in its vicinity that will reflect an unnecessary bright spot anywhere that can be seen by the eyes of the worker.

" 5. It must be protected so that it does not shine in the eyes of some other worker.

" The use of polished brass and nickel should be abandoned wherever it will shine in the worker's eyes. For work done on a flat surface, like the work of a bookkeeper or a reader, the light should be placed where the glare will reflect least in the worker's eyes ; where the work is like the examining of single threads, the relative colour and figured pattern of the background, as well as good light, is important. This is obvious ; so is nearly everything else in good management. Go into the buildings among the

---

[1] " Motion Study," p. 50. (Constable & Co., London.)

workers, the students, [1] and the scientists and see how rarely
it is considered. All of this is not a question of getting the
most out of the light. Light in a factory is the cheapest
thing there is. It is wholly a question of fatigue of the
worker. The best lighting conditions will reduce the
percentage of time required for rest for overcoming fatigue.
The difference between the cost of the best lighting and
the poorest is nothing compared with the saving in money
due to decreased time for rest period due to less fatigued
eyes. . . .

" The sub-variables involved make the problem as to
exactly what lighting is most desirable difficult of solution.
The proper solution will have such a beneficial effect, not
only upon the man's work, but also upon his welfare, that
no time or effort expended upon it can be too great."

Major Gilbreth's admirable call for efficient lighting,
and his statement of the tests that good lighting must pass,
should be carefully considered. In all lighting matters
public opinion badly needs educating, for go wherever we
may—in the streets, in public buildings, in domestic
business and industrial establishments, and particularly in
most country houses—we rarely find anything approaching
efficient lighting. It is true that a few years ago, when the
use of electric light and incandescent gas became general,
the advance from the state of things represented by the
poisonous and flaring gas-jets, or the dismal glimmer of a
few candles, appeared to us as the perfection of lighting ;
but since those days the lighting question has received not
a little attention. Indeed, some years ago, a Society of
Illuminating Engineers was formed, which has since done
very good work in the cause. And we have the Home
Office Departmental Committee's Report on Lighting, [2]

---

[1] The author, on recently visiting the classes of a large Municipal Junior
Evening Institute, was much impressed by the inadequacy of the lighting,
particularly in the rooms devoted to drawing. Owing to the feebleness
of the lighting generally, an atmosphere dismal, inefficient, depressing and
unattractive was created, the very antithesis of what should prevail to
attract the young people.

[2] Cd. 8000, price 11d. (Wyman & Sons.)

published in September, 1915, that deals with defective lighting in factories and workshops and its injurious effects, and suggests minimum standards of lighting. The Health of Munition Workers Committee's Memorandum, [1] No. 9, also deals with the question of lighting factories, etc. It is safe to assume that these official publications will do much to help those who have lighting problems to solve, difficult as some of these are, but it is doubtful whether we shall see any great general improvement until the workers, and other users of artificial light, know what really good efficient lighting is and stands for, and energise until they get it.

[1] Cd. 8215, price 1½d. (Wyman & Sons.)

CHAPTER VII

The Food Question in relation to Waste

So much public attention has been given to this question since the outbreak of war, and so much useful work in the cause of food economy has been done by the authorities and by some of the municipalities, that only the salient features of the subject need be dealt with.

THE CRIME OF WASTEFULNESS

In normal times the amount of food wasted in London alone is notoriously enough to feed all the starving poor of the capital, and it should be brought home to people living in the midst of plenty, even more forcibly than it is at the present time, that the large amount of avoidable waste which is so often permitted in their households should be ruthlessly checked ; but not to these fortunate ones alone should we appeal, as many poor but ill-managed households are extraordinarily wasteful.

Waste of bread even now, it is to be feared, is occurring, but since we have rightly been called upon to ration ourselves, there has been a noticeable diminution in the amount of this objectionable waste. Formerly, even in poor neighbourhoods, one used to see crusts thrown into the gutter, and half-loaves were frequently to be found among the refuse in the dustbins of the well-to-do. There is something peculiarly repugnant at any time in the waste of the staff of life, quite apart from its actual value and present shortage.

Unfortunately, most domestic servants have no idea of economising, and when requested to save food are often openly contemptuous, or they give notice, or they go on wasting. Indeed, they have been heard to make remarks to the effect that they like a bit of waste, and the mistress is far too saving.

EDUCATION IN HOUSEHOLD MANAGEMENT

It has been said that " usually the greatest waste goes on in the houses of the very rich and in the homes of the very poor." The latter are generally excellent buyers, but indifferent caterers and worse cooks. It is admitted that the middle-class woman is generally a careful caterer and a good buyer ; what she has to learn just now is to effect economies, not only in buying less food but by buying economical substitutes for foodstuffs that have increased in price.

In recent years classes in cookery and household management have become increasingly popular, but until such subjects are included in the curricula of all our schools for girls, and are regarded as of primary importance, the nation will not be in a healthy condition. But the folly of using expensive gas cooking-stoves, utensils, and materials in giving cookery lessons to children of the poor (which is a common practice), instead of employing cottage fires and things, is so obvious that the wonder is that it is allowed.

As to the elimination of waste, it is largely a matter of education ; indeed, in all our schools the true spirit of economy and the wickedness of waste, even in its minutest forms, should be instilled into the souls of our young people.

MOBILISING THE HOME

One of the most beneficial effects of the necessity to economise owing to the War is the change that has come

H

over many households. The number of servants has been cut down (generally with the result of increasing the efficiency of those remaining), the mistress of the house taking in hand some of the duties that were previously carried out in a wasteful and inefficient way. Household books have been overhauled, and the quantities of butter, eggs, sugar, tea, soap, bread, etc., etc., used in the establishment have changed the suspicion that too much money was being spent on these things to the certainty that they were being used in a wasteful and extravagant way. In many homes these discoveries have led to shopping by telephone being abandoned, and to the mistress doing her own shopping, paying cash for everything but bread and milk.

An examination of the linen cupboard has perhaps revealed an amount of neglect on the part of the housemaid that was appalling, banks of unmended linen being buried and put out of sight, whilst, on inquiries being made, such things as napkins have been traced on their downward career from the table to the dustbin, qualifying for the latter by rough usage as dusters. Such discoveries invariably lead to the mistress herself taking charge of the linen and seeing that the proverbial stitch in time keeps the contents of her cupboard in usable order. These domestic activities involve a certain amount of labour, but to the true woman they soon become a labour of love, and bring into her life a new pleasure, creating in her a worthy pride in keeping her house in order, and preventing all forms of household waste.

Waste of Food in Camps

This subject has been, and is being, very fully discussed in the Press, and now that the attention of the authorities has been called to the scandalous waste going on in all parts of the country where the requirements of the troops have to be met, doubtless it will be still further reduced. But it must be admitted that the first consideration is the provision of an ample supply of food for our patriotic troops ; further, having regard to their enormous and varying numbers, and to the way in which these numbers have rapidly increased, and to unavoidable causes, the great difficulties in getting the distributing machinery into working order were bound to lead to a certain amount of waste for a time : but a continuance of such waste would be nothing short of criminal negligence.

The Folly of Overfeeding

At the present time, when so many of our habits are being reviewed and corrected, some people are asking themselves whether they are too indulgent where food is concerned. They should know that a famous doctor once said that more people in this country suffered in health from over-feeding than from under-feeding. Other people are curious to know whether, after all, the foodstuffs they favour are the best for them and the most economical. And not only the question of what changes in our food can be economically made, but the regulation of our mealtimes is receiving attention.

On this point Dr. Winslow Hall, M.D.,[1] is of opinion that—

" three meals a day are sufficient ; and between each there ought to be an interval of five hours, in order that due rest may be given the stomach. The common dread of an empty stomach is nought but a bogey raised by greediness. Food while in the stomach is, properly speaking, outside the body ; it is even detrimental, in that it is drawing down nerve energy for digestive purposes as long as it is there ; not until food has been digested and has been passed into the blood and tissues does it become available for work. Anyone who tests this statement will find that

[1] " The Needs of Man," a book of Suggestions.

his best work is done on an empty stomach, and that, should a meal be lacking, the dreaded gastric crave is but a fleeting incident which leaves him as efficient as before."

It is possible for all to economise in food without loss of strength and health if they will " Fletcherise "—that is, perfectly masticate their food. More work can be done on less food providing it is perfectly masticated, and, what is of much more importance, better health is certain to follow.

CHEESE, PORRIDGE, AND POTATOES

Few articles of diet are more wholesome than bread and cheese, the latter having a high food value, about equal to that of beef, weight for weight. In recent years porridge as a wholesome breakfast-dish has become very fashionable. But among the poor classes of South Briton it is strange that the oatmeal of the Scottish peasantry— the national food—is looked upon with so much prejudice, and those who live upon it with so much pity. But the health and strength of the Scottish peasantry are proverbial, and an effort on the part of our food reformers to popularise porridge and to demonstrate to our poor how appetising it can be made for occasional meals might do the State a good turn, since oatmeal contains not only starch, but much nitrogen and a fair amount of fat, although not quite sufficient for the purpose ; but this deficiency is usually in Scotland supplied by adding milk, or a little bacon, to the diet.

According to Mr. Stephens,[1] the quantity of oatmeal that used to be allowed to the ploughman—as his sole food —was two pecks, or $17\frac{1}{2}$ lbs. in a week, exactly $2\frac{1}{2}$ lbs. a day, and he remarks : " I believe that no class of men can endure more bodily fatigue for ten hours every day than

[1] " Book of the Farm," etc., vol. ii., p. 384.

these ploughmen of Scotland who subsist on this *brose* thrice a day."

It has often been suggested that not a little of the intemperance met with is due to the unsatisfactory meals provided for our workers in their homes. Meats and fish bought ready cooked (which are unsatisfying and leave a craving for stimulants), too often appear on their tables instead of appetising home-made wholesome dishes of stew, cottage-pie, etc. Much remains to be done by our educational authorities in these matters.

The Irish peasant thrives on a diet of potatoes, but he requires some 10 or 11 lbs. daily. Potatoes contain chiefly starch (of which he therefore consumes a superfluous quantity), very little nitrogen, and scarcely any fat; hence he obtains, when he can, some butter-milk or bacon or a herring to supply the deficiency.

Vast quantities of potatoes are apparently used in Germany. A considerable portion is dried in factories and used as food for both men and cattle, the dried stock being largely used for making bread during the War. Indeed, the potato crop is the foundation on which Germany has rested its food policy throughout the War. According to official figures, the ordinary requirements are 13 to 14 millions of tons for human food, 20 millions for fodder, and 6 to 7 millions for seed; also very large quantities are used for making alcohol.

VEGETARIAN DIET

A diet that is largely vegetarian has much to recommend it, and there can be little doubt that vegetable foodstuffs would be more popular if they had been advocated with greater moderation : as it is, some of our most worthy and distinguished food reformers are too often regarded as cranks and extremists, but we may reasonably hope that their splendid pioneer work will soon be appreciated. The

Daily Graphic (May 22, 1915) very opportunely published Dr. T. R. Allinson's valuable views on vegetarian foodstuffs. He said :

" To keep a meat-eater takes from 20 to 30 acres ; but on grain food anything from 10 to 20 persons per acre can be kept. If, therefore, the people diminish their consumption of meat, and increase their consumption of fruit and vegetables, our country can support a great many more inhabitants. I anticipate that lots of people now will eat meat only once or twice a week. They will eat more vegetable foods, like Yorkshire pudding, Norfolk dumplings, macaroni, cheese, vegetable stew, pease pudding : and more wholesome bread, breakfast oats, rice, semolina, hominy, etc. Weight for weight, one pound of grain food is equal to about four pounds of fresh meat. Split peas, haricot beans, and lentils are flesh-forming. If you want a mixture of fat and lean beans, mix Soya (the Japanese) beans, which contain a lot of oil, with haricot beans. As to expense, you can live from 2d. a day upwards. An old friend of mine at the age of sixty lived for several months on 1s. a week, and remained a vegetarian to the day of his death at eighty-five."

On the other hand, it has been said that a vegetarian diet is good for one generation, but bad for the next.

Eating to Live, or Living to Eat

Another authority, Professor James Long (formerly of the Royal Agricultural College), has also given his views [1] on the food question with the object of showing how better nourishment with improved health can be obtained for less cost ; and as they have an important bearing on waste they may be quoted. He says :

" Are we in Britain eating to live, or are we living to eat, in this calamitous time ? Are we striving for economy's sake and the nation's, or are we simply pleasing our

[1] The *Weekly Dispatch*, May 23, 1915.

palates ? Let us be honest and have done with our folly
and waste.

" We are feeding our cattle, our horses, and sheep more
sensibly than we are feeding ourselves. There is no branch
of the work in the kitchen in which food is not wasted or
spoiled. Let us eat less and be fitter to work for our
country, and let us study the real needs of the body and
abandon all luxuries, all foods which we do not require,
selecting those only which are sent for our good."

BEST DIET FOR SEDENTARY WORKERS

It is not easy to convince meat-eaters who lead a more
or less sedentary life that they may injure their health
through partaking of a diet largely consisting of meats
which could be consumed with impunity by growing
youths, but all authorities are agreed on the point. Thus,
according to Dr. J. A. Paris, M.D., F.R.S.—[1]

" Persons of sedentary habits are oppressed, and
ultimately become diseased, from the excess of nutriment
which a full diet of animal food will occasion. Such a condition is best corrected by acescent [2] vegetables.

" It is well known that artisans and labourers, in the
confined manufactories of large towns, suffer prodigiously
in their health whenever a failure occurs in the crops of
common fruits." . . . " Growing youths generally thrive
upon a generous diet of animal food ; the excess of nutri-
tious matter is consumed in the development of the body,
and, if properly digested, imparts strength without deple-
tion. Adults and old persons comparatively require but
a small proportion of aliment, unless the nutritive movement be accelerated by violent exercise and hard labour.
In our climate a diet of animal food cannot, with safety,
be exclusively employed. It is too highly stimulant ; the
springs of life are urged on too fast, and disease necessarily
follows."

[1] " A Treatise on Diet," p. 132. A standard work, fifth edition, 1837,
by Sherwood.
[2] Slightly sour.

A Change of Diet should be made Slowly

Further, the following from the pen of Sir Henry Thompson, F.R.C.S.,[1] will give additional confidence and guidance to those who contemplate revising their dietary.

" The meat-eater's digestion is taxed with far less quantity of solid, but that very concentration in regard to quality entails on some stomachs an expenditure of force in digestion equal to that required by the vegetable-eater to assimilate his much larger portions. And it must be admitted, as a fact beyond question, that some persons are stronger and more healthy who live chiefly or altogether on vegetables, while there are many others for whom a proportion of animal food appears to be desirable, if not necessary. In studying this matter, individual habit must be taken into account. An animal feeder may by slow degrees become a vegetarian, without loss of weight or strength, not without feeling any inconvenience in the process ; but a sudden change in diet in this direction is for a time almost equivalent to starvation. The digestive organs require a considerable period to accommodate themselves to the performance of work different from that to which they have been long accustomed, and in some constitutions might fail altogether in the attempt."

Goats' Milk for Cottagers

It is well known that many cottagers in the country experience a good deal of difficulty and find it no easy matter to secure a proper supply of milk, a foodstuff that is so necessary, particularly where there are young children. Cottagers often have far to go for milk, and they can, as a rule, ill afford to get a sufficient supply, whereas if a goat were kept it would materially reduce, if not entirely eliminate, the family milk bill. Goats are proverbially easy to feed, and among the household waste there is usually sufficient greenstuff and other odds and ends to sustain a goat in excellent condition.

[1] " Food and Feeding," p. 12. (Gilbert & Piper.)

HOUSEHOLD STOCKPOT

In every frugal household proper use is made of the stockpot, but it is a notorious fact that the poor of this country have not been trained in the little household economies which are so well understood and practised on the continent ; where in the humblest homes a stockpot is usually to be found for the reception of trimmings of meat, bones, rinds and bones of bacon, scraps of raw vegetables, and potato parings,[1] etc., and such-like odds and ends, including even the water in which vegetables have been boiled, to obtain most nourishing and appetising soup. Too often these useful fragments are considered to be refuse, and are wasted. Very little heat is required to keep the contents of the pot simmering.

The pot may be of earthenware for small households, but a well tinned one fitted with a tap, to allow the stock to be drawn off without admixture with the grease floating on the top, is to be preferred.

HAY-BOX OVEN COOKERY

The principle of the Thermo-flask is well understood : the contents of the bottle are kept hot or cold, as the vacuum of the jacket prevents heat passing into or out of the flask ; in other words, the flask has a non-conducting jacket ; and on similar lines the contents of a saucepan or kettle when brought to the boil can be kept hot for hours away from the fire if surrounded by suitable non-conducting material. A convenient and inexpensive arrangement to give effect to this economy and convenience is the hay-box oven which has come into use. A suitable box can be bought at the grocer's for about twopence, and a lining of felt or flannel, or sacking and newspaper, tacked

---

[1] The potatoes should first be brushed and rinsed thoroughly, then pared, the parings being washed before turning them into the stockpot.

on to its inner surfaces and lid; then a bunch of fresh, clean hay to form a nest completes the apparatus. Its use is easily understood; thus, a saucepan of potatoes after a few minutes' boiling on the fire is rapidly placed in a hollow made in the hay, then hay is spread over the saucepan, the lid of the box is put on, and held down by a weight or strap; then, after about twenty minutes, the potatoes are cooked, whilst the fire has been free for other uses, or, in the case of a gas stove, the gas has been economised. Apparently, in the case of meat, the time the saucepan should be left in the hay-box is about three times the number of minutes it is left stewing or boiling over the fire.[1] Thus after a little experimenting a woman may prepare her dinner before engaging in other household work, or going out to work, and find it hot and ready some hours later. Dried peas, beans, and porridge, etc., may be boiled and put in the box overnight and be ready for use in the morning.

Economy in Food

A most excellent pamphlet on the economy of food, and some suggestions for simple and nourishing meals for the home, has been published by the Board of Education,

---

[1] From information published by the National Food Fund, dishes, as a rule, take twice as long as if cooked in the ordinary way, but are not spoilt if left longer.

It is possible to cook more than one dish at a time, but on no account must the box be opened until the food which requires the most cooking is ready. All meat dishes require a good start.

A calculation should be made as to the length of time they would take in the ordinary way; they should then be cooked for half that time on the gas or fire, and finished in the box. After a little experience many things can be left on the gas one-third or even less than the time required in the ordinary way.

The following are some of the things which may be cooked in the hay-box—

Boiled Chicken.—Half the usual time on the fire, three hours in the box.
Stew.—Prepare in the usual way, stew gently for forty-five minutes on the gas or fire, leave in the box for three or four hours.
Boiled Beef.—Half the usual time on the gas or fire, and in the box as long as possible.
Potatoes.—Put into cold water, boil one minute. Leave in the box for two or two and a half hours.

price One Penny. Its title is "Economy in Food" (Circular 917). It gives notes on some specially nourishing forms of food, by the use of which a large reduction may be made in the quantity of meat usually eaten. A wealth of valuable information is given, which if intelligently used would greatly increase the variety of meals, reduce their cost, and eliminate the elements of waste which at present represent a great national loss.

THE NATION'S FOOD BILL

In pre-war times we were importing food to the extent of some £325,000,000 per annum, and the nation's food bill cannot fall far short of £1,000,000,000 per annum. At every turn we are now being wisely told that it is a patriotic duty to economise, particularly in food and things that are imported; and there is strong evidence to prove that the universal adoption of some of the commendable economies practised in German households, as a matter of course, would save the nation tens of millions a year, and set free cargo space in merchant vessels. But where are our national organisers and practical educationists? We badly need a few domestic economists such as Frau Heyl, who is energetically assisting the German Government in dealing with the food question and in preaching the gospel of the prevention of waste.

CHAPTER VIII

Waste due to Adulteration

THE notorious adulteration of foodstuffs and beverages which continues in our midst can only be regarded as a scandal. It is popularly supposed that we are protected against adulteration of our foodstuffs, beverages, and drugs by inspection under the Food and Drugs Acts, but many of those who have given attention to the matter believe that through one cause or another the Acts are practically, to a large extent, a dead letter. In not a small proportion of the detected frauds the Laws or Bye-Laws are apparently not strong enough to be of service, or some loophole exists by means of which the guilty escape punishment. Be this as it may, it is quite certain that something more must be done by the authorities ere long to protect the health and pockets of the people. It would be a great boon if standards for all articles of food could be laid down by competent authorities ; so much progress has been made in food analysis that no difficulty exists to prevent this.

FRAUDS WHICH COST THE PEOPLE MILLIONS A YEAR

The economic aspect of the matter should not be overlooked, as the loss due to adulteration in the aggregate must be very great ; but assuming it to amount to an average of only fourpence per head of the population per week, it would represent the huge sum of over £21,000,000 per annum. But loss due to injury to health cannot possibly be estimated.

The scope of the Acts should be extended, if necessary, so as to include in searching inspection, followed by convictions where frauds are detected, oils, malt liquors, wines, spirits, mineral waters, tobacco, etc., snuff, seeds, drugs, patent medicines, textile fabrics, etc., etc.

For some years the trashy, worthless character of many of the expensive patent and proprietary medicines, etc., sold has been exposed in a work entitled " Secret Remedies," a perusal of which makes one wonder why such cruel, heartless frauds are allowed to continue.

ADULTERANTS AND INJURIOUS PRESERVATIVES IN USE

Such deleterious ingredients as opium, copperas, strychnine, Indian hemp, darnel seed, tobacco, extracts of logwood, alum, and salts of zinc and lead are used to adulterate intoxicating liquors, whilst poisonous and anti-digestive drugs that are forbidden by medical men on account of their action on the heart and for other reasons are used as adulterants pure and simple, or as antiseptic preservatives. Boracic acid,[1] salicylic acid,[2] bisulphite of lime, formaldehyde, sodium benzoate and sodium carbonate, for instance, are extensively used in many sorts of food, notably meat, fish, ham, bacon, poultry, butter, milk and cream, etc., and it is believed that it is quite possible for a consumer to take large doses of these dangerous and deleterious substances in a single day. In this way the nation's health suffers, and the people are defrauded ; whilst, so far as foodstuffs are concerned, there appears to be no good reason why the above deleterious antiseptics and others should be used, as few possess any advantage

---

[1] Various preparations of boracic acid, such as glacialin salt and boroglycerin, are used. Boracic acid is a powerful inodorous and tasteless preservative, but in repeated small doses it is said to exercise a specific influence on the excretory organs which must be detrimental to health.

[2] Salicylic acid communicates an unpleasant taste to the substances treated, and there are physiological objections to its use. It has been extensively tried as a food preserver, more especially for milk.

whatever over common salt, which is certain in its action, cheap, abundant, and, within limits, harmless.

DETECTED FRAUDS

The following include some of the frauds compiled by the Pure Food Society (inaugurated about the year 1908), and published in the *Daily Graphic* in June, 1914 :

"**White pepper.**—Husks of black pepper bleached.

Raspberry jam.—Apple pulp and husks. Apple pulp makes the jelly clear-looking, but it costs £8 a ton in place of the £30 a ton charged for raspberries.

Jams.—Most cheap varieties consist mainly of apple, no matter what they are labelled.

Cocoa.—Three parts sago and cream.

Flour.—Plaster of Paris.

Gorgonzola cheese.—Artificial rinds composed of barytes and tallow.

Lard.—Addition of paraffin wax.

Tea.—Exhausted and re-dried leaves and other leaves mixed.

Brandy.—' Plain ' alcohol obtained by chemical processes, usually German potato spirit.

Chocolate.—Foreign fats and starches.

Preserved green vegetables.—Sulphate of copper to give an artificial green colour.

Vinegar.—Coloured solution of wood acid.

Mustard.—Wheat flour and turmeric.

Olive oil.—Sunflower oil is largely sold as olive oil.

Oxtail soup, bottled, has been found to consist of bean-flour and sago.

Lemon-juice and non-alcoholic drinks.—Salicylic acid."

FURTHER FRAUDS

The list might well be continued, as almost everything we consume and use is apt to be tampered with by the fraudulent, to our great loss in health and wealth ; but the following should be included :

Bread is chiefly adulterated with alum or sulphate of copper, for the purpose of whitening it and of giving solidity to the gluten of damaged or inferior flour ; or with chalk or carbonate of soda to correct the acidity of such flour ; or with boiled rice or potatoes to enable the bread to carry more water, and thus produce a larger number of loaves per sack of flour, to the extent of about 5 per cent. ; but the presence of more than 47 per cent. of water would itself cause the analyst to suspect the presence of one or both of these foreign starches. A good loaf should be neither crumby nor sodden, and neither sour nor mouldy. It should keep well, and be easily restored to sweetness by heating it in a closed vessel. The only adulterant of bread which is not practicable in the case of flour is the addition of an excessive quantity of water ; but as the possible adulterants of flour are legion a much stricter inspection is called for.

The way in which bread is delivered to us at our doors requires attention, as it is not pleasant to think of the unwashed basket, the dirty-fingered boy, and the dusty coat of the baker's man.

Butter is adulterated by mixing with it inferior fats, and with water, salt, and farina. Most of these impurities are seen when a sample of butter is melted in a glass, and allowed to stand in a warm place for a few hours, when the pure fat will float as a transparent oil, while the water, salt, farina, etc., will subside to the bottom of the glass. Occasionally, also, too much casein, or curd, is left, which is one cause of butter becoming rapidly rancid ; and this leads to the use of additional salt to prevent rancidity—in fact, to so much as to hide the flavour of the butter. Ordinary fresh butter generally contains as much as from 12 to 13 per cent. of water, and sometimes a little salt and a trace of curd.

One of the favourite butter tricks is to take a pat of

fresh butter, scoop out the inside, fill it with a large lump of margarine, and pat it together again.

Champagne of the cheap kind is produced from rhubarb stalks, gooseberries, and sugar, the product being largely consumed at balls, races, etc. The manufacture of wine from sugar and the refuse husk, etc., of the grape has been largely practised, and a great part of the wines of France and Germany has ceased to be the juice of the grape.

Tea.—Leaves of the willow, sloe, oak, plane, beech, elm, poplar, hawthorn, and chestnut are said to be mixed with or substituted in this country. Sand and magnetic oxide are added by the Chinese.

Coffee is adulterated by roasted peas, beans, or other grains, potatoes, sugar, and chicory. Chicory is itself adulterated with roasted barley and wheat grain, acorns, mangold wurzel, sawdust, and beans and peas.

Flour, Oatmeal, Arrowroot, etc.—Bad flour makes a ropy-looking gluten, which is very difficult of manipulation, and it is of a dirty brown colour when baked. Oatmeal is adulterated with barley meal, and arrowroot with inferior starches.

Baking Powder containing arsenic is responsible for many summonses.

Isinglass is often adulterated with gelatine, the fraud being ingeniously contrived so as to retain to a large extent the well-known character of the genuine article. Immersed in cold water, the shreds of genuine isinglass become white and opaque like cotton threads, and they swell in all directions, whereas those of gelatine become transparent and ribbon-like.

Milk, the support of life for our infant population, is commonly adulterated by the addition of water ; and it is known by the appearance of the milk, the specific gravity of it, the quantity of cream which rises, and the chemical composition of the milk. The usual adulteration is accomplished in one of the three following methods, namely, by the addition of water in quantities varying from about 20 to 50 per cent. ; the skimming of the whole milk and its subsequent sale as new milk ; the addition of skim milk to new milk and the sale of the whole as new milk. Good milk has a rich appearance, and a full, pleasant taste. Its specific gravity ranges from 1,029 to 1,032 (water being 1,000), the average being 1,030. The addition of water tends to lower the gravity of the milk, but in many cases it is not easily detected. In genuine milk the total solids, that is, the casein, the milk-sugar and fat, form at least 12 per cent. of its weight, the remaining 88 per cent. being water. In very rich country milk these solid matters may range as high as 14·8 per cent.

The use of preservatives also demands attention, as it represents a danger. A new preservative, sold under the name " Mystin," for preserving milk and cream, has been advertised as possessing the advantage that its presence cannot be detected by analysis ; but formaldehyde and sodium nitrate have been detected in milk to which " Mystin " has been added, and its amount estimated by appropriate methods, although the substance is prepared in such a way as to prevent detection of this preservative by the tests ordinarily applied.[1] The danger of using any preparation containing a comparatively large amount of sodium nitrate is universally recognised.

Among other preservatives for milk, cream, and margarine that are sold are formalin [2] and " Accoine," found to contain sodium benzoate and sodium carbonate.

A health inspector recently stated that some of the milk sampled is practically coloured water.

[1] " Reports to the Local Government Board on Public Health " (New Series, No. 60), 1912.
[2] On Sept. 1st, 1917, a milkman at Newport was fined £10 for selling milk to which this powerful anti-digestive drug had been added.

I

114   WASTE DUE TO ADULTERATION

Mustard is generally so acrid and powerful in its flavour that it is commonly diluted with flour, or other farinaceous matter, turmeric being added to improve its appearance. The mixture is detected by means of the microscope, when the granules of starch and the colouring matter of turmeric are easily seen.

Spices, such as pepper, ginger, cinnamon, curry powder, cayenne, etc., are more or less the subjects of fraudulent adulteration, which can be readily detected by the microscope.

Potted Shrimps has the addition of boric acid as a preservative, which is condemned.

Artificial Vinegar.—Artificial vinegars as a class are inferior in taste and flavour to vinegars which are solely the products of alcoholic and acetous fermentation of the saccharine liquors usually employed for the purpose, and in ordinary circumstances the nature of these artificial vinegars can be ascertained by chemical examinations.

We are told in the Report of the inspector of foods for 1908 that

"Sulphuric acid is sometimes still added to vinegar. Although, many years ago, when vinegar was taxed, the addition of sulphuric acid was permitted by excise regulations on the ground of its having a preservative action, there is at the present day no need for the use of sulphuric acid as a preservative; since it is cheap and, as far as sourness is concerned, an effective substitute for acetic acid, its presence in any vinegar must be regarded as an adulteration."

Clearly the interests of the consumer should be protected in these matters, and vinegar which has been prepared by colouring and flavouring a solution of acetic acid should not be represented and marketed as merely "vinegar" or as "malt vinegar," but should be sold under some suitable designation which should make the nature of the product apparent; otherwise the sale of such artificial products should be considered fraudulent.

APPLICATION OF FORMALDEHYDE TO FOODSTUFFS

For some years the use of formaldehyde, and solutions of formalin or preparations containing formaldehyde, have been in use for spraying and fumigating such food-stuffs as meat, poultry, cheese, bacon, eggs, milk, etc., with the object of arresting decay or concealing incipient decomposition and to hide any smell of staleness or putre-faction; but it should be generally known that formalde-hyde and its preparations have injurious effects in foods and drinks, and the use of such disinfectants and preserva-tives should be made a serious and punishable offence. Indeed, we are told in the Local Government Board's Foods Report, No. 9, 1909, that

" formaldehyde is a very powerful disinfectant; it may retard digestion even when present in food in compara-tively large dilution; and it readily combines with the protein constituents of foods, forming a compound which is less digestible than the original substance.

" These objections to formaldehyde were considered by the Departmental Committee on Preservatives and Colour-ing Matters in Foods, 1901, which recommended that the use of formaldehyde or its preparations in foods or drinks be absolutely prohibited."

ADULTERATED MATERIALS

A large number of materials, etc., bought by the public are tampered with and adulterated with the object of gaining an illicit profit, to the serious loss of the purchasers. The following are typical examples :

Leather is frequently adulterated with glucose, soluble salts and barytes, whilst treated tripe and compressed

paper are known to be used as poor and fraudulent substitutes for leather.

Rubber Adulteration.—Rubber is often much adulterated with *surrogates* consisting of the products of the
action of sulphur and sulphur chlorides on rape and cotton-
seed oils. These surrogates are gelatinous substances
nearly devoid of mechanical strength, and are simply
diluents of the rubber with which they are mixed. Common
rubber articles made by moulding (called mechanicals)
are also largely prepared from old vulcanised rubber re-
worked. Typical of this class of goods we have goloshes
or indiarubber overshoes so extensively used in America.

Worn-out tyres find their way to the reclaimers' yards
to be manufactured into *reclaimed rubber* goods. Pneu-
matic tyres contain on an average as much as 50 per cent.
of canvas, etc. In the fiscal year ending June, 1914,
America imported from Europe 20,000,000 lbs. of scrap
rubber for reclaiming, but there are now some four large
reclaiming works in England equipped with up-to-date
plant. It is estimated that about 50,000 tons of reclaimed
rubber are annually produced throughout the world.

Weighted Black Silks.—Writing in the *Moniteur
Scientifique*, **M. J.** Persoz shows that weighting—
which began with the modest aim of making up the loss
sustained in ungumming—is now carried to the extent of
100, 200, and 300 per cent. This increase of weight is
produced by treatment with salts of iron and astringents,
salts of tin and cyanides. The bulk is augmented proportionately to the weight. What is sold as silk is a mere
agglomeration of various matters devoid of cohesion, held
temporarily together by a small portion of silk. The
elasticity and tenacity of the fibre are reduced, and from
being one of the most permanent of organic bodies, and
sparingly combustible, it becomes fragile, and burns like
tinder.

CHAPTER IX

Some Important Aspects of the Coal Question

COAL, THE BASIS OF BRITAIN'S GREATNESS

IT is a melancholy and disturbing fact that so few people have correct views as to the basis of Britain's greatness, a basis without which our moral and intellectual capabilities could never make or maintain us as the great factor in international affairs, and the centre of gravity of the world's greatest empire. But economists know that our country's great preponderance is based upon our manufacturing and commercial greatness, and that the secret of this greatness and of our rise to wealth is our precious and magnificent store of coal. For coal is at once the source of heat and of mechanical power ; indeed, it is the material source of the energy of the country, and the chief agent in almost every improvement and discovery in the applied arts. It provides heat for household purposes, and heat and power for our countless industries, our railways, mercantile marine, and Royal Navy ; and our electric plants and gasworks depend upon a free and cheap supply of this wonderful mineral.

Coal is the raw material for our gas industry, which provides residual products for the manufacture of dyes, disinfectants, high explosives, oils, and drugs, etc., etc., whilst by exporting coal we at once provide ideal cargoes of sufficient weight and volume to assist in balancing our cumbersome imports ; thus relieving ships of the necessity of making outward trips in ballast, and thereby performing an economic service of inestimable value in profitably working our vessels both outwards and inwards. The coal produced for these various purposes reaches a colossal amount each year, and year by year we make larger draughts upon a commodity which is almost the sole necessary basis of our material power ; a fuel that can never be replaced, as the phase of the earth's existence suitable for the extensive formation of coal passed away for ever millions of years ago. But the grave fact to be faced is that the ever-increasing consumption of this miraculous mineral will lead to the exhaustion of our main wealth and of what has become the first necessary of life in this country. Attention has often been called to this fact ; indeed, a great many years ago, when the question did not cry out so loudly for consideration as it does now, the eminent geologists, Messrs. Conybeare and Phillips, wrote the following warning :[1]

" The manufacturing industry of this island, colossal as is the fabric which it has raised, rests principally on no other base than our fortunate position with regard to the rocks of the coal series. Should our coal-mines ever be exhausted it would melt away at once, and it need not be said that the effect produced on private and domestic comfort would be equally fatal with the diminution of public wealth ; we should lose many of the advantages of our high civilisation, and much of our cultivated grounds must be again shaded with forests to afford fuel to a remnant of our present population. That there is a progressive tendency to approach this limit is certain : but ages may yet pass before it is felt very sensibly, and when it does approach the increasing difficulty and expense of working the mines of coal will operate, by successive and gradual checks against its consumption, through a long period, so that the transition may not be very violent. Our manufacturers would first feel the shock ; the excess

[1] " Outlines of Geology."

of population supported by them would cease to be called
into existence as the demand for their labour ceased;
the cultivation of poor lands would become less profitable
and their conversion into forests more so."

THE RESOURCES OF OUR COALFIELDS AND OUR RATE OF CONSUMPTION

In estimating the ultimate resources of our coalfields
we have to pay attention to the difficulties of working at
great depths. The chief obstacles to deep working are
high temperature and cost. There is no uniform rate of
increase of the earth's temperature with increase of depth;
it varies under different circumstances and in different
localities according to the inclination and conductivity
of the strata, the presence of water, etc. The information
which is now available points to a gradient of one degree
rise in temperature for an increase in depth of rather less
than 64 feet; further, in this country the temperature of the earth is constant at a depth of 50 feet, and at
that depth the temperature is 50° F. Now, there appears
to be no difficulty in working at a temperature of some
90° F. or more, provided the air is dry and the ventilation
is brisk, so, using the above figures, we arrive at a working
depth of 2,930 feet, some 430 feet deeper than our present
deepest mine, for a temperature of 95°.

Although hitherto no special appliances have apparently been tried or required in order to cool the workings
in deep mines, it is believed that there will be no insuperable
difficulty in working at an additional few hundred feet
below this level; indeed, the Royal Commission on Coal
Supplies (1904) fixed upon 4,000 feet as the limiting depth
of practical working, and upon one foot as the minimum
workable thickness of a seam of coal. The Commissioners
estimated in 1904, after most careful investigations, and
the necessary deductions, the available quantity of

coal in the proved coalfields of the United Kingdom to
be 100,914,668,167 tons.

In addition to this coal within 4,000 feet of the surface,
there are in the proved coalfields considerable quantities
lying at greater depths, and they estimated the amount
of this coal to be 5,239,433,980 tons. Of course, whether
this coal at greater depths or any of it is recoverable or
not depends upon the maximum depth at which it may be
found possible to carry on mining operations in the time
to come. In addition to the proved coalfields we have a
large amount of coal in the concealed and unproved coalfields, at depths of less than 4,000 feet, and these were estimated by the Geological Committee appointed by the Royal
Commission to aggregate 39,483,000,000 tons. Also,
we have further unproved coalfields in the undersea area
lying between five and twelve miles beyond high-water
mark in the Cumberland coalfield, estimated by Lord
Merthyr to contain 383,000,000 tons.

Bringing the above figures into line, we had in 1904,
according to the highest authorities, the following estimated
stores of coal in the United Kingdom [1] in tons of 2,240
lbs. :

	Tons.
In proved coalfields at depths not exceeding 4,000 ft. ...	100,914,668,167
In unproved ,, ,, ,, ,, ,, ,, ,,	39,483,000,000
In ,, undersea coalfields at depths not exceeding 4,000 ft.	383,000,000
Estimated total at depths not exceeding 4,000 ft. ...	140,780,668,167
Estimated quantity in proved coalfields at depths below 4,000 ft.	5,239,433,980
Total quantity, proved and unproved, at all depths	146,020,102,147

Now our output of coal for 1913 (the year before the
War) amounted to 287,430,473 tons. So let us assume

---

[1] It is estimated that the world's total coal reserves in all the known
coalfields amount to over 7,000,000 millions of metric tons. And that
if the wholly unknown coalfields be included the total exceeds 9,000,000
millions of tons.

that our industrial and commercial activities are to stagnate (which is unthinkable, as it would mean the beginning of the end of our prosperity) and the output of our collieries to remain practically unchanged, then it will be seen that, with an average annual production equal to that of 1913, our store of coal in proved and unproved fields at depths down to 4,000 feet would be exhausted in about 485 years. And even if it were found to be possible to mine the coal remaining at the lower depths, it would only last another eighteen years at the same rate of output before it was completely exhausted.

But the actual case is a great deal more unfavourable than this ; as in the past, with occasional fluctuations, the output has tended to increase in a geometrical progression when measured over suitable periods. The average rate of increase per cent. per annum has fluctuated somewhat considerably, for reasons well known to engineers. Thus the highest[1] was apparently for the period 1865-74, when it reached 3·9, and the lowest for the period 1885-94, when it amounted to 1·76. But the rate of increase during the past thirty or forty years apparently averages about 2 per cent. per annum, which at first sight does not appear to be a serious increase ; but we are confronted with the appalling fact that an annual increase of 2·2 per cent. per annum would give a production trebled in fifty years, representing a vast shrinkage in the nation's main capital.

To get a grasp of the economic effect of this prodigal expenditure of a vital substance which can never be replaced, we cannot do better than quote from Jevons' classic work, " The Coal Question,"[2] in which the rate of 2 per cent., or, rather, of $21\frac{1}{2}$ per cent. in ten years, the equivalent of 1·975 per cent. per annum, is discussed.

Take, as starting-point, the figure of 145,000,000 tons,

[1] " The Coal Question," by W. S. Jevons, p. 280.

[2] *Ibid.*, p. 282.

the average output of the ten years 1875-84, and we obtain
the following :

The average yearly production at the assumed rate of increase (12½ per cent. in 10 years), would be—

For the 10 years ending	1884	145·0	millions of tons.
,, ,, ,,	1894	176·2	,, ,, ,,
,, ,, ,,	1904	214·1	,, ,, ,,
,, ,, ,,	1914	260·1	,, ,, ,,
,, ,, ,,	1924	316·0	,, ,, ,,
,, ,, ,,	1934	383·9	,, ,, ,,
,, ,, ,,	1944	466·5	,, ,, ,,
,, ,, ,,	1954	566·8	,, ,, ,,

The figure 176·2 compares with the actual 172·7 in a
decade including the year 1893, when the output fell some
twenty million tons below the normal. The figure 214·1
compares with the realised 214·3. A century hence, at
this rate, the average annual output would be 1,500 million
tons. The table shows that the attainment of figures of
output, which may be at once declared impossible, does
not depend upon the selection of the rate of $3\frac{1}{2}$ per cent.,[1]
but on the maintenance of a steady geometrical progres-
sion. At 2 per cent. per annum advance, the output of
the half-century ending 1954 would be 19,933 million tons,
and of the succeeding half-century 52,776 million tons,
together 72,709 million tons. With an estimated store of
140,000 million tons in proved and unproved coalfields
at depths down to 4,000 feet it is sufficiently clear that a
rate of progress which would exhaust more than half of
this store in a century cannot be long maintained.

It may be readily admitted that the period of the
introduction of the steamship, and such improvements of
the steam-engine as permitted its ever-widening application
in industry, was a period when an unusual rate of increase

---

[1] Jevons, in considering the two years 1854 and 1861 of maxima
rate of increase, giving an average of 3·7 per cent., found that a comparison
of the years 1854 and 1864 would give almost exactly the same result.
He then proceeded to make some calculations on the assumption that the
average annual rate of growth of our coal consumption is $3\frac{1}{2}$ per cent., this
being equivalent to a growth in ten years of 41 per cent., or in fifty years
of 458 per cent., or $5\frac{1}{2}$-fold, say.

in coal consumption might be expected. A rate somewhat below that attained at such a period might not signify a cessation of such prosperity as accompanied its high rate. But can any contention of equal force be set forth in reference to the comparison of the future with the present ? Must not the inevitable slackening of the rate of increase [1] of our coal consumption involve either a decrease of national prosperity, or a change in the nature of the industries on the domination of which in our national life that prosperity has been built up ?

The following table, showing the nation's annual output of coal, and its value at the pit, should be instructive.

The Nation's Output of Coal and its Value

According to Whitaker (1918) the output and value of the coal produced in the United Kingdom in the years 1909-15 were as follows :

Year.	Tons.	Value at Pit.
1909	263,800,000	£106,280,000
1910	264,450,000	108,400,000
1911	271,892,000	110,790,000
1912	260,416,000	117,921,000
1913	287,430,473	145,535,669
1914	265,664,393	132,596,853
1915	253,206,081	157,830,670

Showing an increase in output for the period of five years, 1909-13, of nearly 9 per cent.

A good idea of how our enormous annual output of coal is consumed can be formed from the following table.

[1] The late Mr. R. Price-Williams, C.E., in an Appendix included in the " Report of the Royal Commission " (1905), put forward calculations shewing what the coal outputs would be if the average of the variations in the rates of increase and the decrements in those rates experienced during the thirty or forty years preceding 1905 continued to be experienced in the future. And it is interesting to note that these calculations give the output for the year 2001 as 520,000,000 tons.

COAL CONSUMPTION IN THE VARIOUS INDUSTRIES, ETC.

The Royal Commission on Coal Supplies (1904) reported[1] that the following estimate for 1903 may be regarded as approximately correct :

	Tons (2,240 lbs.)
Railways, all purposes	13,000,000
Coasting steamers (bunkers)	2,000,000
Factories	53,000,000
Mines	18,000,000
Iron and steel industries	28,000,000
Other metals and minerals	1,000,000
Brick works, potteries, glass works, and chemical works	5,000,000
Gas works	15,000,000
Domestic [2]	32,000,000
Total home consumption	167,000,000
Exported (coal, coke, and patent fuel) [3]	47,000,000
Foreign-going steamers (bunkers)	16,800,000
Total raised	230,800,000

OUR OUTPUT OF COAL COMPARED WITH THAT OF AMERICA
AND GERMANY

A brief examination of the official records of coal produced in the United Kingdom, the principal British colonies and possessions, and the principal foreign countries, shows that three countries, the United Kingdom, the United States of America, and Germany, stand out in striking contrast to all the others as being far and away the greatest coal producers in the world. And the relative outputs and corresponding rates of increase over the period 1871-1911 convey a lesson which demands the serious attention of our economists and statesmen.

On inspecting the following table the first thing that arrests attention is that in 1871 we produced over 60 per cent. more coal than was produced by our two principal industrial competitors; whilst forty years later, in 1911, our industrial competitors the United States and Germany

---

[1] " General Report," pt. i., p. 11.
[2] About 15 cwt. per inhabitant annually.
[3] Jevons, " The Coal Question," p. 139.

	United Kingdom.	U.S. America.	Germany.
	Tons.	Tons.	Tons.
1871	117,352,000	41,384,000	29,373,000
1881	154,184,000	76,679,000	48,688,000
1891	185,479,000	150,506,000	73,716,000
1901	219,047,000	261,874,000	108,539,000
1911	271,892,000	443,025,000	158,164,000

Sum of the outputs of the United Kingdom, U.S. America,
   and Germany   873,081,000
Output of all the rest of the world   179,799,000
                                                        ——————————
   World's output.............................   1,052,880,000

produced between them nearly $2\frac{1}{4}$ times the amount we
did. Now, in a rough and general way, the consumption
of coal is a measure of industrial progress—a progress
that is only possible with a free supply of good and cheap
coal ; and this brings home to us forcibly that although
we have enjoyed years of ever-increasing prosperity, the
recent rate of the increase of that prosperity cannot be
compared with the giant strides made by our rivals—the
United States, in particular, as it will be seen that her
production of coal in 1911 was over ten times what it was
forty years before. That great country, with practically
an inexhaustible store[1] of good coal and iron, an enormous
amount of which is almost on the surface, is, with her
vigorous and efficient workers, destined, there can be little
doubt, to dominate the industrial world, and to probably
displace English coal from almost every foreign market.

As to our own store of coal, however much the decrement
in the rate of increase of production may vary, we are
confronted with the alarming fact that in a few generations
England will cease to be a coal-producing country on an
extensive scale. Of course long before complete exhaustion
takes place the gradual check to the expansion of our
supply, owing to the increased cost of production (a check

[1] Estimated to be nearly forty times more extensive than ours.

which will be accelerated should the present increase in the
cost of labour continue),[1] will be the first manifestation
of the decline of our coal power and of our greatness and
glory, for British wealth is based primarily upon coal power,
as we have seen.

The Future Decline of Britain.—There is no Substitute for Coal

We are constantly confronted with arguments, often
put forward by unscientific men of great ability, intended
to prove that when our precious store of coal is exhausted
we can make use of some substitute for it. Such suggestions are not tenable, as everyone who takes the trouble
to carefully examine the question is satisfied.[2] Indeed,
the Royal Commission (1903) reported—

" We are convinced that coal is our only reliable source
of power, and that there is no real substitute. There are,
however, some possible sources of power which may slightly
relieve the demand for coal."

In the past, great improvements have been made in
the manufacture of iron and steel that have tremendously
reduced the amount of coal required for their production.
Although it is believed that we cannot hope to effect further
important economies in this direction, there is great scope

[1] In the period 1886-90 the tons of coal produced per annum per person
employed by us were 312, compared with 400 in America. The corresponding figures for the year 1912 were : United Kingdom, 245 ; America, 660 ;
Germany, 269 ; and Australasia, 522. But, as we have explained, a great
deal of coal is mined near the surface in America, whilst we are working
deeper and deeper levels. Further, the average value of coal per ton at
the pit's mouth in the United Kingdom in 1886 was 4s. 10d., against
6s. 4½d. in America, but the corresponding figures for the year 1912 were :
United Kingdom, 9s. 0¾d. ; America, 6s. 1d. These figures speak for
themselves, and should set us thinking.

[2] It is beyond the scope of these pages to discuss this fascinating
question, but it can easily be shown that the tides and the direct radiant
heat from the sun are the only two great sources of natural energy which
man could harness as substitutes for coal, if it were commercially worth
while. Advanced scientists look forward to the time when through new
discoveries the boundless energy stored in the molecules of matter which
exist everywhere may be harnessed for the use and convenience of man.

THE COAL QUESTION

in the more perfect utilisation of the by-products of coal,
and of the waste gases, and waste heat, and still greater
economies due to the bulk supply of electricity from
stations near the coalfields; and it is rather in these
directions that we must work. And we ought to realise
that the time has arrived when we should eliminate every
form of waste, in our manufactories and in our households,
of that material which represents the priceless inheritance
of our descendants; for, as we have seen, the time must
come when they will find it impossible to compete with other
countries enjoying a free supply of cheap fuel; and then
the past period of wasteful extravagance will be rightly
branded the " age of folly."[1] No one better understood
this than Jevons, and the following eloquent but sad
reflection from his famous work, " The Coal Question,"[2]
should be read with interest :

" When our main spring is run down, our fires burnt
out, may we not look for an increasing flame of civilisation
elsewhere ? Ours are not the only stores of fuel. Britain
may contract to her former littleness, and her people be
again distinguished for homely and hardy virtues, for a
clear intellect and a regard for law, rather than for brilliant
accomplishments and indomitable power. But our name
and race, our language, history, and literature, our love of
freedom, and our instincts of self-government will live in
a world-wide sphere. We have already planted the stocks

[1] Ruskin, in his " Seven Lamps of Architecture " (chap. vi), eloquently
says : " The idea of self-denial for the sake of posterity, of practising
economy for the sake of debtors yet unborn, of planting forests that our
descendants may live under their shade, or of raising cities for future
nations to inhabit, never, I suppose, efficiently takes place among publicly
recognised motives of exertion. Yet these are not the less our duties ;
nor is our part fitly sustained upon the earth unless the range of our
intended and deliberate usefulness include, not only the companions, but
the successors, of our pilgrimage. God has lent us the earth for our life ;
it is a great entail. It belongs as much to those who are to come after us,
and whose names are already written in the book of creation, as to us ;
and we have no right, by anything that we do or neglect, to involve them
in unnecessary penalties, or deprive them of benefits which it was in our
power to bequeath."
[2] P. 459.

of multiplying nations in most parts of the earth, and, in spite of some discouraging tendencies, it is not to be doubted that they will prove a noble offspring.

"The alternatives before us are simple. Our Empire and race already comprise one-fifth[1] of the world's population ; and by our plantation of new States, by our guardianship of the seas, by our penetrating commerce, by the example of our just laws and firm constitution, and above all by the dissemination of our new arts, we stimulate the progress of mankind in a degree not to be measured. If we lavishly and boldly push forward in the creation of our riches, both material and intellectual, it is hard to overestimate the pitch of beneficial influence to which we may attain in the present. *But the maintenance of such a position is physically impossible. We have to make the momentous choice between brief but true greatness and longer continued mediocrity.*"

To those capable of thinking in generations and centuries, the certain decline of the industrial and material prosperity of our beloved country must inspire them with feelings of sadness ; but such feelings in turn give rise to the proud reflection that the wane of Britain's power will march with the ever-increasing splendour of the Empire ; for the Dominions beyond the sea (with their mineral wealth, their vast agricultural possibilities and boundless potentialities), fair lands peopled by our race, a sturdy stock with our traditional love of freedom and justice, and with our energy and enterprise, must surely represent all the essential elements for a future of unsurpassed grandeur and greatness.

But we are here more concerned with coal power as the primary source of industrial supremacy, and we happily have in fair Canada, and in Australia in particular, colossal stores of iron and coal of high quality at depths under 4,000 feet. Indeed, it is estimated that in New

---

[1] In 1915 over one-fourth.

South Wales there is a store of 140,000 million tons of
coal, in Queensland 83,000 million tons, and in Victoria
33,000 million tons—a grand total of 256,000 million
tons, in addition to large quantities known to exist in
Western Australia and Tasmania ; so who can tell whether
in the ages to come the centre of power and control of
our glorious empire may not gravitate to the antipodes ?

In the centuries to come, the so-called Yellow Peril
may be something to reckon with ; as apparently there
are in China stores of coal available that are practically
inexhaustible. Indeed, it has been estimated that in
Shansi there are 350,000 million tons, and in Taitsau
630,000 million, a total of 980,000 million tons. This
too, according to many accounts, in addition to other
mineral riches beyond estimation. Such a country peopled
by races whose many sterling qualities are well known
and highly appreciated (for John Chinaman has the reputa-
tion of being a fine fellow) will probably in the time to
come reach a degree of development that will destroy
the world's balance of power as it exists to-day.

WICKED WASTE OF COAL IN THE PAST

The total quantity of coal that has been wasted in
this country will be never known, particularly that which
was wasted before the Royal Commission of 1871 sat,
when so many sources of almost criminal waste were brought
to light. Indeed, the investigations brought out the fact
that vast quantities of coal had been left in the pits by
prodigal modes of mining, coal that is not likely to be
recovered : vacant spaces being left in the gobbing, on
each side of which the refuse was piled up to support the
roof ; and mountains of slack burnt at the pit-mouth ;
but it is only fair to say that in those days the possibility
of utilising this useful fuel was not realised. Even in the

K

present-day practice far too much waste occurs in mining coal, although in the best managed pits there is apparently not much to complain about.

THE INDEFENSIBLE SLIDING-SCALE CONTRACT SYSTEM

which is being worked in the coal trade is a most objectionable one : but fortunately it came under the notice of the " Committee appointed by the Board of Trade to inquire into the causes of the present rise in the retail price of coal sold for domestic use," and the Committee reported that : [1]

" The mechanism by which prices are fixed and the sum paid by the purchaser is divided between the merchant and the colliery owner presents one curious feature peculiar to London. Some of the best kinds of household coal coming from the Midlands (Derbyshire and Nottinghamshire) are largely sold by the collieries to the London merchants on what is known as a sliding-scale contract. A pit-head price is fixed corresponding to a fixed retail price in London ; the colliery owner never gets less than the fixed pit-head price, but when the retail price in London rises above that mentioned in the contract, he receives half the increase. For instance, a contract is made at 10s. 9d. pit-head price corresponding to a retail price of 25s. If the latter falls to 24s. the colliery owner still receives 10s. 9d. per ton ; but he will receive 11s. 3d. if it rises to 26s., 11s. 9d. if it rises to 27s., and so on. The colliery owner has, during the past winter,[2] automatically received 4s. 6d. per ton out of the rise of 9s. from the summer price of coals sold under this kind of contract. It is obvious that this arrangement gives coal owners and merchants a common interest in high prices, while there is no sharing of the loss if prices are low. The merchant is not assisted to reduce prices to the consumer when supplies are abundant by any reduction in the price he

---

[1] Cd. 7866, 1915 ; price 1½d.   [2] 1914-15.

pays to the colliery for his contract-coal. The arrangement has moreover an important effect on the amount
by which London prices must be raised to recoup either
colliery owner or merchant for an increase in his costs.
If they rise 6d. per ton, the consumer must be charged 1s.
per ton extra ; for the party whose costs have risen receives
only half the increased price. Such a system appears to
us indefensible."

Evidence was also given as to how this system is worked
in practice on the London Coal Exchange :

" A few leading firms decide upon increased prices
which, without more ado, become the ' public prices ' of
the day, and are advertised next day in the newspapers.
Sliding-scale contracts are made on the basis that the
price to be paid to the colliery owner varies, not with
the retail price actually received by the merchant to whom
he supplies the coal, but with these ' public prices ' as
advertised. The pit-head price rises 6d. per ton on each
1s. advance of the ' public price ' for all buyers alike,
and does not fall for any buyer until the ' public price '
falls. Thus, without any system of penalties or under-
cutting, the leading merchants in fixing the prices are
secured *pro tanto* against competition by the fact that any
reduction made by an outside competitor in his retail
price gives him no corresponding reduction in the price
which he pays to the colliery owner under the sliding-
scale contract."

In the year 1910 nearly 17,000,000 tons of coal were
consumed in London alone, and probably the quantity
for the twelve months, August, 1914, to July, 1915, will fall
little short of 16,000,000 tons. Now, an examination of
the Committee's Report seems to show that there was an
average rise in price during this period of something over
8s. per ton above the inflated prices of the preceding year,
corresponding to a total increase of £6,400,000 paid by the
coal users of London—a huge sum.

The Committee's Report, already referred to, should

be read by all interested in the great coal question. It is true that it does not carry us as far as many were hoping it would, but the following grave warning with which it practically concludes will doubtless do some good :

"We trust that the measures which we have recommended above will prove practicable and efficacious in reducing the price of coal ; but in the event of prices not shortly returning to a reasonable level, we think that the national interests involved are such as to justify the Government in considering a scheme for assuming control of the output of the collieries of the United Kingdom, with a view to regulating prices and distribution in accordance with national requirements during the continuance of the War."

The Purchase of Coal on a Scientific Basis

Well may it be said that coal is almost as necessary to maintain life as bread, for when this indispensable fuel is fairly cheap the poor can enjoy the warmth in their homes that they need to make life worth living or even possible. With coal at anything like its normal price the industrial life of the nation in all its ramifications can be sustained in a healthy condition ; but the alarming increase in the price of this necessity of life which has taken place since the War broke out is a matter causing grave concern, for since February, 1915, the cheapest coals have been retailed at the ruinous price of 34s. per ton ; and coals are now (December, 1917) being sold in the streets of London at 2s. per cwt., that is, at 40s. a ton. It would be bad enough to have to pay such excessive prices if there was some guarantee that the quality was up to a recognised standard, and that the coal was fairly dry, but, as it is, much of it retailed to the poorest of the poor contains a large amount of rubbish and often about 10 or 12 per cent. of water ; indeed, only the very largest consumers, taking some thousand or more tons a year, can afford to apply efficient tests to make sure that they get value for their money.

Some years ago we heard a great deal about " standard bread," but surely a much stronger case can be made out for some kind of standardisation of coal. But unfortunately the matter is not such an easy one as it may appear at first sight, as the quality of coal varies within such wide limits ; for even coal from the same seam and the same colliery often varies considerably. But surely the buyer should be insured against the delivery of poor and dirty coal. Fortunately, the municipalities are beginning to move in the matter. And, opposed as many are to municipal trading, there can be little doubt that a great weight of public opinion would be in favour of steps being taken to protect the people in this vital matter, and to encourage the municipalities to purchase coal on a basis of analysis and heat value, so that good coal could be retailed at reasonable prices, and at a profit sufficient to cover all the charges and working expenses. Indeed, the following recommendation made in the Board of Trade Committee's Report[1] (previously referred to) should be welcomed, and should receive serious attention.

" We also recommend that the Government should at once consider the question of inviting the London County Council to arrange that the Council itself and any other public bodies which already possess or can secure the necessary facilities should, during the coming summer, acquire and so far as possible store within easy reach of London, large stocks of household coal, to be sold during the winter at prices and under conditions to be fixed in consultation with the Government, to traders engaged in supplying small consumers. Such a step would, we believe, have a salutary effect in steadying prices."

[1] " On the Causes of the Present Rise in the Retail Price of Coal sold for Domestic Use." Cd. 7866, 1915.

It is to be hoped that should effect be given to the above recommendation the authorities concerned will organise a department for the systematic purchase of coal. The problems involved are too technical in character to be discussed here, but it might be explained that from time to time they have received a good deal of attention and that the United States Government has instituted a system which is applied in the purchase of coal for Government use, which has much to recommend it. The contractor is paid a bonus for coal delivered which is of better quality than the standard set in the specifications. For deliveries of coal which fall below that standard, deductions are made from the contract price, proportional to the decreased value of the coal.

This system has advantages and disadvantages, but the complexity of the combined bonus and penalty system is avoided in the procedure followed by the Department of Water Supply, Gas and Electricity for New York, which may be applied with slight modifications to meet any case. Before drawing up definite specifications a careful investigation is first made of the character of the various coals supplied in the buyer's area, and from these results a diagram is plotted giving the moisture, volatile sulphur, ash, and combustible matter ; and any coals falling within the limits so outlined are put in the list of eligibles as to quality, or not open to a penalty. Coals lying outside these limits and below them are penalised with respect to weight but not as to price, so that the buyer should not buy water or incombustible mineral matter and pay for them at the rate agreed upon for good coal.

Our municipalities are already large buyers of coal for their electric lighting departments and for other purposes, so it would not be a difficult matter to organise a system for the purchase, inspection, and sale of coal ; and in cases where the sale and delivery were not practicable, the municipality could purchase in bulk and inspect and market the coal of guaranteed quality through the existing merchants.

Something must be done to protect the public, at least the poor, for, as things are at present, the veriest rubbish is often foisted on to those least able to bear the burden of high prices and poor qualities.

FUEL ECONOMIES IN THE HOME

The annual consumption of coal for domestic purposes in the United Kingdom cannot be much less than 40,000,000 tons ; it was 32,000,000 tons in 1903. It is common knowledge that a great deal of this enormous quantity is very wastefully burnt in grates, only a small proportion (about 13 per cent.) of the heat of combustion being given off in an open fireplace and more or less efficiently used for heating the rooms. It is true that the open fire is pleasing to look upon, and that it is most useful in ventilating the room ; on the other hand, the combustion is usually so imperfect that vast quantities of smoke are emitted from the chimneys, and this vitiates the air, blackens household effects, and tends to destroy vegetation. But the careful tests carried out by Dr. Des Voeux many years ago, with the assistance of the Office of Works, have established the fact that grates which emit the least amount of smoke are also the most economical consumers of coal ; and there can be little doubt that the best modern grates consume some 20 to 25 per cent. less coal.

The increasing use of *gas for heating and cooking* is doing something to abate the smoke nuisance and to economise coal, and if it were found possible to supply gas for such purposes at a lower charge, doubtless the use of gas-stoves would receive a further impetus. But for anything like an important economy in the use of coal for domestic purposes we must look to a considerable extension of *central heating* in houses, the open fire or an electric radiator being merely used as supplementary to the general warming by hot-water pipes or stoves. A general adoption of this system would, in the opinion of the Royal Commission on Coal Supplies (1903), lead to halving the present consumption of coal for domestic purposes. It is true that decided progress has been made in this direction, but it may be that the absence of proper provision for ventilation in connection with some of the systems in use accounts to a great extent for the prejudice which exists against them.

There are also many minor economies that deserve the attention of small householders. For instance, all domestic grates should have a backing of firebrick ; blocks of firebrick in a wide range of sizes suitable both for the backs and sides of grates are usually stocked by ironmongers and the oil-shop people. These reduce the quantity of coal required to fill the grate, and the blocks once heated give the fire a bright and cheerful appearance, and tend to prevent the escape of heat to the iron back and sides. Better still, a good backing of fireclay, plastered on to the back of the grate in its plastic state, and well perforated with small holes to reduce the tendency to crack when baked, will with care last for years, but it requires to be gradually dried and heated before using the grate, to prevent cracks appearing. Pieces of *chalk* laid in the grate at the back of the fire, forming about a third of its contents, are a fairly good substitute for the above.

Most coal contains a good deal of *slack*. This can be most economically burnt by forming it into *fire-bats*, which may be done by filling paper sugar-bags with the slack, tying them up with string, soaking them in water, and draining them, when they are ready for use. One of these, placed at the back of the grate when the fire is made up from time to time, will burn brightly for an hour or two,

Further, a mixture of *coal slack and clay* made into large balls will burn for hours and give out a great heat.

The last thing at night partly consumed coal should be taken off the fire and put to cool on the hearth for further use.

COKE AS A HOUSEHOLD FUEL

In coking, coal loses about one-third of its weight, but increases one-tenth in bulk. The average weight of coke is 45 lbs. per cubic foot, or, in round numbers, 50 cubic feet weigh a ton. The calorific value of coke is about 12,500 BTU per lb. A good quality house coal should have a calorific value of about 14,000 BTU. So, on a heat value basis, such coal at 28s. per ton would equal in value coke at 25s. per ton. But coke will not burn freely in an ordinary grate, and at the best it is not a clean fuel for household purposes, owing to its large amount of ash, etc. However, when broken to the size of a chestnut and mixed with about an equal amount of coal it burns very well, and a certain amount of economy ensues, as coke can very often be bought direct from the gas-works at about two-thirds the price of coal. It burns very well in the ordinary anthracite closed stove, and on economic and patriotic grounds it should be used instead of anthracite coal, as in its manufacture valuable by-products are produced for which there is a great demand for munition work.

HOW TO LAY AND LIGHT A FIRE

The price of firewood is steadily going up, whilst the size of the bundle is coming down, so economy in wood in lighting fires is becoming necessary. As it is, in many households a whole bundle of wood is thrust in where half, or even a third, would do. And then, too often, through want of skill in arranging the paper, wood, and coal, the fire has to be relit, with the wastage perhaps of another bundle and more paper. This being so, the following extract from a little pamphlet issued by Messrs. Charrington, Sells, Dale & Co., giving hints on lighting fires, may with advantage be read :

" In laying a fire, shake free the ash and remove all old cinders on a shovel. Fold half a sheet of newspaper and press it down into the grate, allowing the edges to protrude. Place a small lump of coal in the centre, and lay the wood in a conical shape all round it. Place half a sheet of newspaper around this, pressing it well down in the grate, and cover the whole with the residue of the wood. Then place on top of this only sufficient coal to cover the surface, and put the cinders on top of this, principally at the back of the grate. As soon as the wood is well alight remove the burnt paper by gently passing the poker along the bottom of the grate so as to clear the air passages and enable the wood to heat the bottom plate.

"If these directions are carried out it will be found that the fire will require no more attention for two hours at least.

"Most people choke their grates with too much paper over the air apertures and wonder why the fire does not burn. The ash-pan must be cleared daily or the fire will not draw properly."

It may be added that if the coal to be used for lighting fires be well dried before a fire the night before, and two or three of the sticks of wood be pointed and used with the pointed ends downwards, the wood and coal easily ignite with the use of very little paper and wood.

Waste due to the Smoke Nuisance

In winter some 50,000 tons of coal are daily consumed in domestic fireplaces in London alone. This, in certain states of the atmosphere, produces clouds of smoke resting for days over the central districts, shutting out the sun, even when it does not descend in foggy weather as a thick, impenetrable, and partly poisonous mass of darkness. The evil has been greatly increased in recent years by the installation of great power stations for the production of electricity in the London district, with their hideous chimney shafts belching forth clouds of grimy smoke.[1]

During the fogs of 1879-80 it was noticed that asthma increased 220 per cent., and bronchitis 331 per cent., with a considerable rise in the death-rate. The injurious effect of smoke upon household property and upon the contents of houses is well known ; and the mere expenditure occasioned by the nuisance in London alone was some years ago estimated, after very careful consideration, as amounting to the huge figure of over £5,000,000 yearly.[2] Since 1881 a great deal of attention has been given to the problem of smoke abatement, which really resolves itself into the problem of the production of perfect combustion. With perfect combustion it is believed that one-sixth the coal at present used in domestic fires would produce the effects ordinarily obtained, with a great gain in cleanliness and public convenience; we should no longer have sooty chimneys, and the atmosphere would no longer be polluted by unburnt carbon—in fact, the "London fogs" would lose their distinctive character of grimy opacity, although they would not become any less frequent than now, as it is an error to state that these fogs are caused by the smoke which blackens them.

The sulphur of the coal (oxidised ultimately to

---

[1] It has been estimated that 70 tons of soot fall every month on each square mile within the precincts of Manchester. Of course in London the quantity is not so great ; but, assuming it to be only 45 tons per month per square mile, some 120 tons of soot would fall every day during the winter on the London area.

[2] Probably if the soap and other cleaning materials used, and the cost of laundry work and of domestic work involved in the daily household cleaning be taken into account, the sum would be nearer £20,000,000 at the present time.

sulphuric acid), and not the carbon, is the active non-preventable and destructive agent, the evil effects of which on town air, on human lungs, and on plant life, etc., are well known ; so the abolition of smoke would mean an enormous gain in health and in cleanliness, whose value cannot be over-estimated.

All the methods that have been suggested for the abolition of smoke fall into two classes, namely (1) The use of some other kind of fuel, and (2) the improvement of the appliances for the burning of bituminous coal.

The possible substitutes are (a) anthracite, (b) patent fuels, such as coalite, (c) gas, and (d) coke. Of these, without question, coalite is to be preferred ; gas, of course, is the most convenient, and when efficiently installed there is little to complain about, but for continuous burning, day by day, it becomes expensive.

The number of different domestic grates and stoves that have been invented and used with the object of securing complete combustion is so great that we are precluded from discussing them here ; it will suffice to explain that the exhaustive trials carried out at the South Kensington Smoke Abatement Exhibition many years ago, on a great number of domestic grates and stoves of different types, established the fact that the class of air heating open grates with downward, backward, or lateral draughts is, on the whole, the most efficient.

Now the *scientific essentials for complete combustion* are, a sufficient but not too great supply of air, the thorough admixture of this air with the products of the destructive distillation of the coal, and the maintenance of a high temperature within the fire.

But in the ordinary crude domestic fire these desiderata are invariably absent; large masses of fresh fuel are thrown on the top, which cool the fire just at that part where the highest temperature is required ; then the products of the distillation of this fresh fuel, heated from below, do not get properly mixed with the air till they have been drawn up the chimney, thus large volumes of cold air are continually being sucked up through the fire, cooling it and carrying its heat away from where it is wanted. The object aimed at by the improved methods are regularity of supply of both fuel and air, so as to maintain a steady temperature, a steady evolution of the products of distillation, and a steady and complete combustion.

HEATING, LIGHTING, AND POWER FROM THE PIT-HEAD

The ultimate solution of this colossal problem, one of the greatest of the age, is to practically abolish the use of coal in all our cities and towns and consume it at the pit-heads and other convenient places for the generation of electrical energy, distributing the electrical current to every city, town, and village for traction, power, lighting, cooking, and heating purposes. The cost, of course, would be enormous, but so would be the saving in countless directions, particularly in the utilisation of the coal's valuable by-products, such as gas, tar, oils, spirit, pitch, and sulphates.

Such a gigantic scheme presents no insuperable difficulties, and would, if carried out by the State, be an economic proposition that would transform our populated centres from the begrimed places we know them to be to centres of sweetness and light. Further, it would greatly help to solve the domestic servant problem ; and the elimination of so much waste of kinds too numerous to particularise here would have far-reaching economic effects, and would enable the nation to recover the cost of the scheme in the course of a few years ; and, it has been estimated, make it possible to supply power throughout the country at as low a price as one-eighth of a penny per Board of Trade unit.

GREAT SCHEME FOR ELECTRIC SUPPLY FOR ALL PURPOSES

Since the above lines were written the Coal Conservation Sub-Committee has issued (December, 1917) an interim report to the Ministry of Reconstruction regarding electrical power supply in Great Britain. It proposes, briefly, to supply all our industries with electrical power generated at big super-power stations, not more than sixteen in number for the whole country, and to eliminate or combine all smaller stations.

The object of the scheme is to economise our coal supplies. The amount of coal used in the United Kingdom for the production of power is estimated to be 80,000,000 tons, at a cost of, say, £40,000,000 at the pit-head. By an up-to-date and national scheme of electrification, 55,000,000 tons of this (£27,000,000 a year) could, it is believed, be saved.

It has been settled conclusively during the past fifteen years that the most economical means of applying power to industry is through the electric motor.

At the present time the supply of electricity in Great Britain is split among about 600 companies and municipal undertakings. The reform proposed by the Sub-Committee is to supersede all these relatively small undertakings by laying down throughout Great Britain main trunk lines, to be fed by some sixteen super-power stations.

CHAPTER X

The Coming Agricultural Revolution

" All original wealth comes from the soil."—ADAM SMITH.

THE HOME-GROWN FOOD QUESTION

IN 1913 we imported foodstuffs to the total value of £324,308,770, a truly colossal sum ; on the other hand, we have seen almost throughout the length and breadth of our fair land a marked absence of that agricultural activity and enterprise that have so much enriched some of the small countries of Europe. Old countries like our own are apt to repose more or less upon the accumulated advantages derived from the labours of past generations, until they are stirred into action by some strong impelling force to encourage in every possible way scientific research and invention, and to adopt well-established discoveries and improved methods.

The progress of science is ever revealing new wonders, such as the inoculation of unfertile soils with the constituents of good earth taken from superior land, the cross-fertilisation of different kinds of wheats achieved at Cambridge, M. Flammarion's method of stimulating plant growth, the extraordinary increase in productivity due to the use of Prof. Bottomley's bacterised peat, the extinction of insect pests preying upon fruit-trees by the introduction of its enemy discovered in some foreign land, and the magic of continuous cropping and intensive cultivation. Well may we look forward to still greater marvels, and be encouraged to spare no efforts and expense to discover them.

We are using the whole strength of our Empire for war. We need it quite as much to provide ourselves and our Allies with foodstuffs; and after the War our efforts cannot be relaxed, owing to the world shortage of foodstuffs, so our master-words must be Progress and Organisation; with the mobilisation of our engineers, chemists, and agricultural experts and workers, never forgetting that although we are an industrial nation, agriculture is still our greatest industry. That our available agricultural land is not fully cultivated is apparent to the ordinary observer, who can see up and down the country tens of thousands of acres either under-cultivated or lying in a waste condition. Indeed, there are good reasons for believing that the agricultural productivity of the country could be easily doubled and trebled by more intensive cultivation, by the application of scientific knowledge, by the utilisation of waste lands, and by the general adoption of modern methods; whilst co-operation in the purchase of requirements, and in the transport and marketing of foodstuffs, would enable our farmers to compete with the foreigner, who is well aware that we have it in our power to become practically independent of him. Indeed, the author some years ago heard a speaker, at a meeting held in the London University, explain that when on a visit to Denmark he remarked to a native agriculturist that we could quite easily produce in our own country all the hundreds of millions of eggs and the enormous quantities of other produce we imported from his country. The reply was, "Yes, we know you could, but we are quite certain you never will, as you are too conservative and easy-going."

Such remarks should acutely bring home to us our past folly, and inspire us to develop our agriculture to the utmost possible extent without let or hindrance, and encourage us to do all that is possible to forward the campaign to turn 3,000,000 acres of grass land into arable land for 1918. Of course such an extensive turnover of pasture land raises the question of our milk supply, but some advanced agriculturists believe that if farmers would keep their cows in stall, and feed them on maize and other crops grown on the land now under pasture, they would produce three times more milk and meat for the nation.

Our agriculturists would be wise if they studied carefully the wonders that Sir Horace Plunket has worked for Ireland. Britain badly needs the priceless services of a few Plunkets.

Farming a Highly Technical Industry

If we are ever to make a success of our agriculture, by intensively working the land for all it is worth, to raise its productivity to the maximum, we must radically alter our views as to the type of training our young farmers should receive. As things are at present (or rather were in the immediate past), we too often have the sons of the larger class of farmers loitering about without any definite occupation, attending markets and fairs, and often the hunting-field and race-course. It is true that some of the better type after leaving school are put to farm labour and kept steadily at it, becoming proficient at every kind of work performed on the farm ; but though this is a good professional training as far as it goes, it does not go nearly far enough, having regard to the highly technical character of the matters that require attention in the management of a large farm producing a variety of foodstuffs in the most economical way. Of course the really wise parents send their sons, after giving them a sound education, to one of the well-known agricultural colleges or farm schools, of which we have some twenty-eight fairly well distributed over the country, in most of which an excellent training in the technology of farming can be had.

In cases where the future farmer is specialising in some branch of agriculture, such as fruit, poultry, cattle, or forage, etc., the training required is, of course, greatly simplified ; but we shall never get all that is possible out of the soil until the country has an adequate supply of thoroughly trained men capable of farming on a large scale, who are masters of agriculture, in the sense that a captain of industry (such as a general manager of a large engineering works) is the master-mind that intelligently controls all the multitudinous activities of his staff and workers.

Before an adequate idea of the highly technical and varied character of the training such agriculturists should undergo can be formed, a brief survey of the qualifications of an ideal superintendent of agriculture might be attempted. It must be admitted that he should be a good business man with a great capacity for work, a knowledge of simple book-keeping, and a sound grip of farm economics ; and that he should be able to tactfully manage men, and be familiar with the laws affecting agriculture and relating to land ; further, his training, which never really ends, should, it must be conceded, embrace the following subjects, which are more or less included in the curricula of our agricultural colleges :

Farm buildings, principles of their arrangement, etc. Farm arrangements generally. Large and small farming. Draining, levelling, and trenching, and measurement and preparation of the land for tillage operations. Benefit of fences ; varieties of fences. Chemistry of soils. Manures and foodstuffs. Cultivation of grain, roots, herbage, and forage, and crops of limited cultivation. Sequence of crops. Influence of climate on the productivity of the soil. Influence of the proximity of cities, towns, and of populous villages upon the demand for produce. Live stock, horses, cattle, sheep, goats, hogs, and poultry of different breeds. Farm management of live stock. Modern engines, machines and implements of husbandry, their use, cost, and maintenance. Elementary veterinary science. Rough carpentry. Advantages of co-operation for transport, the purchase of requirements and the sale of produce, etc. Improvement of waste lands, etc., etc.

Now, having regard to the catholicity of the qualifications as outlined above, it goes without saying that the raw material for our agricultural colleges cannot be too good ; fortunately, we have in our young men reared in the country in an agricultural atmosphere, an adequate supply of the very finest to draw upon, and if the State, in its wisdom, sees to it that in our colleges there are farm classes, and assists in the foundation of a sufficient number of additional colleges and farm schools to give us in every agricultural centre a college, with suitable museums, laboratories for research, apparatus and experimental and illustrative farms ; and the State and county authorities offer sufficient inducements in the direction of bursaries, scholarships, and free studentships, we should soon have available a supply of young agriculturists who would in due course, with proper enterprise on the part of all concerned (and a great extension of the arterial or trunk drainage of the country, and a reduction of the evils due to the excessive preservation of game), raise the agriculture of the country by intensive methods to a degree of prosperity undreamt of in pre-war times.

This undoubtedly would carry us a long way in the direction of being self-supporting in foodstuffs. We have all the fundamentals concerned : an excellent soil when scientifically used, the finest human material and live stock in the world, a capacity for the production of most of the fertilisers required, the capacity to manufacture the most perfect agricultural machinery and labour-saving appliances, etc., in any quantities required, the ability and means required for arranging an efficient transport system, an unlimited market for every kind of agricultural produce at our doors ; and last, but not least, unsurpassed organising powers to carry anything through to a successful issue that we seriously put our hand to.

But we must be on our guard against encouraging anyone to prepare for an agricultural career who is not qualified by intelligence and a good capacity for work ; for too often parents resort to an agricultural calling for their sons whose inability to progress in other callings shows clearly that they are unfitted to prepare for a strenuous career, in which success can only be secured by unremitting labour, and by a training in highly technical matters ; for it has been truly said by J. Hain Friswell that " the British are kept up to the mark by a land which is very kindly if one will only feed it, cultivate it, and work it thoroughly, and by a climate which does not permit the farmer to make mistakes. It is no use for him to plough when he ought to be clearing his crops, nor for him to look after his weeds when he should be harvesting his wheat."

The remarkable achievements of our farmers at their best show how wrong it is to regard them as a dull, plodding sort of people, inferior to urban dwellers in intelligence and energy ; so in the coming agricultural revolution we may well trust them to rise to the great occasion and to loyally and enthusiastically co-operate with engineers and scientists in increasing the fertility of the land to its utmost limit. But, having regard to the experience and knowledge that are required for success in agriculture, we must be on our guard against any movement which would lead to inexperienced men being settled on the land in the capacity of responsible farmers or agriculturists. On the other hand, there should be an unlimited demand for men of the right type to qualify as farm hands.

LABOUR-SAVING MACHINERY FOR INCREASE OF TILLAGE

That any substantial increase in the production of food must rest upon a greater output from the soil is well established, and we are informed by a Government Report[1] that

"Speaking generally, the land of England is being kept at a comparatively low level of cultivation, and that it might be made to produce a greater amount of food without the withdrawal of labour from more profitable industries. In particular, the conversion of arable land into grass, which has taken place to the extent of nearly 4,000,000 acres during the last forty years and is still going on, must necessarily be attended by a diminution in the amount of food produced. We received evidence that a great deal of this land would produce twice as much meat and milk when under the plough as when in permanent grass, and that more, and not less, stock could be maintained on it if it were restored to arable cultivation, while it would also be producing corn for human consumption. It does not, however, follow that the larger grass returns from arable land, beneficial as they would be to the nation, would always be attended by a corresponding profit to the farmer. His labour bill would be greatly increased, and account must also be taken of the greater capital required, the increased risk, and the call for more skill and management. We were, however, assured that for some years prior to the War arable farming had been remunerative on all but the heaviest of soils, that it affords opportunities for profit not open to grazing, and, particularly, that it can be intensified and cheapened by the employment of machinery in such a way as to render it possible to pay a higher wage to the agricultural labourer.

[1] "Final Report of the Departmental Committee on the Home Production of Food." (Cd. 8095, Oct., 1915.)

" A larger supply of agricultural tractors and ploughs would be of great assistance to farmers, but, owing to the priority which is necessarily given to goods required for war services, the manufacturers of agricultural tractors and ploughs are unable to turn out machines, owing to the shortage of labour and material."

Thus we are confronted with a most unfortunate condition of things ; but there can be little doubt that if the Government could before long arrange to give greater facilities to farmers to hire tractors and ploughs (say of American make) and labour-saving machinery, and to help them with seeds and fertilisers, a great and much-needed increase in the production of foodstuffs would result.

INEXPENSIVE MOTOR PLOUGHS AND AGRICULTURAL MACHINERY REQUIRED

Although for some years steam and oil tractors for direct-traction ploughing have been efficiently used, they are expensive machines, ranging in price from some £500 for those of about 30 horse-power, to some £1,000 for more powerful machines up to about 70 horse-power. Of course, to these sums a considerable amount must be added for engine gang-ploughs and accessories, to complete the ploughing plant. Such machinery renders good results and is an excellent investment when operations are carried out on a large scale, but if we are to see a great agricultural development, with every possible acre efficiently utilised, we must produce well-designed general purpose motors, fitted for road work and goods haulage as well as all-round work on the farm and estate ; and also, in enormous numbers, inexpensive mechanically propelled ploughs capable of doing similar work on five- or ten-acre fields to that done by implements pulled by animals, machines that can also be effectively used for inter-cultivation, capable of scarifying, hoeing, and scuffling between

trees in orchards, hop gardens, vineyards, and generally
for cultivating between rows of growing crops.

Such ploughing machines are being imported from
America in fairly large numbers, and are being made in
this country, but on a small scale ; they are built on the
lines of a horse plough and are sufficiently powerful to do
the work of three or four horses, the fuel used being petrol
or paraffin. The work done is similar to that done by
implements drawn by animals, but the motor machines
have several advantages over the latter, for they do not
require rest and are always ready for work. There is also
absence of padding of the subsoil from hoof pressure ; and
as the operator has only to turn on the fuel and oil taps,
start the engine, and control the running of the machine
by means of one lever actuating a friction clutch, an
unskilled worker can soon be trained to operate it. Further,
as the driver may ride on the seat when the plough is at
work (provided that the engine is not overloaded), instead
of struggling to keep the plough straight, carrying several
pounds of soil on his feet, it can be easily worked by female
labour, or by a slightly injured soldier. The power is
usually obtained from a single-cylinder motor of about
10 horse-power, automatically controlled by means of a
sensitive governor, giving a constant engine speed, whether
running light or under the load. The price of such machines
at present is about £175 to £350, cultivator and harrow
accessories and parts, and parts for scuffling and hoeing,
or parts for belt-driving for small mills, chaff-cutters,
pumps, grinding machines, etc., being extras. Hundreds
of thousands of such machines will be required if we are
to have a great agricultural renaissance, and there can be
no doubt that standardised machines could be produced
in such numbers at a fraction of the above cost, if we
utilised after the War the vast plants of machine tools
that have been specially put down to manufacture

munitions of war. We have spent tens of millions on this machinery, and the nation must see that there is no whole-sale scrapping after the War, as by judicious rearrangements and scientific organisation practically the whole of the prodigious engineering and industrial equipment laid down, and much of that commandeered for war purposes, could be utilised in some way or other for the regeneration of our agriculture and industries.

Even the distilleries and gas-works, that are now being used in connection with the production of high explosives, could be extended and utilised for the production of home-made fuel for the motor implements and transport vehicles, etc., as we shall see. Fortunately, after the War, there will be an enormous number of motor vehicles, that are at present used by the Services for transport and other purposes, available for the conveyance and distribution of raw materials and of agricultural and other produce.

For working out the great problem of the complete organisation of the industries of the country, we shall need for one purpose or another every man who can do his bit. Indeed, every man should be where he is wanted in peace time as in war.

WE MUST STANDARDISE AGRICULTURAL MACHINERY AND REQUIREMENTS

On most farms there is a serious waste of mechanical, animal, and manual power continuously going on, largely through the want of efficient implements and machines, or the imperfection of those in use. It is commonly known that in the past each important invention in agri-cultural machinery has led to enormous savings ; thus the American reaper effected thirty men's work, and, in pre-paring corn for man's food, the introduction of the steam threshing-machine saved two-thirds of the former expense ;

and so it can be easily shown that the introduction of modern implements and machinery in cases when the conditions are favourable has always led to great economies, despite the high cost of such plant.

But the question of cost is one of vital importance, and no matter how much the State may be prepared to help, through agricultural banks, or how much manufacturers assist through the hire-purchase system, no great progress can be expected until machinists, by adopting the most modern systems of manufacture, including standardisation, considerably bring down the selling prices of all farmers' requirements. It can be done. In fact, it must be done to enable us to recover our financial equilibrium after the War. Firms should be encouraged or directed to specialise in fewer implements or machines, and to lay themselves out for the production of them in enormous quantities, for it is primarily in this direction that costs can be reduced.

The enterprise and output of our leading agricultural engineers are probably unsurpassed, but there are up and down the country far too many manufacturers who have not kept pace with the great progress that has been made in manufacturing processes in recent years. For example, some years ago the author looked over a flourishing works, in an agricultural district not a hundred miles from London, in which ordinary ploughs were being manufactured, and was astonished at the antiquity of the plant used. It might have come out of the Ark ! Indeed, it is safe to say that if this particular implement had been produced in sufficient numbers, and by the use of the most up-to-date plant and processes, it could have been turned out at a cost not greatly exceeding that of the raw materials from which it was made. It is to be feared that this is only too typical of much that is being done in this country, representing a state of affairs that could be radically altered by organising the various factories, and arranging that each should specialise in the production in great numbers of such things as they are best able to turn out. A committee recruited from the ranks of the leading agricultural engineers, the Royal Agricultural Society (which in the past has done so much in raising the standard of agricultural machinery), the Board of Agriculture, and the leading agricultural colleges, presided over by an organising genius, if appointed soon enough and endowed with suitable powers, could work wonders before the War is over in the directions indicated, if sufficient labour could be secured.

DEMOBILISATION AND FARM WORK

When hostilities cease some millions of men will be free to engage in industrial work of some kind or other, and it is reasonable to suppose that the open-air life they have led in the field will tempt a large proportion of them to take a hand in agricultural work ; and should this synchronise with a great extension in the use of labour-saving machines and of implements used upon the farm, the new condition of things would tend directly to elevate the condition of the rural workers, as there would be a reduction in the drudgery heretofore imposed upon human thews and sinews, with an equalising of employment throughout the year, and a better and steadier rate of wages. Further, however we go about it, we have to see that after the War there are not hundreds of thousands of unemployed crying for work and food.

Farming on the most economical lines requires a good deal of capital, for besides the costly and bulky machines and implements used, every farm must be provided with a large assortment of tools and hand implements. These, although not individually costly, absorb in the aggregate a considerable amount of capital, and when not in use

require to be well looked after and securely stored. The
capital required to work a farm depends, of course, upon
many things in addition to the machinery, implements,
etc., and it would be interesting to know how far modern
conditions would be met by the old sum of £10 per acre,
which used to be regarded as sufficient in the case of land
of fair quality, on which the alternate husbandry is pur-
sued, and the rents payable as the produce is realised.

Apart from machinery, etc., much could be done to
reduce the cost of agricultural developments by deciding
upon standard forms of farm buildings, homesteads,
cottages, barns, drains, etc., and greatly extending the
use of concrete and ferro-concrete for such purposes.

THE GREAT VARIETY OF AGRICULTURAL IMPLEMENTS IN USE

Engineers and others who are at present engaged on
munition work should be turning their attention to the
problem of finding work after the War for the machinery
they have laid down to cope with the extensive orders
they are executing. They might with great advantage
turn their attention to the certain great demand for
agricultural requirements that will spring up in the near
future, but few have any idea as to the very wide range of
engines, machines and implements, etc., that are in use,
from which they can make a selection to suit their plant ;
most of which are capable of being improved and perhaps
simplified, if not standardised, and certainly greatly reduced
in price if produced on a sufficiently large scale in the most
up-to-date way.

Without attempting to make the list complete, the
following will give some indication of the extensive variety
of requirements that may be catered for :—Motor and other
ploughs, portable engines, road engines, threshing machines,

hocs, scarifiers, grubbers, harrows, field rollers, land-pressers, manure distributors, seed and manure drills, turnip-thinners, cutters, and pulpers, gorse mills, sheep shears, mowing and reaping machines, haymakers, sheaf-binding harvesters, rakes, loaders and stackers, wheel-carriages for the cartage of crops, manure, etc., winnowing machines and screens, straw elevators, corn-bruisers, grinding-mills, cake-crushers, potato washing machines, chaff-cutters, hay and corn drying machines, grain cleaners and separators, steaming apparatus for cooking cattle food, live-stock furniture, milk strainers, churns, cream separators, cheese presses, dairy refrigerators, weighing machines, sawing machines, stack-stools, fencing, water wheels and windmills, etc., etc. But, as explained in the previous article, there must be organisation to prevent overlapping in production.

Colonial and Foreign Competition

Colonial agriculturists visiting the Old Country with the object of examining our methods in different branches of the farming industry—methods of production and distribution, methods adopted in the purchase of requirements—and of seeking information as to the cost of labour and land, and generally examining all the economic factors which enter into the problem of making a profit out of an agricultural industry, have been often puzzled by the apparent anomaly that a colonial or a foreign farmer, paying higher wages, using machinery that is imported, and in some cases paying a higher rent for his land than is paid for similar land in England, can send his produce thousands of miles from where it is grown, and undersell the British farmer in his own market. The puzzled one often seeks in vain for an explanation, for he rarely has time to sufficiently investigate matters and arrive at any definite conclusions : and, although it is beyond our purpose to discuss them in these pages, many readers will be able to give an explanation.

It is true that during the past two or three decades a fair amount of progress has been made in agriculture ; but it is notorious that whilst for the previous hundred years or more every other industry in the country has been making the most marvellous and rapid progress, the agricultural industry nowhere kept pace with the others. This was probably due partly to the farmers' distrust of experts, and of the applications of science, but to a greater extent to the want of security in the tenure of the land.

It is only natural that a man who has an uncertain interest in a property, and is not sure but that if he improves it others will reap the benefit, can never be expected to improve it, as he would if certain to realise the benefit himself : but even so, great agricultural developments seem possible if progressive methods are more freely adopted, for we must agree with Professor James Long,[1] that

" Not only do we need improvements in our methods of production, but of securing what we grow. Our cultivated area needs expansion, broad acres still employed as sheep-runs or utilised for sport must be reclaimed, sandy moors and peat land all respond to kindly treatment and to the ingenuity and skill of man. Our live stock could be doubled in number and the quality commensurately improved, and our crops might be increased by one-half. What is done by a few can be accomplished by all, where the conditions are equally balanced ; and there are British farmers who accomplish great things, while others achieve nothing at all."

[1] " Making Most of the Land."

What Co-Operative Societies can do

On the Continent Co-Operative Societies and agricultural banks have worked wonders, but the fact is well established that although there are a great many Co-Operative Societies in this country, the majority of British farmers have not come under the spell of co-operation ; they do not understand its magic as the Danes do, for instance, with the result that we are spending hundreds of millions a year on foreign produce, most of which could be quite easily grown at home, to the great economic advantage of the nation. It is true that the farmer has not the assistance of the agricultural banks—as the continental farmers have—in procuring the most modern machinery, implements and plant, particularly steam and motor tractors and ploughs. Indeed, very little effort is made by our great agricultural implement and machine makers to bring their specialities to the notice of farmers in their own towns. There can be little doubt that if in every agricultural town they, or the State, had showrooms, with assistants to explain and advise—such as our gas and electric light companies have in most large towns—and there were greater facilities offered for the purchase of machinery on the hire system, a great and beneficial development would take place in the use of labour-saving implements, machinery, and appliances. But the development the country most urgently requires is a more general adoption of the co-operative principle for the purchase of requirements and the sale of agricultural produce.

If more powerful Co-Operative Societies came into being, the great problem of economic distribution could be tackled ; the standardisation of grading and packing arrangements, collective bargaining with railways for the conveyance of produce in bulk, and the establishment of railway clearing systems, and systems of motor transport in districts badly served by railways, would bring down the cost of carriage considerably, and make it possible to successfully compete with foreign producers, thereby reducing our imports, to the great advantage of the nation.

FORTUNES IN EGGS AND POULTRY

In the year 1913 we spent the enormous sum of £9,590,602 on imported eggs (2,580 millions in number) alone, and now, when efforts are being made to reduce in every direction our imports, the folly of allowing foreigners to provide us with such necessities, in the past, as could quite well be produced in this country by well-directed organisation and co-operation, is brought home to us. Many years ago it was a saying, " Dear as eggs a penny a-piece," now new-laid eggs are being retailed at 4½d. each, and the price of poultry is still advancing. Indeed, as things are developing prices must still further advance. Fortunately, the Government has realised that something must be done to promote the production of eggs and poultry, and it has projected a new scheme through the Board of Agriculture to be put into operation with the assistance of the various County Councils. The proposal is, to establish in the several selected counties breeding stations for the distribution to cottagers and small-holders of sittings of eggs laid by pure-bred stock. A similar course adopted in Ireland, and more recently in Scotland, has given excellent results and has done much to increase the volume of the output and the quality of the produce.

" The sittings of eggs[1] are to be available for those small occupiers, the assessment of whose holdings does not exceed £50 per annum. Names are asked for by the different County Councils of poultry keepers who are willing to sell not less than sixty sittings at a price of 2s. per dozen,

[1] *The Poultry World*, Nov. 26, 1915.

between 1st December and 1st April, stocking at least twenty-four pure-bred hens and two cockerels.

"Occupiers who are approved for this purpose, and become station holders, will be paid a bonus of £5 by the Board of Agriculture—upon proof of the distribution of the sixty sittings—to cover expenses or any possible loss by the deal. Station holders will be required to conform to certain rules and requirements. Their birds and methods will be subject to the inspection of the officers of the Board of Agriculture. On the other hand, in addition to the official recognition and subsidy, the County Councils, through which the scheme will be operated, will advertise the names of the station holders free of cost— application for the supply of eggs being made to the station holders direct, who will sell the eggs at a fixed rate.

"The number of stations will, of course, vary according to local conditions and needs, more being allotted to some counties than to others. The classification into laying and table poultry stations will entirely depend upon what stations may be found available, and will also be relative to the character of the locality and the possible demands."

In Ireland splendid service is being rendered by women in this branch of farming, both as teachers and workers; in fact, the Irish poultry industry is apparently a woman's industry, with the result that during the past decade the exports have increased enormously. So it is now up to our own women-folk to emulate the enterprise and industry of their fair sisters of the Emerald Isle, and do their share in increasing our poultry and egg supply, and at the same time to pocket a share of the millions that are going a-begging.

The time has undoubtedly arrived when everything possible should be done to encourage poultry-keeping by the masses. The restrictions put upon the breeding of poultry in urban and suburban areas by landlords should be swept aside, to the great advantage of the country and all concerned. That some of the most unlikely places can be utilised is shown by the case in the City, where for three or four years, it is said, poultry have been kept on the roof of a building between Mark Lane and Mincing Lane, with good results.

THE PROLIFIC PIG

The present famine in pig meats, and the high prices ruling, should cause agriculturists, small-holders, cottagers and others, to turn their attention to pig-breeding and rearing as the quickest possible way of adding to our meat supplies. It has been claimed that it is possible for a single pig to produce 2,000 pounds of meat in a year. Think of it—nearly a ton of succulent pork and bacon, for which there is a great demand.

The number of pigs in the United Kingdom in 1915 was apparently nearly 4,000,000, but the number of sheep was over 28,000,000. Strangely enough, there was an increase in the number of sheep over that for the previous year, but a decrease in the number of pigs. Doubtless in recent years the bye-laws in force in urban and a few rural districts, which provide that pigs shall not be kept within a prescribed distance of dwelling-houses, has in the past kept down the number of pigs grown ; but by a recent regulation these bye-laws may be considerably relaxed in suitable cases, thus allowing pig-keeping in the neighbourhood of towns and villages, and thereby (1) utilising refuse food remnants, offal, etc., and (2) saving the cost of transit.

It is said that a sack of barley can make 30 lbs. of pork.

PIG-RAISING IN LONDON

Pork and Profit from Table and Kitchen Waste

According to the *Star* of January 19, 1918, Mr. T. K. Bowman utilised a stable behind his shop in Camden Town in January, 1917, by installing two four-month-old pigs,

M

a feeding trough, and a bundle of straw : the capital outlay being 50s. Feeding a staff of about sixty people, Mr. Bowman found that the refuse from the tables and kitchen was sufficient to feed the pigs until they were well grown, when the cabbage-leaves, potato-peelings, and scraps from his own establishment were gladly supplemented by similar waste from one or two neighbouring eating-houses. Shortly after Christmas, 1917, when the pigs were killed, they weighed over 46 stones each, and at the Food Controller's fixed price they fetched £44 12s. 4d. All that they cost for feeding, apart from the waste food they consumed, was the price of one half-sack of " middlings." So they yielded over £40 profit, and something towards the food supply of the country.

We must have a Home-made Fuel for Motor Ploughs, etc.

We have seen that the fuel used in motor ploughs is either petrol[1] or paraffin oil, both of which are imported, to our great economic loss, and their cost has been steadily rising for years ; but, fortunately, we have in benzol (a spirit distilled from coal-tar) and denatured alcohol—the only other fuels that can be employed as substitutes—home-made fuels that can be used with great economic advantage, with a little modification of the valves, the carburettor, and the compression of the motors.

Benzol alone could never hold the field, as its supply is regulated by the amount of coal-tar (a by-product in the manufacture of household gas) available. Therefore, the only spirit we can rely upon for extended use is alcohol, which can be made in any quantity required, so long as the sun continues to shine ; in fact, it is the only one illimitable fuel. Strangely enough, it has long been known that a mixture of alcohol with a small proportion of benzol makes

[1] And, to a small extent, benzol.

an excellent motor fuel ; indeed, it was disclosed by the late Professor Vivian B. Lewes, at a Society of Arts lecture in the early part of 1915, that Germany escaped a fuel famine by substituting such a mixture for petrol, using 80 per cent. alcohol, 20 per cent. benzol, with an addition of about 200 grammes per gallon of naphthalene, a solid hydrocarbon that is easily soluble. The naphthalene and benzol act as enrichers, and the latter gets over the starting difficulty resulting from the low vapour pressure of the alcohol. This mixture is said to give nearly the same consumption and power as petrol, and all that has to be done to the engine is to fit an exhaust heating jacket to each carburettor.

Thus we happily have in this mixture a fuel that can be entirely home-made, one that can be economically produced in any quantities we are likely to require, not alone for agricultural purposes, but for our increasing requirements for road vehicles and many industrial engines. Indeed, we shall see presently that the use of such a fuel would cause several economic factors to conveniently hang together, and be interdependent, the agriculturist providing the raw material for the alcohol, that could in turn be used by him to provide motive power to cultivate the land and drive his machinery and transport vehicles ; whilst the plants that have been extended and put down to provide benzol for munition purposes could be fully utilised in due course to supply that spirit for the new fuel, and for other purposes.

PRODUCTION OF INDUSTRIAL ALCOHOL

As is generally known, alcohol can be produced anywhere, in any quantity, from any vegetable matter containing starch or sugar, such as Indian corn (maize or mealies), potatoes, millet, beets, sugar-cane, rye, oats, barley, wheat, peat, cellulose, and sawdust, etc., etc.

Thus there is the important advantage that alcohol can always be made in the locality of demand, and become a home-made fuel ; unlike petrol, which requires transportation from distant countries, and the supply of which must sooner or later become exhausted. There is the additional advantage that agricultural interests would greatly profit from the vastly increased markets for cereals, if the legislature made it possible to use alcohol for industrial purposes. It is known that 50 bushels of Indian corn [1] (nearly 2,800 lbs.) will furnish 1,960 lbs. of fermentable matter, that is, starch and sugar together, and that 45 per cent. (882 lbs.) of this will be obtained as absolute alcohol, 95 per cent. pure. Further, assuming an acre to yield 300 bushels (18,000 lbs.) of potatoes, as an average crop, it would produce 3,600 lbs. of fermentable matter, equal to 255 gallons of commercial alcohol, and there is reason to believe that by using a grade of potatoes especially suitable for alcohol production, the output could be increased to 500 gallons per acre. [2]

PLANT FOR THE PRODUCTION OF ALCOHOL

In countries where industrial alcohol is produced, such as the United States, Germany, [3] and France, particulars relating to the cost of plant are well-guarded secrets : but the author (who was for many years consulting engineer to the Alcohol Syndicate), when called upon some years

[1] Spooner's "Motors and Motoring," p. 224.
[2] Should Professor Bottomley's method of increasing the yield of vegetables by the use of bacterised peat prove to be commercially sound, these figures would be greatly increased. The author, in the fourth edition of his "Motors and Motoring" (1909, and subsequent editions), fully discussed the question of a *home-made fuel*. About 600,000 acres in Ireland are at the present time under potato cultivation.
[3] In Germany there are 30,000 distilleries producing alcohol, chiefly for industrial purposes. Eighty per cent. of her industrial alcohol is made from potatoes.

ago to submit an approximate estimate for a plant in
South Africa, where they have excellent raw material
in the second-class mealies (which is not allowed to be
exported), succeeded in getting some data from a reliable
American source, which went to show that where there is
a plentiful supply of good water, a 3,000-bushel house
could be installed at a cost of from £40,000 to £50,000 ;
and that the cost of production, including the mealies,
would work out to about 7d. to 9d. a proof gallon,
depending upon the cost of fuel and labour. A few years
ago German potato spirit was selling in London at about
this price per proof gallon.

For many years the author has strongly advocated,
in his lectures and writings, the use of alcohol as a substitute for petrol, and, fortunately, for some time there
has been a growing movement on the part of a large body
of influential men in favour of the substitution.

VALUE OF AGRICULTURAL PRODUCE IMPORTED BY THE
UNITED KINGDOM IN 1913 AND 1915

The following foodstuffs were imported, to the extent
of the values given, from foreign countries and British
Dominions during the years 1913 and 1915. Only those
which might almost equally well have been raised in this
country are given :

	1913	1915
Butter	£24,083,658	£27,022,745
Cheese	7,035,039	11,107,100
Eggs	9,590,602	6,123,326
Fruit	12,397,521	12,145,501
Lard	5,552,462	5,783,260
Margarine	3,917,701	5,751,253
Vegetables	6,500,159	5,572,128
Total	£68,582,142	£73,505,313

VALUE OF OTHER FOODSTUFFS IMPORTED BY THE UNITED
KINGDOM IN THE YEARS 1913 AND 1915

It would only be possible to produce a part of each
of the following foodstuffs in this country :

	1913	1915
Grain and flour	£85,494,628	£112,357,768
Wheat	43,849,173	57,306,499
Barley	8,077,100	6,029,866
Oats	5,671,957	8,488,539
Wheatmeal and flour	6,347,771	8,310,853
Meat	56,726,411	86,830,036
Animals for food	305,063	—
Bacon	17,428,881	25,441,460
Hams	3,068,251	5,280,316
Beef, fresh and frozen	16,181,908	25,839,544
Mutton, fresh and frozen	10,907,992	14,102,141
Pork	1,667,495	1,010,284
Total	£255,726,630	£350,997,306

We thus imported in the year 1913 the above foodstuffs to the total value of £324,308,770, and in 1915
£424,502,619, truly colossal sums, showing what need
there is in this country for increasing our production of
such articles. It is true that the extent of the United
Kingdom is comparatively small, but this fact need not
prevent our raising, particularly in Ireland, a far larger
amount of produce than we do now, if we go the right way
about it. For with the adoption of modern scientific
methods and co-operation, a considerable portion of these
foodstuffs could be raised, much of it even on small areas
of land, with the happy result that we should be conserving our gold reserves by reducing our enormous imports.
Indeed, the expense of the terrible War will impose upon us
the duty of fully utilising all our energies and every possible plot of land to assist in the steady reduction and
amortisation of our gigantic creation of credit.

CHAPTER XI

Utilisation of Waste Land

" The man who makes two blades of grass or two ears of corn grow where but one grew before, deserves well of his country."—SWIFT.

WASTE LAND IN THE UNITED KINGDOM

AT a time when the country is faced by the grave problem of maintaining our food supply and of preventing further inflation of prices, attention is properly drawn towards our waste lands, amounting in the aggregate to millions of acres up and down the country, doing good in the main to neither man nor beast.

Now let us be clear as to what may be properly called waste land; the term " waste land," we are told by Mr. Sampson-Morgan, F.G.L., " means, from an agricultural point of view, land such as we have by the mile in the form of hills and valleys at Chobham Common in Surrey. In fact, the waste common lands of this country may very appropriately be referred to as being the most comprehensive illustration of what is meant by the above description. If ever there was waste land in England we have it here."

It is estimated that we had in the United Kingdom, before the War, 21,000,000 acres of land remaining waste, but of course a large proportion of it, estimated at 6,000,000 acres by Sir J. S. Stirling-Maxwell, could only be profitably utilised for forestry.

Now although an immense amount of energy, skill, and capital has for many generations been brought to bear

167

upon the improvement of our soil and the maintenance of its fertility, there are, as statistics show, in addition to the waste common lands, still large portions of the surface of our country that we usually class as waste lands (to distinguish them from those which are under tillage or have at some time been subjected to the plough) lying in their natural state.

It is true that only a certain portion of this so-called waste land is absolutely unproductive, as large tracts of it are used with great advantage as sheep-walks (and could be used with still greater advantage if planted for timber) ; but there is a growing belief that much of it is capable of being converted by modern methods into arable land to still greater advantage ; indeed, it is a serious fact that only about 5 per cent. of the cultivated land in the United Kingdom is devoted to wheat production.

Of course those hilly and mountainous parts of Great Britain which, from their uncongenial climate and steep and rugged surface, are unfit for tillage, are most profitably used as pasturage for innumerable flocks, and even for this purpose it is believed that much of it is susceptible of economic improvement. Indeed, whether lands be uncultivated owing to natural poverty of the soil, to wetness, or to the degrees to which they are encumbered with stones, whether they be so near the sea level as to be more or less liable to be submerged, or whether they remain uncultivated due to bogs, morasses, or blowing sands, they can be in many cases improved and reclaimed by up-to-date methods, as we shall explain in the chapter that follows.

UNUSED LAND IN THE VICINITY OF TOWNS AND VILLAGES

Too much attention at the present time cannot be directed to the waste spaces in the vicinity of our cities, towns, and villages awaiting development, or lying derelict from some cause or another : even in the London district the total area of such lands amounts to 14,000 acres. The "Report of the Committee on the Home Production of Food" (Cd. 8095, Oct., 1915) deals with the matter, and the following extract deserves consideration :

"Our attention has been called to the possibility of increasing the production of vegetables and other foods by the cultivation of plots of unused land in the neighbourhood of villages and the suburbs of towns. The Board of Agriculture and Fisheries have advocated the formation of societies for this purpose, but representations have been made to us that owners of vacant building sites and other waste land are often unwilling to let them for cultivation at an agricultural rent, and that difficulty has been experienced in acquiring the use of suitable land. The council of any borough, urban district, or parish has power, under the Small Holdings and Allotments Act, to acquire land compulsorily, but the procedure under this Act involves at least six months' notice, and is unsuitable under present circumstances.

"If the Government were to announce that it was desirable that all vacant land suitable for growing crops should be brought under cultivation, this announcement would probably enable societies formed in villages and in boroughs to obtain land at a fair rent. But it may be necessary that the local authorities above mentioned should, for the duration of the War, be empowered, in the event of a properly constituted society failing to come to an agreement with the owner of a portion of unoccupied land, to take over such land forthwith at a rent to be determined by a valuer appointed by the Board."

Poor Land can be Economically Utilised

It might be suggested that the unused lands in thickly populated districts are not favourable for the growth of vegetable foodstuffs : but it has been proved beyond question that any ground, however poor, on which the sun can shine for a few hours daily in the summer, if it be not swept by chemical fumes that are deadly to vegetable life, is capable of yielding a profitable return for organised labour ; which need not be of a skilled nature, as, although horticulture in its highest form is a complicated science requiring special training, experience, and knowledge, the simple operations which are performed in producing vegetables can be easily understood and practised by the man in the street, if he secures a copy of the literature relating to *Vegetables for Allotments and Gardens*, patriotically published by the Royal Horticultural Society, Vincent Square, London, S.W. The pamphlet is prefaced by this paragraph :

" The following short notes have been prepared to assist holders of small plots of land, allotments, etc., to cultivate them with a view of bringing them into a good state of production to meet the special needs of the country during the present year."

The pamphlet gives detailed instructions relating to digging, manuring, and instructions for sowing and planting potatoes, seeds of all varieties of cabbage, savoys, kales, brussels sprouts, cauliflowers, broccoli, and leek ; also, peas, beans, turnips, beet, carrots, onions, and spinach, etc. ; and the proportions of seeds which should suffice for the same, and the best seed-sowing times, etc., are given. Attention is called to the great household economy that can be effected by bottling rhubarb, gooseberries, currants, cherries, raspberries, plums, damsons, apricots, apples, and pears ; and full instructions are given, with the intimation that a pamphlet on the subject can be obtained by application to the Board of Agriculture, 4, Whitehall Place, London, S.W.

The Royal Horticultural Society has also had a series of eight small pamphlets drawn up by an eminently successful practical gardener, fully describing in detail the best methods of cultivation ; and the Society very strongly recommends correspondents to purchase a set of the pamphlets, which will be sent post free on receipt of 1s. 6d. at their office, Vincent Square, London, S.W.

Dust-Heaps to Productive Gardens

All students of home food production are familiar with the work of the late Joseph Fels,[1] in the utilisation of vacant building plots in London : how townsmen who knew nothing of gardening work have been provided with land, tools, and seed, and have turned many of the most desolate-looking dust-heaps in the London area into pleasing and productive gardens. Indeed, a few of Greater London's rubbish-heaps and vacant building sites (only a very small fraction of the spaces available), some **23** acres, produced crops and foodstuffs in 1915 of the value of £1,810. These are matters that might well enlist the assistance of some of our municipal workers, who so patriotically give their services in caring for the interests of their fellow-citizens. A little co-operative organisation in arranging schemes and recruiting the activities of men, women, and children would help in cultivating the 14,000 acres of waste land in the London area, and would turn many a dreary-looking rubbish-ground into a productive beauty-spot.[2]

[1] Who founded the Vacant Land Cultivation Society, Buckingham Street, in 1908, under whose care odd lots of land of all sorts and sizes in all kinds of places are being tilled by working-men under the supervision of the Society's superintendent and instructor, Mr. G. W. Butcher. There are in all 361 plots under cultivation, producing food of retail value *equivalent to £78 9s. 0d. per acre.* The land is worth nothing to the owner as it lies, nothing is paid for it, and nothing is charged for it by the Society to the actual cultivators. The Society, moreover, presents the cultivators with most or all the seeds used, fences the land where necessary, and instructs the budding gardeners free of charge. Every week Mr. Butcher inspects every holding for instructional purposes, and so thoroughly effective is the work that not more than 5 per cent. of the Society's tenants have failed to achieve success.

[2] Before the War Wandsworth had 100 allotments ; in May, 1917, it had 2,200. In districts contiguous to London there were at this time upwards of 1,000 acres additional ground put under cultivation. Southall had 2,000 allotments to a population of 30,000 people, or a ten-rod plot for every three houses in the town.

A charming picture in the *Daily Graphic* of May 22, 1915, appeared over the words "Germany makes sure of the potato crop.' The picture shows a party of about twenty boys with spades and food baskets, apparently in charge of two teachers. A striking feature is the extreme youth of some of the party, as their ages look like ranging from seven to fourteen years. The picture is described as follows :

" In Germany all waste land has been seized by the Government for growing potatoes, and during the recent weeks it was a common sight in the big cities to see schoolboys marching off to their appointed plots intent upon preparing the ground for planting."

What a fine object lesson for our own people ! It is true that to a limited extent our children have during the past summer or two engaged in such garden and field work ; and as it is the kind of healthy work that most children delight in when it is well organised, we may hope that for the duration of the War their services after school hours and during holidays will be more extensively utilised.

INTENSIVE CULTURE AND THE MARKET FOR FRUIT AND VEGETABLES

We spent in 1913 on imported fruits £12,397,521, and on imported vegetables £6,005,159, a total of £18,402,680. That a large part of these huge imports could have been produced in this country there is no reasonable doubt, as we shall see directly. The amazing results due to intensive cultivation practised in the Channel Islands, France, Madeira, and in other countries, to say nothing of the success that has rewarded the efforts made at home here and there in this direction, should, at a time when the cultivation of every nook and cranny in the country is a matter of supreme importance to the State, receive the most anxious attention ; as, although this country is supposed to be highly populated, there is, as we have seen, at present an enormous amount of waste land lying idle that could be profitably cultivated on scientific lines. In the words of Mr. Sampson Morgan, F.G.L.[1] (Editor of the *Horticultural Times*, etc.): " It is not too much to say, with regard to private land alone, that there are hundreds of thousands of acres which, for centuries, on account of the popular belief of their barrenness, have been unproductive of an ounce of fruit or an ear of corn."

Now, many cases can be cited where such land has been economically utilised, but Mr. Morgan's own experience is well worth quoting. He says :

UTILISATION OF WASTE LAND IN SURREY

" Living for years in the midst of a vast expanse of idle and unproductive acres, on a ten-acre fruit farm nestling under the shadow of one of the highest hills in this county, with its model farmhouse which, on account of its elevated position, could be seen from the country roads around Guildford, nearly ten miles away, I am in an exceptionally favourable position to deal in a practical and comprehensive manner with a question which is undoubtedly of paramount importance to the English landowner. Generally speaking, the soil of the Surrey slopes and hills consists of a very light sand, shallow in some parts, deeper in others, but in most cases lying upon a subsoil of gravel, forming in the majority of cases a hard and almost impervious pan, which has first of all to be broken through before the land can be made fit for cultivation. Of course I need hardly say that such a soil is looked upon by the local agriculturist as being totally useless, hence for ages it has remained in the same state as we find it to-day—unproductive of anything save the peat that is cut from its surface, and the fir trees which spring up in profusion and flourish to perfection midst tangled

[1] In an article in " Land, its Attractions and Riches," p. 490.

masses of wild heather and gorse which cover the hills and valleys as thick as grass.

"Now to prove that such waste, hilly land as I refer to may be utilised in a very profitable manner, in spite of local opinion, I will refer to a case independent of my own—although the crops that were raised on my ten-acre holding, which when taken in hand was a fir wood, were of the most lucrative nature—to show what can be done under improved systems of culture.

"Five years before I had taken up my abode on the Surrey hills, a retired London tailor had bought fifteen acres of the same land, of which he had ten acres laid down with fruit. After this was done, he and his wife and one regular man kept the place in order without any other help except during busy seasons. I need scarcely add that in a few years he obtained regular and profitable yields of fruit, which met with a ready sale at Aldershot, every peck, in fact, being disposed of there. The weight of the crops was extraordinary ; the fruit itself was clean and very fine, and he was enabled to make money in fruit-growing on the proverbial waste and barren land of the Surrey hills. I anticipate the objection—first, that high winds on hill slopes would be fatal to fruit culture ; and secondly, that the dry nature of the soil on the light waste lands referred to would prevent the adoption of such a system.

"To the first I reply that, by the medium of the dwarf instead of the tall standard tree, and the protection of a bank of earth on top of which a hedge is planted—by making which we secure a ditch for surplus rains—we are enabled to meet the difficulty referred to ; and secondly, I assert that perfect and thorough drainage is positively essential to successful fruit culture. I am now referring to sloping areas of land in elevated positions. . . . On both fruit farms were raised the finest strawberries, raspberries, currants, apples, pears, plums ; also asparagus, marrows, peas, beans, potatoes, spinach, and various other products that could be grown in the open air. . . . I might here mention that the farmers of the district never dream of raising in their best fields anything except the usual round of root crops and corn.

" *Intensive or Petit Culture* is the panacea for which I plead, and the advantages that may be derived from the introduction of improved systems are evidenced in the case of a Mr. Rogers, near Petworth, in Sussex, a tenant under a twenty-one years' lease, on the estate of Lord Leconfield, whose little fruit and nursery plantation I have inspected, and which proves in the most striking manner what can be done with the land in this country. Originally, Mr. Rogers was a carter at Deptford, and in due course, without any agricultural knowledge whatever, found himself at an insignificant Sussex village, surrounded by the most beautiful scenery in England. His first start, I believe, was with a cottage and one or two acres of land, which he cultivated with his brother. Industrious and energetic to a degree, steady and economical, he worked on and on, until at last, when I visited his holding, he held about five acres in all, he had erected five glass-houses, mostly with his own hands, and had one of the most perfect little nurseries I have ever seen. . . .

" The productive nature of this little place is seen at a glance when we learn that it finds occupation and a living for five workers regularly, besides which Mr. Rogers and his brother have kept themselves and their two families of sixteen, all told, from this little fruit farm, and have a banking account besides. He propagates all kinds of nursery stock, including fruit trees, for the district, and his miniature orchard is planted with apple, pear, plum, and nut trees. The trees are planted in rows, first a half-standard tree, then a pyramid tree, with bush fruits between all.

" Where available he raises in the land between the rows of trees, early potatoes, strawberries, violets, etc., and I am convinced that he thus obtains from one acre more in money value than the neighbouring farmers do from twenty acres at least. The specimens of fruit raised are of high quality.''

The Soil is not Everything

It is proverbial that in places where the soil is comparatively poor, good crops can be produced by those who have the necessary skill ; for instance, Professor Bottomley claims to have grown radishes and tomatoes in sand by means of his new plant food made from bacterised peat. Indeed, as Professor James Long truly says : " There is nothing in romance or ancient story more thrilling than the fact that by the employment of artificial fertilisers in one case, or by a selection of plants in another, man is now able to clothe the almost barren hills with rich verdure." [1]

In fact, we may turn to one authority after another and find them agreed that nearly all soils are grateful for judicious, generous treatment, if science, industry, and intelligence prevail. [2]

" Generally speaking, with regard to the soil," says Mr. Morgan, " I find that much of the soil of what is termed our waste land is quite equal to that of the Channel Islands. Besides which I am convinced that many fields I have passed through, especially in the vale parish of Guernsey, would at first be designated poor soil by the majority of English farmers. The soil is not everything. With stony and light soils the Channel Island growers have by intelligence and skill made their productive little islands famous all the world over for the quality and quantity of their productions. By the same means, by the utilisation of the same methods, the same results can be secured at home."

[1] " Making Most of the Land."
[2] The competition for prizes for the best war allotments in Yorkshire has revealed an extraordinary triumph over terrible disadvantages. Fine crops of potatoes and turnips have been produced under the very nose of dye-works' chimneys. The ingenuity of the amateur cultivators has defied the blighting effect of the most deleterious fumes.

WASTE LANDS AN ECONOMIC FACTOR

The practicability of utilising waste lands, of course, depends upon the cost of labour and of fertilisers, etc., but even so there is good reason to believe that if the problem of developing these lands were sensibly taken in hand, means could be found to make them productive. In some cases they could be let to small-holders for a period of years at a nominal rent, or such holders could be subsidised until the land paid its way. In other cases use might be made of our prisoners of war and perhaps of convict labour. Certainly the problem should not be dismissed without it being seriously and sympathetically examined with due regard to its importance to the State and to recent developments in agricultural science and technology.

We have seen what success can be secured by individual effort alone, unaided by exceptional circumstances in any shape or form ; but much must be put into the land if much is to be got out of it. Unfortunately, the intensive system of farming in all its branches, which is believed to be the only one which can generally be counted on to pay, necessitates the expenditure of a certain amount of capital on the part of the occupier, and this is where the State through agricultural banks, and through help in instituting Co-Operative Societies and Joint-Stock Land Companies, could forward a great movement. Such agencies would be able to bring a large proportion of our waste lands under cultivation, and to purchase estates as they come into the market, divide them into assorted farms—large, medium and small—and sell them to those willing to purchase for the purpose of developing the agricultural and piscatory resources of the country. To break up overgrown sheep farms, and to substitute sheep for deer in the Scottish Highlands. To afford the farmer of small means and

N

great enterprise the opportunity of rising from the smaller to the larger holding, and the labourer of intelligence and energy of rising to the position of tenant farmer. To afford the amateur farmer and others opportunities to possess a few acres, and generally to help in restoring the balance between the agricultural and the manufacturing industries; encouraging suitable people, particularly our soldiers, after the War, to become associated with the land, and in so doing to relieve the cities that are overcrowded, and to greatly increase our production of foodstuffs.

Great are the possibilities in these directions; indeed, it was computed by the Agricultural Committee (about 1850) that the cultivation of waste lands would yield to the nation an income of above £20,000,000 a year.

And in the Third Report of the Emigration Committee (about 1850), it was estimated that we had in the United Kingdom 15,000,000 acres of waste land capable of improvement, and nearly 16,000,000 acres of land unprofitable. Of course, much of this land has since those days been cultivated.

CHAPTER XII

Reclamation of Waste Land

" It is a poor art that maintains not the artizan."—OLD PROVERB.

VAST SCHEMES OF RECLAMATION CARRIED OUT

IT is commonly known that an enormous amount of land that at present is absolutely useless, owing to it being water-logged or subject to flooding, could be made valuable for the production of foodstuffs by suitable embanking and drainage to bring it into a state fit for cultivation. So far back as 1844 it was computed that in the British Isles some 600,000 acres were available for this purpose. Of course the question of reclamation is largely an economic one, but in the history of this country vast schemes of reclamation have been beneficially carried out. The drainage of the Fens[1] has engaged the attention of several generations of engineers, with the result that large areas of what was formerly morass have been converted into exceedingly fertile land. This result has been attained, in the first instance, by cutting large arterial drains which discharge the water into the rivers, all of which discharge into the Wash.

The rivers which receive the waters from the Fens are the Witham, the Welland, the Nene, and the Ouse,[2]

---

[1] The Fens occupy a vast area about 70 miles in length, and from 3 or 4 to 30 or 40 miles in breadth ; upwards of 1,060 square miles, or 680,000 acres.

[2] The river Ouse, which is the outfall for the drainage of 1,936,000 acres of land, is perhaps one of the most interesting of the rivers in the Eastern Counties from an engineering standpoint.

and these rivers also drain uplands in the counties of
Lincolnshire, Northamptonshire, Huntingdonshire, Cam-
bridgeshire, and Norfolk. These rivers have from time
to time been diverted and straightened, so that the waters
are discharged into the sea more rapidly than they formerly
were. The reclamation and drainage of the Fen lands from
their former condition of morass are to-day a monument
to the perseverance and industry of the people who in
former years carried out these, at that time, great works,
converting vast tracts of waste land into fertile plains,
under a high state of cultivation.

Although these great engineering works were carried
out with the assistance of the State, many schemes of
reclamation, by which thousands of acres were embanked
off the estuaries of rivers or snatched from sea-shores
on almost every coast, have been promoted and executed
by individual enterprises during the past century.

Also on the Continent much has been done in this
direction. For instance, in the province of Farara, Italy,
200 square miles of land have been reclaimed and drained,[1]
at a cost of some £700,000.

UTILISATION OF THE RIVER OMBROME FOR RECLAMATION OF MARSHLAND NEAR GROSSETO

This scheme [2] is a fine and novel example of how
engineering skill can utilise natural forces to do useful
work. A large tract of marshland is being gradually
reclaimed by utilising a river which in the time of flood
carries about 10 per cent. of silt : a portion of the silt-
laden flood is diverted by means of one of the largest
artificial channels in the world, capable of discharging
8,000,000 gallons per minute, the gradient being one

---

[1] " Giornale del Genio Civile." Rome, 1911. Vol. xlix.
[2] *Ibid.* Rome, 1914. Vol. lii.

in 2,400. About six floods a year are expected to be used, and it is estimated that the deposit from the diverted portion of these will raise the tract of land about four inches per annum.

Loss of Land due to Erosion

Problems of great public interest relating to land have in recent years received a deal of attention, and it would seem that a serious attempt to compensate the country for the shrinkage of its shores by erosion, which is constantly going on, should be made in due course by reclaiming land wherever it be possible ; but, of course, it should not be overlooked that although denudation is daily taking place along our coasts, there are accretions at other parts which tend to equal them, as was some year or two ago pointed out by Lord Headly. [1]

" He believed that the Wash would one day add at least 100,000 acres to the land of England. So also at Dungeness, where the shingle bank is pushing gradually towards Gris Nez. At that particular spot there are 60,000 acres which not long since were under the sea. At Dingle Bay also he had noticed that the banks, which formed a bar, were steadily increasing. At the same time, the erosion in another part was most marked. When any alteration occurred in the formation of a bank, there must be a corresponding alteration in the ocean currents. He had in his possession an interesting plan of Dover Harbour, marked with all the schemes put forward by eminent engineers, but the result of the work done could not have been very satisfactory, as some sea-captains had told him that in storms it was impossible to make the harbour. At the present time there is no official or reliable record of the changes taking place round our coast, changes which must eventually affect buildings erected at a large expenditure

[1] A lecture before the Société Internationale de Philologie, Sciences et Beaux-Arts.

of private and public money. In his opinion all shores should be closely watched by the State. A great deal of money was often wasted by local authorities attempting preventive measures on too small and niggardly a scale. Unless remedial works were properly carried out they were useless, and the small sums voted occasionally by municipal authorities could often be spent to greater advantage in the purchase of bathing-machines and in planting trees."

Doubtless in due course much more attention will be given by the authorities to the problems due to erosion ; they certainly call for attention, particularly on some parts of our coast, such as those at Holderness, where, as Mr. Matthews, borough engineer of Bridlington, points out,[1] " the erosion was 11 feet a year, and 73,780 acres, or 115 square miles, had been lost on this coast since the Roman invasion." Mr. Matthews also explained that " the changes at Spurn Head had been enormous ; it had been alternatively island and mainland. Flamborough and Lowestoft Ness had been rapidly receding ; at other points there had been enormous reclamation."

WASTE DUE TO OVERFLOWING RIVERS

From time to time some of our most important rivers overflow their banks, flooding large areas of land, streets, and dwelling-houses, causing much damage to crops, produce, and property, and in the aggregate causing enormous losses to landowners, their tenants and others ; to say nothing about the serious and irritating inconvenience dwellers near the river-banks in particular are subjected to. The amount of waste due to the flooding of the Thames is a scandal, and adequate remedial measures are long over-due. Of course it is purely a matter of cause and effect, and Mr. Alexander Ross, C.E., lucidly dealt with the

---

[1] Discussion of Mr. C. Read's paper on " Coast Erosion." British Association, York, 1906.

matter in his presidential address to the Institution of Civil Engineers, November, 1915. He explained that—

"It is first of all essential to effective drainage that surplus water should have a free outward flow. All water must, sooner or later, find its way into the running brooks, streams, and rivers by which it is conducted to the ocean. It therefore follows, as a condition precedent to good drainage, that the streams and rivers should themselves be so regulated and controlled as to afford a free and uninterrupted flow. We cannot shut our eyes to the fact that in many cases our rivers and their tributary streams are not only unable to take the flood waters, but on the contrary their condition is frequently the cause of the damming back of water on the lands adjoining. We need not go far for examples. The river Thames, flowing past our doors, now and again rises in flood, and notwithstanding many improvements carried out by the Thames Conservancy above Teddington, in dredging, renewing and widening locks, weirs and sluices, and in regulating the discharge of flood water, still at times it overflows its banks and floods large areas of land, streets, and dwelling-houses, causing much damage to produce, crops, and property. The Thames is by no means an exception. There are large areas of land in the valleys of numerous rivers in England, Scotland, and Ireland which in times of exceptional rainfall are deeply flooded, causing in the aggregate enormous losses to landowners and their tenants.

"The largest agricultural areas subject to floods are on the east side of England, and are included in the valleys of the Waveney, the Bure, and the Yare, all discharging into the sea through the narrow channel of the Yare at Yarmouth, and in the valleys of the Great Ouse, the Nene, the Welland, and the Witham, flowing into the Wash through separate channels. In many cases measures for improvement would meet with difficulties and the works might be costly, but in not a few instances a quick return might be expected, while in others the improved value over a period of say twenty-five or thirty years would be sufficient to redeem the capital expenditure."

Fortunately legislative machinery now exists by which improvements in rivers may be brought about under the pressure of public opinion, as, with the object of facilitating and making feasible works of improvement, an important Bill was promoted in Parliament in 1914 by the Board of Agriculture for the purpose of creating an authority in any river valley by Provisional Order, conferring the power on this body to undertake certain specified works of improvement, and, in order to provide for the costs, to issue precepts to the authorities to levy rates in certain proportions according to benefit on their rateable areas. The Act received the Royal Assent under the title of the " Land Drainage Act, 1914."

Utilisation of Land Affected by Blowing Sands

In the aggregate, much good land adjoining extensive tracts of blowing sands on many parts of our sea-coasts (especially in the Hebrides) has been practically ruined by the sand deposited on it by the winds ; but a beautifully simple and effective process is available to prevent the mischief, namely, planting the sand-banks with sea bent-grass (*Arundo arenaria*), the matting fibres and stems of which not only bind the sand but clothe it with a herbage which is relished by cattle and furnishes a valuable winter forage in those bleak situations, as the grass is able to resist the severest winter weather.

The bent-grass can be propagated by seed, but in exposed situations it is found better to transplant it. This operation is usually performed between October and March, as it succeeds best when the sand is moist and evaporation slow.

ADDENDUM.—Refer to the Memorandum on the " Reclamation of Land," by Mr. A. D. Hall, M.A., F.R.S., in the Third (and Final) Report of the Royal Commission on Coast Erosion, 1911 [Cd. 5708].

CHAPTER XIII

Waste due to Neglect of Afforestation

THE TIMBER PROBLEM

OUR national needs, as revealed and emphasised by the War, have brought to the front the wicked neglect of many of our national resources, but none of greater importance than afforestation. In 1913, the year before the War, we imported[1] wood and timber to the extent of £33,788,884, between 80 and 90 per cent. of which consisted of coniferous or soft woods, of which a large proportion could have been grown in this country. For the year 1905 the sum was some £24,000,000, showing an increase of nearly £10,000,000 in eight years, despite the fact that the use of steel and ferro-concrete have immensely displaced timber in building and other work. But, on the other hand, timber is now used for many purposes for which it was not used in the past. To mention only a few : enormous quantities of timber are used for street paving, telephone poles, and for temporary purposes in connection with ferro-concrete work, etc. Also there is the large standing demand for wood in the shape of pit-props, and of the harder woods for furniture, etc.

---

[1] Of the timber imported, roughly one-fourth comes from the British Dominions, chiefly from Canada, and the remaining three-fourths from the United States, Norway, Russia, Sweden, Austria, and Germany. According to Messrs. Fay, Morgan & Co.'s annual wood report, the nation paid about £10,000,000 more in 1916 for wood imported into the United Kingdom than for a similar quantity in 1915, and £16,500,000 more than in 1914, the additional burden of costs being mainly attributable to the enormous increase in freights.

Then we have immense quantities of the smaller soft wood trees, spruce and others, converted into pulp[1] for the manufacture of paper ; the requirements for the average circulation of a popular daily paper amounting alone to 200 trees for pulp. This rapid increase in the use of timber is unfortunately not confined to our country ; indeed, it is taking place in all the civilised countries, and the world's consumption is increasing at a greater rate than the world's growth. Further, vast areas are being denuded by fire and reckless destruction without adequate reforesting, particularly in Canada, and during the War the loss has been unnaturally increased owing to the destruction of standing timber by artillery fire. In short, if afforestation is not taken in hand on a much wider scale than at present obtains both at home and abroad, the time is not far distant when we shall be faced by the calamity of a timber famine.

LAND UNDER TREE PLANTATION IN DIFFERENT COUNTRIES

Strangely enough, we have the smallest percentage of land under tree plantation in the whole of Europe, as the following shows :

Austria	32 per cent.
German Empire	26 per cent.
France	18 per cent.
Belgium	17 per cent.
Spain	17 per cent.
Italy	14 per cent.
Great Britain	4 per cent.

But it is not denied that our percentage of land under tree plantation could with great economic advantage be increased, and its productiveness considerably enhanced by the elimination of waste and by skilful forestry. On the other hand, we must not be led to believe that we could ever become self-supporting in the matter of timber, as

[1] In the year 1912 we imported wood pulp to the value of £4,418,000.

some writers suggest we might, for certain of our requirements, such as mahogany and other finer woods, can only
be met by using foreign timber.

FOREIGN TIMBER *versus* HOME-GROWN

Another phase of the question has been clearly explained by Mr. Charles E. Curtis, Professor of Forest
Economy, who says :

" There is, and always will be, a great demand for
foreign timber, and under present circumstances home
timber cannot compete with it. This is because the foreign
timber is fully matured and has grown under favourable
conditions, unlike our own, which has either been felled
in its infancy or after maturity has been passed. The
timber merchant knows well that our ordinary home-grown
produce is unfitted for many important purposes, and
buys chiefly to meet a local demand or for the few well-
defined purposes which it is fitted for. If the foreign
supplies were to cease we could not find in our woods the
class of timber which is needed. To some extent this may
be met by the spread of the true principles of forestry,
but under the most approved rules and principles we
cannot expect perfection. The chief reason is that private
individuals cannot be expected to allow their trees to
reach a perfect growth. States alone can achieve this.
Under no circumstances, therefore, can we become a timber-
growing nation, but we may, nevertheless, do much to
improve both the quality and quantity of our timber
supply. The matter rests with the landowners, and until
they recognise this the teaching of forestry will avail but
little.

"There is one link almost entirely missing in our system,
and that is the natural reproduction of trees. True, in
many cases blanks become filled up by the germination of
self-deposited seeds, but this natural planting meets with
no encouragement. In France and Germany it is the
keystone of the success which they so justly enjoy. This

power of natural reproduction is not simply permitted, it is encouraged and promoted, so that there is a regular rotation of a set period.   This natural power is, of course, aided where necessary by planting, and temporary nurseries are made in the various blocks to which the forester has access for this purpose. . . . The landowner who plants wisely will do more to increase the capital value of his estate than he who expends large sums on doubtful agricultural improvements."

Serious efforts should be made to decrease our ever-growing imports of foreign timber, and no pains should be spared in devising substitutes for timber where it is used in large quantities.   Many attempts have been made in this direction by the Railway Companies, who consume enormous quantities of timber.   For sleepers alone millions of pieces 10 inches by 5 inches and 9 feet long are used annually, but the efforts that have been made in the past to find a substitute for them have failed to give complete satisfaction. Still, success in this and other directions must not be regarded as hopeless.   Although apparently the problem of finding a substitute for pit-props has not been tackled seriously, it may be that some form of concrete or ferro-concrete props could be evolved.

WASTE DUE TO DECAY OF TREES

When woodland trees pass the period of maturity, whether this arrives from old age or from causes that bring about pre-maturity, the effect is that of disease and initial decay ; and therefore if trees are not felled and realised before this period has been reached it means waste, and this permissive waste is often one of the greatest sources of loss to the landowner.   As the loss is not apparent it is usually borne with indifference ; indeed, there is apparently an inherent feeling in landowners, not easy to overcome, that certain areas of woodland must not be reduced in

size, and thus trees are allowed to live on for years after
their value to the merchant has ceased.   Of course large and
beautiful trees should be permitted to remain to preserve
the sylvan beauty of a place, although they may be rapidly
deteriorating in value ; but this preservation should not
apply to woodland areas, where no such waste should be
allowed.

Coming Developments in Forestry

In May, 1916, an important statement was issued by
the Royal Scottish Arboricultural Society as a reason why
the Government should now seriously consider the question
of Scottish afforestation. The Society has passed this
resolution :

" That it is necessary, in order to provide for the nation's
future requirements of coniferous timber and such hard
wood timber as can be economically grown in this country,
and also to afford suitable and healthy employment for a
large and ever-increasing rural population, that the Government should now create the promised Department of
Forestry in connection with the Board of Agriculture for
the Development of Forestry in Scotland, with an adequate
annual grant for the purpose, and should instruct the
Department to prepare, without delay, schemes of afforestation, combined with small holdings and other rural industries ; to be put into operation as soon as the War is over,
so that advantage may be taken of the unique opportunity
when returning soldiers, sailors, and others are desiring
work, to induce a proportion of them to settle on the land
by offering them immediate and suitable employment
in comfortable and congenial surroundings.

" The Council of the Society point out that the area of
woodlands in Scotland is about 868,000 acres, or only
about four per cent. of the whole land area, being the
lowest percentage of the countries of Europe. . . .

" While the demand for home-grown timber is likely

to continue long after the conclusion of the War, and large areas of home woods are being cleared to meet the present demand, it is improbable that all or even a large proportion of these areas will be voluntarily replanted, with the result that the already relatively small extents of woods in this country will be alarmingly decreased. It is claimed that large areas of comparatively poor land in the country would be more economically used in growing timber crops than as at present used."

At a later period, July 4, 1916, a deputation of the Society attended a meeting of the Scottish Liberal M.P.s at the House of Commons to urge the necessity for adopting measures to promote afforestation, and Lord Lovat said he estimated that there were

"at least 2,000,000 acres in the Highlands on which afforestation would make it possible to settle one man for each 200 acres. Thus, should it be decided to plant this large area, there would be a working population of 10,000 woodmen and their families."

There can be no doubt that such developments would be economically sound if properly carried out. Indeed, it was estimated by the Commission on Coast Erosion and Afforestation (1909) that we could grow timber to the value of about £20,000,000 a year if we had 9,000,000 additional acres under timber. And according to the Report of the Commission the scheme of planting 9,000,000 acres[1] could be accomplished not only without any eventual loss, but, on the contrary, after the lapse of eighty years, all expenses having been repaid, the State would be in possession of a very large asset, about £107,000,000 in excess of the total cost, calculated at 3 per cent. compound interest.

---

[1] Sir J. Stirling Maxwell, at a meeting of the British Association, 1916, said that " probably not more than 6,000,000 acres were available for planting."

GERMAN STATE FORESTS PAY

As we have seen, with the exception of Austria, Germany has the largest percentage of public and private lands under tree cultivation in Europe. The State forests alone occupy 17,000 square miles. As might be expected, they yield a handsome revenue. Professor Fraser Storey, at the 1913 meeting of the British Association, in a paper on " German Forestry Methods," said that

" the average gross income from the State forests in recent years amounted to about £6,000,000 per annum, and the cost of management was rather more than £2,500,000. He thought that in England we might with advantage copy almost precisely the German methods of sowing, planting, soil cultivation, tending, regulation of density, and protection."

The above is well-deserved praise for what is believed to be the most scientific forestry in the world.

AFFORESTATION OF PIT BANKS

A remarkable illustration of what is possible in forestry, even under the most unpromising conditions, was explained by Mr. P. A. Martineau in a paper he read on " The Afforestation of Pit Banks," at the British Association (1916). It was a review of actual operations in the Black Country. Although no real income has yet been derived, considerable quantities of wood were well developed. He claimed the greatest successes for the experiments with black alder, but also claimed successes with birches and sycamores. The experiments ranged over eighty acres of high-lying bleak shale heaps, which, being burned out, were composed of red friable soils. He explained that the necessary preparations of the soil were practically nil. He had been able to utilise the casual labour of the district, and the cost, including supplies, would not exceed £7 per acre.

AN EXPERIMENT IN COMMERCIAL AFFORESTATION

The estate of Glencruitten, near Oban, has been bought by Mr. Alexander Mackay, C.A., Dundee, according to the *Daily Graphic* of October 13, 1917, for the purpose of experimenting in afforestation.

" The estate extends to 2,200 acres. The Crown Forester has visited the place, and the first 120 acres of plantable ground has already been staked off, and it is intended to begin the planting of trees about the middle of February. The idea of the purchaser is to demonstrate that trees can be grown advantageously on commercial lines, and to keep that part of the ground in such a way as will furnish an object lesson."

ARBOR DAYS

Even America, with its vast forests, has for some years been gravely concerned about the shrinkages of its timber resources, and wisely stipulates in all cases where the construction of a railway necessitates the felling of trees that others should be planted on a suitable scale. Mr. Roosevelt had the happy idea of helping to correct this shrinkage by instituting Arbor Day, a yearly ceremonial which encourages children in the planting of trees.

This is an institution we might well adopt, but something on a bigger scale is needed if we are to utilise our waste lands to their full advantage. It is true that arbor days are not unknown in this country, as the Kentish village of Eynsford a few years ago celebrated its " Arbor Day " by planting along 250 yards of roadway thirty-nine trees, the initial letters of the names spelling out the line from Browning—

Who keeps one end in view makes all things serve.

A walnut tree denoted the W, a holly the H, an Oak

the O, and so on. Then, again, the Browning Settlement in Walworth marked its coming of age by " tree-planting."

THE GOVERNMENT COMMITTEE

The Government (1916), it is stated, has decided to appoint a Committee to inquire into the needs of afforestation throughout the United Kingdom, and to propose a practical scheme on a large scale. The Committee will be appointed without delay, and its deliberations will be speeded up.

Fortunately, the folly of our neglect of timber cultivation is at last realised, and much good to our economic position should result from the activities of the Committee. In the first place we have to utilise to the full the resources we already possess, and this will probably mean the establishment of co-operation among landowners and estate agents, and readjustment of the cost of railway transit. Such organisation might well have a lasting effect on our timber supply problem, and prove to be one of the most beneficial results of the War ; but we must never forget how many years it takes for afforestation to become even moderately profitable, for although Douglas fir reaches maturity in about 40 years, according to Dr. Nisbet the best period for felling larch, scots pine, ash, elm, sycamore, and spruce, so as to procure the highest remuneration, is 50 to 60 years, and for oak 120 to 150 years.

Although, as we have seen, this country can never grow all the timber it requires, we may well believe that with organisation and science the Empire could become, with great economic advantage, self-supporting.

PART II

GLOSSARY

INTRODUCTION

" Thus Time brings all things, one by one, to sight,
And Skill evolves them into perfect light."
LUCRETIUS, Book V.

As many of the miscellaneous wastes that have received attention cannot be more conveniently grouped, they have been brought together and dealt with in three sections under the headings of I. The Romance of Waste, II. Miscellaneous Household Wastes and Economies, III. Miscellaneous Trade, Industrial, and other Wastes.

Probably no better way of exciting interest in the general subject of waste can be suggested than to relate some of the triumphs of past workers in this field, showing how great the rewards for success have been. This has been briefly attempted in Section I.

In Sections II and III notes have been arranged pointing to wastes that appear to demand attention, either with the object of utilising things that are ordinarily thrown away or destroyed, or with the object of focussing attention on problems and possible economies, the neglect of which is a measure of our past folly and extravagance. It is true that since war broke out we have been compelled to devote attention to some of these matters, but very much remains to be done before we view every kind of waste from the standpoint of economy and patriotism.

SECTION I

The Romance of Waste

NOTES ON HOW WASTE SUBSTANCES HAVE BEEN UTILISED,
AND WASTE OF PERISHABLE THINGS PREVENTED

IF our efforts to utilise every kind of refuse and waste products and things are to be successful in the highest degree, we must stimulate in the rising generation of workers imagination and the inventive and creative faculty, and foster skill in research ; as developments in these directions lead to greatly increased national prosperity. Probably there is no better way to kindle latent ability than to review, as we have attempted to do in this section, some of the successes of past workers in a field that has yielded such marvellous results and such rich rewards, often to the inventors and pioneers themselves, but always to the State.

The notes give short accounts in simple language of how such unpromising substances as sweepings, scourings, dross, dregs, scum, scoriæ, flue-dust, sediments, lees, offal, etc., etc., have been economically utilised, and of how in many cases the exercise of common sense, inventive ability or scientific research, has led to great economies and to the establishment of new industries by the utilisation of waste substances that have often been encumbrances—achievements that might well suggest to many an alert mind further triumphs.

The field of waste-prevention is a large one, and signal triumphs have been won by inventions that prevent the waste of perishable things—of which refrigeration and ensilage are typical—whose economical value it is not possible to estimate.

No attempt has been made to arrange the notes in order of their technical or commercial importance ; they are roughly grouped and more or less arranged alphabetically for convenience' sake.

FABRICS FROM WASTE

Alpaca from Waste Wool

Mr. (later Sir Titus) Salt, who had been for some years connected with the woollen manufacture, happened one day to notice at Liverpool some three or four hundred sacks of alpaca wool that had been imported from time to time from South America, in the hope of finding a manufacturer who might buy them for some purpose. Several men had tried to work up this new material, but without success, so there it lay for years, no one seeming to want it, till in 1836 Mr. Salt came across it, and after a number of trials, in which he modified his wool machinery to suit the stuff, adapting it afresh and overcoming many obstacles, he finally solved the problem by adopting cotton warps, and soon after put on the market a new material, ALPACA, a soft, glossy, elegant fabric, which so took the fancy of the public that in some fifteen years Mr. Salt amassed an enormous fortune ; and this enabled him to become a great philanthropist.

Utilisation of Cotton Waste

Cotton waste, suitable for spinning into yarn, is divided into two classes, " soft " and " hard." It has been effectively used in this country and on the Continent during the past thirty or forty years for the production of inexpensive cloths ; but the refuse of cotton, wool, etc., from spinning-mills and sheds is largely used as swabs for cleaning machinery, etc. ; the best of it is also, when of cotton only, and picked, cleaned, and bleached, used for the manufacture of gun-cotton. The refuse waste, which is usually dirty and somewhat greasy, is boiled under pressure with dilute caustic soda, then bleached and finally dried. In some cases the cotton waste is first treated with a solvent, such as carbon bisulphide, for the removal of grease.

Shoddy and Mungo from Woollen Rags and Cloth Clippings

Shoddy is a cloth made from worn woollen things, old stockings, druggets, etc., which were formerly only used for the production of inferior paper, wallpaper, etc., but which were more often thrown on the *waste-heap*. These odds and ends are now raw materials for inexpensive clothing fabrics. The woollen things are torn to pieces by a machine having spiked rollers (termed a devil), cleansed, and the fibre spun with a certain proportion of new wool, the yarn being afterwards woven into the full-bodied but flimsy fabric termed shoddy. Tailors' clippings and remnants of fine woollen goods, such as broadcloth, etc., are devilled and spun into yarn for making cloth of nicer quality, called *mungo*.

The portions of the devilled rags which cannot be utilised for shoddy and mungo are available as manure. They contain from about 3 to 13 per cent. of nitrogen, and are widely used in hop-gardens, the finely divided condition of the stuff being a valuable feature.

Battlefield Waste [1]

Scheme by which Millions will be Saved

A big enterprise has been built up at Dewsbury by the War Office, by which discarded uniforms and other articles of clothing collected on the battlefields and in home camps are dealt with in such a way as to save the nation hundreds of thousands of pounds.

[1] Extract from the *Evening News*, Oct. 13, 1916.

Since the work has been in progress about 45,000,000 separate articles have been dealt with, including—

- 4,100,000 jackets.
- 4,500,000 pairs of trousers.
- 620,000 great coats.
- 903,000 pairs of riding breeches.
- 2,700,000 puttees.
- 3,500,000 shirts.
- 856,000 caps.
- 1,800,000 cardigan jackets.
- 18,000,000 socks.
- 2,700,000 pairs of drawers.
- 6,000,000 other articles.

This part-worn clothing comes to Dewsbury in bags (says the *Daily Chronicle*), and is run in trucks straight into the huge sheds at the three railway-stations.

Here the bags are ripped open, and the contents spread out amongst the " pickers," whose nimble fingers and trained eyes quickly discover which garments should be set aside for renovation and which are only fit for disposal to rag-merchants and others, who put them through their special machinery preparatory to their being made up again into Army cloth in the local factories. As many as ninety truck loads have been received in a day.

300 Women Sorters

There are about 300 women sorters, who do their work so thoroughly that nothing is wasted. Garments which are beyond repair are carefully scrutinised, and sorted into woollens, linseys, angolas, etc.

Articles capable of being restored are sent to a local firm of dyers and cleaners, by whom they are cleaned. Then they are repaired and re-issued to the troops or for the use of German prisoners of war.

In ten months the value of produce received and disposed of at Dewsbury has been £658,650, while the two-thirds value of garments recovered for re-issue at all depôts has been £340,502, making a total of £999,152.

Against this, expenditure, including enlisted men's pay, civilian wages, cleaning and repair, etc., has amounted to £67,308, showing a net credit balance of £931,844.

Up to date, sales of rags to merchants and manufacturers in the heavy woollen district have amounted to £1,000,000. As showing the completeness of the arrangements to save, it may be explained that cotton rags are sent to Woolwich Arsenal to be used as wipers and cleaning rags.

Cardigan jackets are repaired with tape taken from old puttees, and darned with wool found in discarded " housewives," which also provide the needles and cotton used by the repairers.

Plush, Imitation Sealskin, Poplin, etc., from Silk Waste

Mr. Samuel Cunliffe Lister of Bradford, created Baron Masham in 1891, who had made a large fortune by inventing and introducing wool-combing machinery, happened one day to be at a certain warehouse in London, where he noticed a heap of rubbish, and on inquiry was told that it was " silk waste," sold as rubbish to get rid of it, as it was impossible to do anything with it. He began to think, and finally bought the heap at a halfpenny a pound, and had it sent down to his mills.

He started to solve the problem of how to make into beautiful fabrics the dirty, sticky mass of silk rubbish, consisting of the floss-silk or outer covering of the cocoons, badly formed or otherwise defective ones, the bottoms of cocoons when the usable filament has been wound off, scraps of twigs, dead leaves, and even dead silkworms, forming altogether a large proportion of the total weight of the cocoons, which was at the time considered as waste all the world over.

First the mass was sorted by boys, who picked it over and shook out the knots and twists ; next it was thoroughly washed and afterwards dried and introduced to Lister's machinery, which was specially altered, arranged and improved in various directions as he noticed would be necessary from the peculiar nature of the stuff. He continued to think and try to overcome the various difficulties that one by one revealed themselves. Some machinery suitable for his purposes he bought, some he had to invent, some he altered, and finally, after many years of patient improvement wherever he detected imperfections, he in 1857 produced the great variety of beautiful silken fabrics, satin, plush, poplin, shawls, stockings, handkerchiefs, ribbons, imitation sealskin, carpets, etc.—all made by the enterprise and mechanical genius of the great inventor out of waste rubbish, hitherto considered a nuisance, but now forming the raw material for an important industry, giving employment to thousands of hands.

The portion of the silk waste which cannot be utilised as above is of value as a manure, containing as it does about 14 per cent. of nitrogen, and being finely divided.

PRODUCTION OF OILS, ETC.

Paraffin Oil from Shale

When James Young, of Glasgow, succeeded in producing paraffin oil by the distillation of shale or cannel coal, he made vast waste heaps of shale, which were almost a nuisance, into a valuable raw material. This coal was all but worthless at most of the mines where it turned up ; in fact, in some cases money had to be spent in carting it away ; and such large quantities were found at other mines that it rendered them financial failures. There is something romantic about the history of Young's invention. He was brought up as a carpenter, but took a great fancy to chemistry, and, after much study, became a demonstrator at some classes, from which he went at the age of twenty-two to be manager of a chemical works. A spring of an oily substance being noticed in a coal mine of Derbyshire, and Young being recommended as the right man to attempt its utilisation, he succeeded in working up the stuff into two kinds of oil, one for burning, and the other for lubricating. The spring running dry, he was thrown out of employment ; but he had formed the idea that the oil was somehow distilled from the coal by the

heat of the earth, which led him to experiment and try
to imitate the processes of nature. This problem he worked
on for two years, when by heating a mixture of shale and
soda-ash just sufficiently to make it emit a gas, he found
that this when liquefied yielded paraffin. Suitable plants
were erected to give effect to this invention, and soon
after Young's patent paraffin oil was marketed all over
the world. This success soon brought him money enough
to buy up mines and adjacent tracts of land that were
dreary wastes, and that had previously been almost worthless, and by working his process these increased in value
a hundredfold, creating an important industry, which in
the course of about twenty years made him a millionaire.

Petrol once a Waste By-Product

Petrol was a waste by-product for which science had
found no use up to the time that the petrol motor was
invented. It is now used in enormous quantities in all
civilised countries, the world's production in 1911 being
over 50,000,000 barrels.

Oil from Sunflowers

Nothing is wasted in Germany, absolutely nothing.
One of the war-time economies practised there is the
utilisation of the narrow strips of ground along all fencing
for the growth of sunflowers, so that they may have the
oil from the seed—a very useful substitute for olive oil—
for cooking, or for oil-cake as cattle food, and the husks
for feeding poultry. Germany, it appears, has hitherto
imported sunflower-seed to the value of £150,000 per
annum, and in pre-war times apparently exported the oil
to this country as olive oil.

Oil from Cotton-Seed

Cotton-seed, which was formerly utterly useless,
became a valuable raw material when the means of ex-
tracting oil from it was discovered. The utilisation of this
oil has assumed a distinct industry in the United States.

In India cotton-seed is used more as a cattle food direct than as a yielder of oil. But when crushed in the native mills it yields about 25 per cent. of good oil, the cake remaining, after the expression of the oil, being used as a cattle food, and as a fertiliser. Egypt exports large quantities of seed to English and French ports ; but the seed cannot be shipped with safety without undergoing preliminary cleansing to prevent it heating and deteriorating in bulk on the voyage. The gumminess of cotton-seed oil limits its use for lubricating purposes, but it is used in large quantities by soap-makers in combination with other oils and fats. It is also largely used for adulterating other oils.

Oil from Cocoa Refuse

The refuse of cocoa manufacture, when treated with carbon bisulphide, yields a good oil, suitable for use in the manufacture of soap.

CENTRIFUGAL EXTRACTORS AND SEPARATORS

Recovery of Used Oil and Grease, and Wiping Materials

In many of our industries oil is used in vast quantities for lubricating purposes, for cooling and lubricating the taps and dies and the cutting tools used in screw ng and automatic machine tools, and such-like purposes in particular. Formerly, beyond allowing the oil to drain from the articles machined and from the screwings and turnings, no attempt was made to recover the oil adhering to them ; but in all works where proper attention is given to economy and high efficiency centrifugal extractors are now employed to recover the oil to the last drop for filtration and re-use. The methods employed are also applied to the recovery of waste oil and grease from the cotton waste and cloths used for cleaning machinery. These materials, which were formerly burnt or thrown away after first use, are now often of greater value than the new materials, owing to the oil contained in them.

The wiping material is repeatedly reclaimed for re-use
and the oil recovered therefrom for putting into service
again.

The centrifugal extractor or separator primarily consists of a perforated cage, into which the oily waste, cloths,
turnings, or articles are placed, and it is rotated at a
peripheral speed of some 5,000 to 7,000 feet per minute
by an electric motor or steam turbine. The cotton waste
and cloths if very dirty require washing after they have
been through the extractor, but if they have only been used
for wiping down engines, mopping up oil, and similar
jobs they are ready for further use after the oil has been
extracted. Mr. A. Grison, chief engineer of rolling stock
of the Orleans Railway, in giving an account[1] of a process
for enabling the lubricating oils and pads employed on
rolling stock to be re-used, explains that when the wheels
were removed from the bogies of the vehicles of the American
type they have running, so that the tyres may be re-turned,
the wool waste and oil had to be removed from the boxes
and were a serious loss, as they could not be re-used owing
to the sand and dust which collected in the boxes, even
with the greatest care in keeping the covers closed. But a
plant has now been installed to treat these materials
(to the extent of about 1,000 lbs. of waste per day), consisting of a centrifugal extractor heated by steam, two
purifying tanks, a small pump, a drying stove, and a
carding machine.

The temperature of the extractor is kept at 80° C. by a
steam coil, the dirty oil runs from the extractor into the
first tank and is then decanted into the second tank,
heated by a steam coil, and finally filtered. The oil can
be re-used by mixing with three times its volume of new
oil, and the carded waste is ready for re-use. The cost
of the installation at the Paris depôt was £280, and it has
effected a saving of £80 to £120 per month.

The Lancashire and Yorkshire Railway Company
use some 6,500,000 sponge cloths annually for cleaning

purposes,[1] the use of cotton waste being discarded by them some years ago. These cloths, which are saturated with different kinds of oils, such as ordinary lubricating, rape, and heavy petroleum cylinder, with small quantities of yellow grease and tallow, yield in the extractor from one to one and a quarter gallons of crude oil per gross of cloths.

In the Wolsey Motor-Car Works 1,200 gallons of cutting oil are recovered a week, to be used over again, with only 10 per cent. of fresh oil to make up for the wastage. Another interesting example is the following. A firm manufacturing cycles treated in six months 834 cwt. of metal turnings, 8 cwt. of rags, and 134 gross of sponge cloths, and recovered a total of 2,440 gallons of oil, weighing approximately 10 tons.

Another method of recovering the grease and oil from cotton waste and cloths used only for wiping machinery is by the use of carbon bisulphide, which is an excellent solvent for fats. The greasy articles are very lightly and loosely introduced into an air-tight iron cylinder arranged with a false bottom, care being taken to ensure the porosity of the mass and its freedom from more than a very small percentage of water. The bisulphide is pumped in from below, and as it rises through the mass it dissolves the fatty matters, which flow away from the top through a still. It is there distilled off by steam and condensed. When all the grease has been extracted from the materials, the bisulphide retained by the latter is drained off for re-use, its loss in each operation, when stringent precautions are taken to prevent leakage, being only trifling. Care must be taken in using the bisulphide, as it is both inflammable and poisonous.

We thus see how wasteful the burning of greasy waste and rags as fuel is, as some 90 per cent. of the oil can be economically recovered, and the rags, etc., made fit for re-use.

[1] Abstracted from a paper read by Mr. G. H. Ayres before the Graduates Association of the Institute of Mechanical Engineers.

Recovery of Oil from Metal Turnings, Swarf, etc.

Centrifugal extractors are also very largely employed
for the recovery of oil from metal turnings, chips, cuttings,
etc., as well as from small finished work made in the auto-
matics, lathes, and other tools, about 98 per cent. of the
oil being easily recovered for re-use.

The metal swarf being left very dry is in a condition
most suitable for re-melting where desired.

Centrifugal Fat Extraction from Offal, Kitchen Waste, etc.

Centrifugal extractors, usually of the steam turbine
type, are most economically used, capable of dealing with
a wide range of materials, such as kitchen waste, greases,
cracklings, tongue trimmings, scratchings, stockpot residues, dregs, bacon and ham rinds, meat offals, cowheel
hair, catch-pit skimmings, tank bottoms, bones, bristles,
barrel scrapings and kettle scraps. The extractors also
eliminate all suspended matter from rendered fat, lard,
tallow, etc. These extractors are also extremely useful
for the recovery of fat from filter and hydraulic press
cloths and bags, mutton cloths, printers' rags, etc., and
for the full recovery of liquors remaining in all classes of
extract residues.

USEFUL MATERIALS FROM RESIDUES
AND REFUSE

Beeswax from Residues

The residues from beeswax manufacture, which formerly were worth about £8 per ton as manure, are now made
to yield an excellent yellow wax by treatment with carbon
bisulphide.

The Recovery and Re-use of Manganese in the Production of Bleaching Powder

The recovery of manganese in the production of chlorine for the manufacture of bleaching powder by Weldon's beautiful process is an excellent example of what science has done in preventing waste. Formerly for every 100 lbs. of bleaching powder made, about 100 lbs. of the native oxide of manganese were required. Now this manganese is recovered and used again and again in the process, the amount of fresh manganese ore requisite to replace that lost being only 1 per cent. of the bleaching powder made. The earlier methods of recovering manganese were not nearly so perfect, and therefore were not much used. The comparative costliness of manganese has made its recovery essential, in order that it may again serve as an oxygen carrier.

Aniline Dyes from Coal-Tar

The dark-coloured resinous substance obtained by distillation from coal, known as coal-tar, was formerly of little value, but science has made it possible to derive from it a vast host of extremely valuable substances, such as carbolic oils, benzol, toluene, phenol, anthracene, creosote oils, naphthalene, benzene, pitch, etc., etc., but, commercially the most important of all, the beautiful aniline dyes. In the year 1856 Perkin, while searching for a cheap method of preparing quinine from nitro-benzol, obtained a beautiful solution of mauve colour. This was found to be such an effective dye that exhaustive experiments have been made on this substance, with the result that over 300 of the most beautiful colours of the spectrum have been discovered for dyeing purposes. But unfortunately we allowed the development of an important industry to drift to Germany, where astute business men saw the vast possibilities of the discoveries, with the result that our staple textile industries, representing an annual turnover of more than £300,000,000, have until recently been practically dependent upon the foreign

P

dye manufacturers.[1] However, fortunately a supreme
effort is to be made by us to establish on a firm and lasting
footing the industry in the land of its origin. The production of coal-tar in Germany increased enormously in
the five years 1908-13, and it is now claimed to be sufficient
to also render that country independent of imported
petroleum. The output of coal-tar in Germany increased
from 120,000 tons in 1906 to 450,000 tons in 1911, an
enormous rate of expansion. One of the most important
distillates of coal-tar is benzol ; its calorific value is about
18,000 BTU per lb., nearly the same as that of petrol,
and in Germany very large quantities of this spirit, mixed
with alcohol, are now consumed in petrol-motors ; indeed,
the production in that country increased from 59,598 tons
in 1909 to 87,214 tons in 1910.

Synthetic Indigo—Utilisation of a Waste that was a Nuisance

For over 5,000 years the indigo plant was the sole
source from which this valuable dye-stuff (indigo) was
obtained. The dyers of ancient Thebes employed it for
ornamenting the garments of the living and the burial
cloths of the dead. But in 1866 Von Baeper began his
researches, which, by laying bare the innermost structure
of the indigo molecule, not only completely revolutionised
the industrial manufacture, but also disclosed a limitless
vista of artificial dyestuffs, sharing the valuable properties
of indigo, but capable of dyeing every colour of the rainbow.
Having elucidated its structure, the chemist proceeded
to build up the dyestuff artificially, from products con-

[1] The result of our past folly in allowing ourselves to become dependent
on Germany for an adequate supply of dyes is now severely felt, as some
of them are almost unprocurable, the prices of others having romped up
to prohibitive figures ; thus malachite green crystals, formerly 3s. per lb.,
sold at 30s. in November, 1915 (a price that can only be paid by makers
of distempers, who use one pound of the crystals to about 2 cwt. of dis-
temper) ; and black aniline, formerly sold at 8d. per lb., rose to 6s. 8d.
per lb. At the Midland Railway lost property sale at Derby on
November 3, 1915, a keg of methylene blue, weighing about 1½ cwt.,
realised £310, which works out at 36s. per lb. Before the War the keg
would have been worth about £12 to £15.

tained in coal-tar. The starting material in the most successful processes was naphthalene, at one time regarded by the tar distiller as a waste and a nuisance, but now recognised as a valuable product. In the first stage of the synthesis of indigo, naphthalene is converted by oxidation into phthalic acid ; next the discovery was made that the direct oxidation of naphthalene could easily be effected by fuming acid in the presence of mercuric sulphate. Cheap fuming acid was therefore a necessity, and it was successfully produced by the " contact process " after a great deal of patient research, and by the year 1907 the synthetic manufacture of indigo had become a firmly established German industry.

A works installed in this country by the Germans to work this process is now happily in the hands of an English Company.

Utilisation of China-Clay Wastes

In the production of china-clay there are waste or pseudo-waste products which are now produced in very large quantities. Among these we have the following :

Fine Mica, deposited in the " micas," was formerly washed away, but it is sometimes now collected, dried in the manner of clay proper, and sold at a low price to the makers of soft paper, pasteboard, inferior pottery, etc.

Sand.—This consists of broken quartz crystals ; when washed clean it is the finest building sand procurable, as the angles are all sharp. It forms a concrete as hard as stone when mixed with one-eighth of portland cement.

Discoloured Clay.—Has to be dug out from among the good white clay in many places. It is used in the manufacture of white tiles and bricks. When mixed with the above-mentioned sand it produces an excellent fire-brick.

Utilisation of Cork-Cutters' Waste, and of Used Corks

In making corks there is a large amount of waste, amounting to some 35 to 40 per cent. These refuse cuttings are utilised in the manufacture of linoleum, and form the larger part of its bulk. They are first passed through a breaker, which they leave in pieces about the size of peas, and then through mills, resembling those used for grinding corn. The ground cork on leaving the mill-stones is passed through a sieve, the finer particles falling into sacks, while the coarser residue is returned to the mill. The sacks of powdered cork are placed in a drying stove, and allowed to remain at a temperature of about 100° F. for about twenty-four hours before being placed in the mixing machine, where the powder is roughly mixed with the cement which is used to unite the particles of cork forming crude linoleum.

On a smaller scale, the waste from cork-cutting is used for other purposes. It is considered the best material available for stuffing mattresses to be used at sea, as it is light and damp-proof, and forms a raft in case of accidents. Being a good non-conductor of heat, it is a useful material for lining ice-houses, etc., and it is also used for filling cushions and horse-collars, whilst in France it is utilised in the manufacture of pasteboard, the ground cork being thoroughly incorporated with paper pulp. The least economical way of utilising waste cork is to burn it as fuel, as is done in some cork factories. When wet, the waste cork is not easily dried, and it is therefore not readily disposed of in that condition. It should be known that cork dust and air in certain proportions is highly explosive. It would appear that in establishments where a great many corks are drawn they should be worth storing for sale, instead of being thrown into the dustbin.

Utilisation of Granite Waste

In shaping and dressing granite paving-stones as much as three-fourths of the rock quarried is, in some cases at least, wasted. This waste is apparently in many cases only partially utilised for road-metal, and in small chips for granolithic pavements.

Utilisation of Grindstone Waste Swarf

The waste " wheel swarf " or grit, worn away in grinding cutlery wet, has a certain value. It is used in the formation of a cement for sealing the cementation furnace boxes used in the conversion of wrought iron into steel ; and some manufacturers not only employ all their own waste sand for this purpose, but have to purchase that of others.

New Glass from Glass Waste

In the manufacture of glassware, all broken glass is carefully collected and sorted ; the best is mixed with the raw material and remelted ; the poorest qualities are worked into coloured glass, or into tiles and transparent bricks. There is also a large quantity of final waste which has become so mixed with clay and dirt as to be unfit for use as transparent glass ; this waste is in some works collected, sifted, ground into an almost impalpable powder, and spread upon clay tiles, then placed in a kiln until the glass is partially melted, to give an opaque, exceedingly hard surface to the pieces, making them suitable for pavements or wall decoration. By the intermixture of metallic oxides almost any colour can be obtained. Another use to which glass waste is put is as a grinding material for the rims of buffs, and as a partial substitute for emery in emery wheels. It is also used in the manufacture of glasspaper. The prosperity of glass-works, needless to say, depends upon the reduction of actual waste to the smallest limits.

Glue from Refuse Parings

Although the best glue is obtained from the " soundings " of sheepskins and cattle-hides, known as fleshings, very good glue is made from the refuse parings and scraps produced in trimming hides, horns and hoofs (refuse that was formerly considered a waste), which are washed in limewater, boiled, skimmed, strained, evaporated, cooled in moulds, cut into convenient pieces, and dried on nets.

Ivory-Black from Ivory Turnings, Chips, and Dust

Ivory turnings, chips, and dust are utilised for the production of the beautiful black pigment known as ivory-black, which is employed by copperplate printers in the preparation of their ink. When mixed with white lead it also makes a rich pearl-grey pigment. In preparing the ivory-black, the ivory fragments are exposed to a red heat for some hours in crucibles; when quite cold the crucibles are opened, and the contents pulverised, the richest coloured fragments being collected for the best quality. The powder is levigated on a porphyry slab, washed with hot water in a filter, and dried in an oven. The product is a beautiful velvety black stuff, free from the reddish tinge which so often mars the quality of bone-black.

Paper from Rags, etc.

Vast quantities of rags, etc., are gathered from our dust-heaps annually, and used in paper-making. In 1875 it was found that as many as 3,761 men and women in this country gained a livelihood in connection with the dust-heaps, collecting rags, bagging, ropes, tarpaulin, string, hair, paper, etc., for all of which there is a ready market for various kinds of paper making. There are master-men even in this industry, and it is on record that one rag and bone collector always employed ten hands, and collected about 250 tons of rags per annum. Dewsbury is the important centre of the rag trade. There are also rag depôts and auctions in Leeds, Huddersfield, Wakefield, Bradford, Batley, and other towns. Rags are used as the raw material for shoddy and paper-making. In paper-making, the rags, linen or cotton[1] as the case may be, are sorted by hand into various qualities proper for different kinds of paper; the best and finest, of course, being selected for the stock from which the better qualities of writing-paper are to be made. The sorted rags are

---

[1] Paper has been made from cotton from a very early date, apparently **first at Mecca**, about the year 706.

divided into shreds and are washed in hot water and boiled
with caustic soda, and are afterwards reduced to pulp
by the rag engine.

As a further economy the fine particles of fibre recovered
from the waste liquor of paper mills by settlement can
frequently be used again for the manufacture of slightly
coloured paper.

There are also many materials (besides those we have
mentioned) used in the manufacture of paper, that are not
all exactly waste materials, but were more or less unde-
veloped substances before they became so largely used in
paper-making ; and among these may be mentioned flax
and jute mill waste, and paper scraps from printing-houses
and binding works, etc.

Slag-Wool and Garden Rollers from Furnace Slag

Blast furnace slag, the scoria or refuse from the blast
furnace, which was formerly *waste* material, with a bulk
some three times that of the iron from which it had been
separated, is now utilised in several ways in different
countries for such things as road material, garden rollers,
and slabs for pavements, etc., or it is granulated, ground
fine, and used as building sand ; or in its coarsely granular
state made into bricks. An incombustible non-conducting
fibrous material is also prepared by blowing a jet of steam
through a thin stream of viscous molten slag as it falls
from a narrow gutter on leaving the blast furnace. This
stream is so manipulated[1] that it causes the molten slag
to take the form of downy silicate of cotton, with delicate
fibres resembling asbestos or spun glass, which from its
appearance has received the name of *slag-wool*. This

[1] The jet of steam in springing on the molten slag scatters it into a
stream of shot, which is projected forward near the mouth of a large
tube, in which a couple of steam jets cause an induced current of air. This
tube opens into a receiving chamber, composed chiefly of wire gauze. As
each shot leaves the stream of slag it carries a fine thread or tail with it.
The shot, being heavy, falls to the ground, while the fine woolly fibre is
sucked through the tube and deposited in the chamber. The appearance
of this chamber after a charge had been blown into it is singularly beautiful.
Not an inch of floor or roof but is covered with a thick layer of the downy
silicate cotton. After each blowing the wool is removed by forks, and
packed in bags ready for use.

material, being a good non-conductor of heat, is used as a covering for boilers, steam pipes, etc. At some furnaces on the Continent the slag is sold ; it is run directly into waggons, or it is prepared by granulation in water, and is used for making cement, artificial stone, and in the manufacture of ground and other glass.[1]

Other kinds of slag on the sites of ancient smelting-works have in modern times been again put through the furnace to extract the metals left in them, with profitable results.

Lead-Pencils from Waste Graphite Cuttings

For a great many years the graphite used in making lead-pencils (consisting almost entirely of carbon and containing no lead) was obtained almost exclusively from the Borrowdale mines in Cumberland, being mined in compact grey-black masses, cut into thin plates, then into rectangular sticks and cased in wood. When the best quality was exhausted (early in the nineteenth century), the manufacturers turned their attention to the utilisation of the accumulations of waste from cuttings of the original masses, which they finely ground and mixed with varying proportions of clay, and in this way were able to produce pencils in fourteen degrees of hardness and softness, making them superior to those formerly made from the entire graphite, which was never uniform in colour and hardness.

PRODUCTS RECOVERED FROM WASTE LIQUORS

Glycerine from Soap Lees

Glycerine may be derived from all oily or fatty substances by various processes, the object being to detach it from its combination with the acids stearic, oleic, and

[1] The vitreous character of slag indicates a resemblance to glass in its composition. It does, in fact, contain the principal components of glass, but not in proper proportions, and those in which it is deficient have therefore to be added. The metal so produced is largely used for the manufacture of wine- and beer-bottles.

margaric, to which it is united as a base. The refuse from soap-making (the spent lees), which was formerly run to waste (often into our rivers) in enormous quantities, contains a large proportion of glycerine, which is now most economically recovered by the vacuum evaporator process, the annual saving in a works producing 10 tons of soap per week being about £1,200, as estimated by Mr. R. D. West. The enormous development in its production and use is one of the most wonderful things in the history of the chemical industry, and a scientific achievement of far-reaching importance. Glycerine is most largely used now for the manufacture of the powerful nitro-glycerin explosive ; it possesses remarkable solvent properties on some substances, and it can be used wherever a substance requires to be kept more or less moist. Owing to its low freezing point it is used with water in gas meters, and in floating compasses, also in the cylinder jackets of petrol engines in cold weather to prevent the water freezing, the mixtures of glycerine and water having lower freezing points than either constituent. Its uses are constantly increasing, and its applications in pharmacy are almost endless.

Fat Recovered from Soap-Suds

Soap-suds contain a certain percentage of fat combined with alkali as a soap. Formerly in certain mills in which soap is used this fat was allowed to run to waste, but it is now largely recovered, especially in the woollen-manufacturing districts. The suds from woollen-mills contain a large quantity of fat derived from the wool itself in addition to the soap employed in washing or fulling the wool. The suds are first strained and then settled to remove extraneous matters, after which they are treated with steam and sulphuric acid to liberate the grease, which is passed through filter presses to separate the oil ; the latter is transferred to a lead-lined vessel and treated with strong sulphuric acid to remove any water that may be in it, after which it is barrelled for sale. The residue in the hot press (called " sud-cake ") is treated with carbon bisulphide to extract any remaining traces of grease, and is then used for manure-making. Even the waste liquor is sometimes beneficially used for irrigating pasture, after being neutralised with lime, or made slightly alkaline.

Soda from Waste Liquors

Formerly the liquors in which rags, wood-pulp, esparto, and other paper material had been boiled were run into an adjacent river or stream, tending to pollute it ; but now all such liquors are evaporated and treated for the recovery of the soda originally used as caustic soda ; and a Füllner apparatus is used for the recovery of fibre.

The caustic soda is used to remove grease, dirt, etc., and to break down the structure of the grass by removing the resinous or gummy cementing matters.

In paper-making, the spent caustic liquor from the grass or rag boilers contains much organic matter. To remove this the liquor is first concentrated in a multiple vacuum evaporator, using steam, and is then incinerated in rotary furnaces, which drives off the water remaining in the concentrated liquor and burns out the organic impurities, the soda being discharged in the form of a black ash, which is largely carbonate of soda. This ash is easily converted into caustic soda solution, which is again used in the process of boiling.

The recovery is from 80 per cent. to 90 per cent. of the soda used, and the approximate saving in a works using 20 tons of solid caustic per week is said to be about £4,000 per annum. Indeed, it is one of the most valuable improvements in modern paper-making.

Soda Recovery from Mercerising Process

John Mercer in 1850 discovered that if cotton be treated with a strong solution of caustic soda the fibre changed from a hollow flattened form to approximately a solid round thread, with increased dyeing capacity and increased strength.

Many years later it was discovered that when yarn

or cotton goods were treated with caustic soda whilst stretched in frames to prevent shrinkage, the fibres retain their original length and strength, and when the caustic is removed by washing, the fibres acquire a beautiful silk-like lustre ; but the process was attended by an enormous wastage of the soda in washing.

Eventually a process was devised which effected the recovery of the soda liquor at a sufficient strength to enable concentration in multiple effect vacuum evaporators to be carried out economically, the resulting liquor being perfectly suitable for re-use and the recovery being from 75 per cent. to 90 per cent. of the caustic soda used.

The estimated saving in a works using 10 tons of caustic weekly, due to this remarkable process, amounts to about £3,000 per annum, according to Mr. R. D. West.

Grease from Wool-Scouring Waste

Wool as taken from sheepskins, or sheared from live sheep, is excessively greasy with dried perspiration, and has, besides, adhering to it, more or less, seeds, dirt, and excrement. Practically all this has to be removed before the wool can be carded. The process [1] of removal is termed wool-scouring, and it consists in passing the wool through a hot solution of soap, and sometimes carbonate of soda, the mixture being kept agitated. The dirty solution usually has 3 per cent. of solid matter and 1 to $1\frac{1}{2}$ per cent. of fats, and when run off constitutes one of the most polluting of trade wastes.

Wool suds vary in quality, some being much more greasy and concentrated than others, according to the kind of wool that is being washed. Australian wool yields the most greasy suds. At some wool-scouring works the greater part of the fat in this waste is recovered, but the recovery is incomplete. In the process for degreasing raw wool, devised by Smith's Patent Vacuum Machine Company, Ltd., it is claimed that the potash, as well as the grease, can be profitably recovered. The raw wool is treated with petroleum naphtha under diminished pressure,

[1] " Report of the Royal Commission on Sewage Disposal," vol. i., 1915.

and afterwards the naphtha is recovered from the grease solution by distillation. The degreased wool is then extracted with a small quantity of water, which dissolves out the potash. The wool then requires very little further cleansing.

The method at present in use at most of the wool-scouring works in this country consists in " cracking " the wool suds, in tanks holding about 4,000 to 5,000 gallons each, with slight excess of sulphuric acid, and allowing the fats to separate at the top and bottom of the tank. The acid liquor is then run off, either to the sewers or into a stream, while the crude fat magna is made into " puddings " in pieces of sacking and hot-pressed for grease. The grease (known as YORKSHIRE GREASE) recovered is at present apparently about 60 per cent. of the grease in the original suds,[1] but it is believed that a better yield is possible by using the modern steam-jacketed filter press, and that there should be a market for the practically de-greased cake ; further, that efforts should be made to also recover the potash and nitrogen which are lost. Crude wool-grease is used for the manufacture of LANOLIN, which owes its therapeutical value largely to the fact that, unlike fats, it readily emulsifies with water and is rapidly absorbed by the skin.

The cleanings of *wool-cards* when acted upon by carbon bisulphide give about 30 per cent. of fatty substances, useful for the production of soap.

Candles from Waste Fats

All sorts of waste fats, such as those from wool-washing and glue-making, are now used for making candles, the free acid being extracted by treating the fat with sulphuric acid. This industry furnishes an excellent example of the utilisation of waste products.

---

[1] At the Hudson Worsted Company, Mass., the method employed consists of a settling-tank which receives all the wool-waste from the factory, after which it is passed through a cooling-tower. Thence it passes into three treating-tanks, each holding 15,000 gallons, and 800 to 1,000 pounds of sulphuric acid are added. After settling, the sludge containing the grease is made into " puddings " by being folded into squares of wool sacking from which the fat is extracted by hydraulic presses. The resulting effluent contains only 20 parts of fat in 100,000.

Illuminating Gas from Waste Liquids

The soap used for cleansing purposes in yarn mills is recovered by precipitating the soap from waste liquids with lime, and pressing the precipitate into briquettes, from which sufficient gas can often be obtained by distillation to light the mills.

Grease from Margarine Liquors

The waste liquids from margarine works are subjected to settlement in tanks, and the greasy matter rising to the surface of the first tank is skimmed off at intervals and sold for use in the manufacture of soap, etc.

Garancine from Spent Madder

Madder, which held a chief place among our dyestuffs till about 1869 (but has since become of trifling importance through the introduction of artificial alizarin), in its spent form at our large dyeworks was years ago suddenly raised from a useless to a valuable material by the use of sulphuric acid, which converted it into the dye called garancine.

India-Rubber from Waste Liquors

The waste liquors from the manufacture of various india-rubber articles contain considerable quantities of acetate of lime (but mixed intimately with hyposulphite of lime) and lead, and they contaminate the product if simple distillation with sulphuric or hydrochloric acid be attempted. It has been proposed to employ chlorine to convert all the sulphur acids and salts present into sulphate of lead, which can be filtered off or allowed to subside.

Potash from Distillers' Wash

The wash from molasses distilleries, which was formerly run to waste, is used to produce potash, which forms the base of so many valuable alkaline salts.

BY-PRODUCTS AND RESIDUES UTILISED FOR FOODSTUFFS, ETC.

Margarine from Suet and Vegetable Fats

This excellent substitute for butter is manufactured from animal and vegetable fats. Very briefly, the process is carried out by exposing the fats to a temperature of about 122° F. and collecting the liquid portion, which is drained away. This liquid is kept at about 77° F. until the glyceryl salts, solid at that temperature, have separated, and the resulting mass (which becomes buttery in consistency at the ordinary temperature) is pressed. It is then churned up with milk to impart a butter-like flavour, a little anatto, turmeric, or saffron being added to give it a yellow colour.

The following are used for the production of the vegetable fats and oils : cotton-seed, ground nut, gingelly (sesame), kapok-seed, linseed, maize, palm kernel, niger-seed, poppy, rape-seed, soy, shea, and sunflower.

Coco-nut is also used, and it supplies a proportion of glyceryl salts of fairly low fatty acids, the characteristic flavour of coco-nut oil being removed by treatment with alcohol and animal charcoal.

The main difference between butter and margarine is the absence or comparative absence in the latter of the glyceryl salts of lower fatty acids.

Margarine of the best quality is about a third of the price of butter, and is only distinguishable from the latter by the expert ; whilst dietetic authorities are agreed that it is as palatable, wholesome, and nourishing as butter, which is becoming dearer and dearer. The prejudice against the use of margarine in this country is steadily decreasing, but still we are a long way behind continental countries in making use of this wholesome and inexpensive foodstuff, the consumption in 1912 for Great Britain being only about 8 lbs. per head per annum, less than a fourth of the consumption per head in Denmark that year. It is true that we only started to manufacture in this country about the year 1890, but happily we are rapidly increasing the number and size of our manufactories ; the special machinery and plant used in refining, bleaching, deodorising, pressing and finishing, or otherwise treating the oils, being chiefly made in Holland. In 1914 we spent on imported margarine nearly £4,000,000 and on imported butter £24,000,000—vast sums to spend upon commodities that with proper organisation and enterprise could be just as well produced in our own country, particularly as we have in the Empire unrivalled stores of the necessary raw materials.

Strangely enough, margarine was invented in Paris during the Siege in 1870 (by the chemist Mège-Mouries) owing to the shortage of butter ; but it was not until about 1880 that it was commercially exploited by the Americans and the Dutch, the Danes entering the market at a later period.

A point not to be overlooked in using margarine is that bulk for bulk it is heavier than butter, therefore if it be spread on bread with the same thickness as when butter is used it will not go so far.

It may be remarked that the use of solid animal oil for this foodstuff absorbs some of the raw material formerly available to the soap-maker, but the deficiency has been made good by the conversion of the plentiful supply of vegetable oils, such as olive oil, into solid fats by hydrogenation in the presence of finely divided nickel.

Utilisation of Blood from Slaughter-Houses and Abattoirs

Blood from slaughter-houses is now a valuable raw material for food, mordants, and manure. When pigs' blood is collected, with suitable precautions to prevent contamination, it is sometimes used for the manufacture of an article of diet known as black puddings ; but blood from any animal should not be wasted, as excellent albumen, used as a mordant in the pigment style of calico printing, is made from it of such good quality as to supersede that from eggs whenever large quantities are wanted.

If well prepared it can be used, it is said, for all but the very lightest and brightest colours.

The Germans claim to be able to make blood albumen perfectly colourless.

Where the supply of blood is small it is sold to a blood boiler, but in public abattoirs the blood is usually collected during the process of killing and taken to a large store where it is manipulated on the premises for the production of a fertiliser. After passing through a process in the stoving-room, it is placed in shallow tin vessels furnished with a tap at one corner, then after a time the drawing-off commences, whereby the albumen is extracted. After the drawing-off is completed, the residue is a peculiar pink coloured matter of the consistency of jelly, which can be divided by a knife ; by another process this jelly is converted into a valuable manure.

In cases where the blood is converted direct into a poultry-feeding meal, or into a fertiliser, the modern process of boiling is carried out in a sanitary manner under a vacuum, the residue being a dry powder.

In London, and in many other cities and large towns, objectionable private slaughter-houses are still retained to a great extent. The operations are so barbarous to contemplate that the wonder is the public authorities do not get such houses suppressed, as they are nuisances which should no longer be tolerated in business or residential parts of towns. There is the further objection that diseased cattle, and cows from dairy sheds, on the point of death can be taken to these slaughter-houses and killed in the night or early morning, in spite of the best system of investigation that can be organised ; whilst, on the other hand, such inferior or diseased cattle would not pass muster on the inspection of a public abbatoir. There should be public abattoirs in sufficient numbers wherever possible, with the means of dealing with the blood and offal, the fat, the hides, hoofs and horns of the animals, and with places for the salting down of the hides in hot weather, and the reception of the fat and tallow , and also a melting-place properly constructed should be provided.

Foodstuffs and Fertilisers from Offal of Animals

The offal of animals is apparently much more used for food on the Continent than it is in this country, and it is placed before the public in a more cleanly way. In Paris you never see anything dirty in a butcher's shop ; the same cannot be said of our own country. In London sheep-trotters are chiefly boiled down for glue, but in Paris they are taken to the tripery, thoroughly washed, then placed in a tank of boiling water to scald off the hair : they are then carried away in a wheelbarrow with a false bottom into an adjacent building, where from 50 to 100 women and children are at work scraping the hair off the feet with a blunted knife : they are then brought back again to the tank, cleansed again, and finally they are put into another tank and thoroughly boiled ; and the oil alone produced from boiling the feet more than twice pays the expense of the manipulation. They are then bleached in running water and sold in different shops at about 1½ francs per dozen. In London these trotters are for the most part carried away with the skins, but it is claimed that a more appetising food cannot be placed before any person ; they are believed to be just as good as calves' feet, very gelatinous and edible.

The refuse, including the viscera, waste fat, condemned meat, etc., is economically utilised by converting it into tallow, meat meal for poultry, or guano. The boiling or rendering being done in vacuum vessels, there are no foul odours to create a nuisance.

The guano is often removed from public abattoirs by barges to waterside farms. Its value is about the same as that of town stable manure.

FERTILISERS FROM WASTE SUBSTANCES

Sulphate of Ammonia from Gas Liquor

Ammonia from gas liquor, formerly lost altogether, is now recovered in the form of sulphate of ammonia in the destructive distillation of coal, and forms a valuable

Q

fertiliser for enriching the soil. Also in shale oil distillation the water from the scrubbers, called " gas liquor," in which the ammonia from the shale distillation has been condensed, is distilled for the recovery of ammonia, a little lime being added towards the end of the operation. The ammonia is condensed in the usual way in oil of vitriol to sulphate of ammonium, the spent liquor being a waste.

The pre-bellum price of ammonium sulphate was about £12 10s. a ton, but the price has gone up to about £14 10s., and the demand for it is increasing. The more general adoption of the low-temperature system of distilling coal would greatly increase the yield and home supply.

Basic Slag as a Fertiliser

Formerly the slag from the converters used in the production of steel by the basic process was more or less a waste material. It is now largely used as a purely phosphatic manure, when finely ground, for certain purposes (for grassland especially), as it contains phosphate of lime in a more or less available condition. It usually contains some 40 per cent. of lime capable of neutralising acids in the soil, though " probably not more than 2 to 5 per cent.[1] is in the form of ' free ' or ' caustic ' lime." Obviously, then, the first thing to be ascertained in buying slag is the percentage of phosphate of lime which it contains. This is roughly determined by ascertaining the percentage soluble under standard conditions in a 2 per cent. solution of citric acid. The slag is very finely ground,[2] and 80 per cent. of it should pass through a sieve having 10,000 meshes per square inch. Samples, 90 per cent. of which will pass through the sieve, are readily obtainable.

---

[1] Leaflet No. 267, issued free by the Board of Agriculture and Fisheries. It contains valuable information on time of application, quantity per acre, effect on soils and crops, etc.

[2] " Powdered Manure." M. Menier (Ann. de Chim.) shows that pulverisation renders the effect of the manure more rapid ; and that in pulverising the manure mechanically, instead of leaving it to be done by the weather, there is considerable economy ; and that phosphatised or potassic minerals, that are useless in the rock-form, become fertilisers when reduced to impalpable powder.

There are great dumps of slag, hitherto regarded as waste, both from the basic Bessemer and from the open-hearth processes, which with further research and experiment may be made available for a wider range of agricultural purposes. The final "Report of the Departmental Committee on the Home Production of Food " states that " in view of the fact that the higher grades of basic clay are not available in any quantity, it is possible that farmers will have to use basic slag with a lower percentage of phosphoric acid than usual, and that, therefore, the export of basic slag of this quality should be prohibited or closely restricted."

Manure from Calf-Hair and Hair Waste

Calf-hair and hair waste, formerly of no commercial value, are used as a manure ; they yield nearly 10 per cent. of nitrogen, and their value is about 50s. to 60s. per ton. Ordinarily the hair is matted in lumps and therefore does not easily decay. Its market value would be increased if supplied in a finely divided state.

Manure from Rabbit Waste

Rabbit waste consists of the ears, tail, feet, and other external portions of rabbits ; it is commercially known as *rabbit flick*. It yields from about 10 to 12 per cent. of nitrogen, and a small percentage of phosphate. It sells at about £6 per ton as a useful manure, but its value depends upon the extent to which it is broken up.

Manure from Hoofs and Horns

Hoofs and horns are largely used as manure, when finely ground or in the form of shavings. They yield from 9 to 14 per cent. of nitrogen and 20 to 25 per cent. of phosphate. This fertiliser is largely used by market-gardeners.

Fertiliser from Tallow and Soap Refuse

The refuse or sediment left in making tallow and soap grease, commercially known as *greaves*, is used as manure and is an effective fertiliser for fruit, wheat, hops, and other crops. The market price varies between 50s. to 140s. per ton, according to the quality. Finely-ground greaves well dried and mixed with bone-meal form a manure known as meat guano, for which apparently there is a good demand.

Fertiliser from Feathers and Feather Waste

Feathers and feather waste make an excellent manure, particularly for hop-gardens, as they yield over 8 per cent. of nitrogen. As small feathers are more easily decomposable, parcels of them command a higher price ; large feathers are slow in action, the shafts in particular taking a long time to decay. They find a market at £1 to £1 10s. per ton delivered.

PRESERVATION OF FOODSTUFFS AND VEGETABLE MATTER

Preservation of Foodstuffs by Refrigeration

It has long been known from ordinary experience that cold checks putrefaction ; and refrigeration, natural or artificial, used for keeping animal or vegetable substances below the point of fermentative disorganisation, has, since about the year 1875, been employed to a continually increasing extent for the preservation of perishable foodstuffs. Refrigeration enables us to ship fresh meats and other foodstuffs from New Zealand, Australia, South America, and other countries in enormous quantities, to largely meet the requirements of our ever-increasing population.[1] It is also used to preserve in a fresh condition

[1] Before the introduction of *cold storage* sheep were worth in New Zealand only 6d. or 1s. each. Refrigeration changed the conditions in that fair country from profitless occupations to prosperity. Such a transformation reads like a fairy story.

provisions for daily use on passenger and other vessels throughout their long voyages. For land purposes, during the warm weather in particular, it prevents immense quantities of food from deteriorating into a condition of waste.

In short, refrigeration has accomplished a perfect solution of the great problem of food preservation and distribution, and it is extensively employed in the manufacture of alcoholic beverages. The somewhat recent introduction of small refrigerating plants, with a capacity of about a half-ton, suitable for dairy produce, sold at about £60, bids fair to still further extend the use of an invention that has an enormous economic value.

The exposure of butcher-meat and poultry in open shops is, for several reasons, objectionable and unhygienic ; the food becomes coated with dust, which is dried filth, and the air and sun greatly accelerate decay. Indeed, it is commonly known that when dead animal matter is exposed it becomes a depository for the ova of flies and other insects, and possibly germ organisms which are more dangerous than insect life, because they are invisible. But, having regard to the exigencies of trade, it is not possible to suggest a practical remedy superior to cold storage in or adjacent to the shop, and the protection given by shop windows, as of course a cool and dark place for such foodstuffs is economically the most appropriate ; and this equally applies to fish and fruit, as the latter loses flavour by exposure to the sun.

Meat is one of the most carelessly handled of food products, not only in transit, but in the kitchen, and we would like to believe that it is wiped or washed before being cooked, although it is true that cooking sterilises it more or less.

Preservation of Perishable Food by Cold Storage

The practice of preserving foodstuffs by the application of cold, the meat or fish being either actually frozen or maintained at a temperature near the freezing point, without actual congelation, is also the result of a knowledge of bacterial life. (See previous article.)

Preservation of Food by Canning

The sterilisation by boiling of meat and fish, followed by the immediate hermetic sealing in cans, is the result of a knowledge of the nature of bacterial life, which has made it possible to ship from distant countries vast quantities of foodstuffs in a portable form, that keep in a wholesome condition so long as the tins remain uninjured, once they are perfectly sealed.

Preservation of Fodder and Vegetable Products (Ensilage)

Ensilage, a mode of preserving fodder and vegetable products in a green state by burying them in pits or stacking them in simple ricks and subjecting them to pressure, was adopted on the Continent and in America many years before anyone dreamt of trying the process in this country.

" The system[1] was at first advocated mainly as a resource when wet weather prevented the saving of the hay crop in good condition, the contention being that it was preferable, under such circumstances, to convert grass and other fodder crops into silage ; and this course was first widely adopted in the year 1888. It has been subsequently claimed, however, that the utility of the system is equally, if not more, marked in a year of drought, or when the root-crop fails, as by its means green fodder may be economised and stored in a succulent state for winter keep. When ensilage was first introduced it was generally considered that the making of silage involved the construction of a silo, namely, a receptacle of some kind with sides of brick, stone, or concrete. This was often too expensive for tenant farmers, and in some cases outhouses, parts of barns, and other buildings were converted for use

---

[1] Leaflet No. 9, issued free by the Board of Agriculture and Fisheries. It gives valuable information relating to the construction of stacks, etc.

as silos at comparatively small cost. A considerable stimulus, however, was given to the system by the discovery that good silage could be made in stacks and clumps by a comparatively cheap and simple process.

" All classes of herbage upon farms may, if necessary, be utilised for silage, even weeds and nettles having been successfully employed. The margins and sides of hedges, and other waste places, may be brushed and the material so obtained ensiled. The leaves and young shoots of most hardwood trees may also be utilised. If the material is too coarse for actual silage it will be useful for topping up the silos, stacks, or clamps. Coarse grass in meadows, pastures, and under trees in orchards and elsewhere, which stock frequently reject, may be made into eatable silage. Hop-bines may be utilised directly the hops have been picked, before the sap has disappeared.

" Many stock-owners make silage regularly, and use it as a valuable addition to ordinary food for stock. In one instance an owner of forty-five dairy cows for some years kept his cows almost entirely upon silage made in stacks, with an allowance of oil cake."

A great advantage in making ensilage is that the farmer is quite independent of the weather. The wetter the material is when stacked the better, as it presses more easily wet than dry, and in pressure lies the chief art of making. There are many seasons when half the hay in the country is more or less damaged by rain, at least it is so far damaged as not to make wholesome diet. This loss might be saved if crops were converted into ensilage instead of hay. Another advantage is that there is not nearly the expense in making ensilage as in making hay, and this is of great importance now that labour is scarce. The cost [1] of cutting, carting, and stacking only comes to about 1s. per ton, and from 12 to 15 tons of green materials are got to the acre.

[1] John Walker, in "Land, its Attractions and Riches," p. 611. Published by Dowsett & Co.

" Ensilage is wholesome food for cattle and sheep, but is not good for cart-horses in work, and is totally unfit for nags doing fast work. . . . As silage goes in very small compass, it is not wise to make stacks to contain less than 100 tons of green herbage ; if 200 or 300 be put in each rick so much the better, as the larger the bulk the less proportion of waste in tops, bottoms, and outsides."

Notwithstanding the progress which has been made in this country in recent years in the installation of silos, the want of enterprise in this direction on the part of so many of our smaller farmers must represent in the aggregate a vast amount of waste.

MISCELLANEOUS

Heat and Light from Sewage

For some years the production of gas from sewage sludge has received considerable attention in America, France, and Germany. At Worcester, Mass., U.S.A., the sewage is precipitated with lime and eventually made into briquettes. These briquettes are heated and the products of distillation passed through a red-hot iron coil. Laboratory records show that 6,850 cubic feet of gas were obtained from each ton of treated sludge. The by-products are 27 per cent. of ammonia, 13 per cent. of tar, and 58·3 per cent. of black residue.

Frankfort-on-the-Main has decided to convert its sewage into heating and illuminating gas, and anticipates considerable profits on the process ; whilst a scheme has been under consideration for its introduction generally into French towns.

Separation of Oxide of Cobalt from Nickel

About 1840 Mr. Askin of Birmingham discovered a method of separating cobalt, in the form of oxide, from nickel—two substances which were very difficult to separate. This oxide of cobalt was at first a waste product, but before long it was put into the hands of potters, who readily bought it up as a pigment to produce a blue colour on their ware, at the then rate of two guineas per lb., and a large fortune was very quickly amassed.

Utilisation of Old Iron Articles, etc.

A great many of the old iron and miscellaneous metal and other articles collected by the marine-store and other dealers find their way to the Caledonian Fair, held in the Islington Cattle Market on Fridays; and in France to the Old Iron Fair held annually in Paris. Extraordinary displays of the most varied kinds are to be seen, ranging from bits of machinery, bedsteads, old plated ware, pictures, bedding, books, jewellery, screws, bolts, etc. etc., the last named usually in great profusion, for when a bolt drops out of a motor vehicle it is picked up by some keen-eyed roadsweeper, put away until it is joined by others, and finally it appears in one of these fairs, where it may appear again and again until some purchaser comes along. In fact, in these matters waste is to a noticeable degree avoided, as sooner or later these oddments are put to a new use, instead of finding their way to the ironworks as scrap, to be worked up into new material, as the contents of the scrapheap of an industrial works periodically does.

Gun-Barrels from Old Horse-Shoe Nails

These are made of superior soft iron, and after use are utilised with other high-grade scrap-iron in the manufacture of soft malleable iron for English fowling-pieces.

Vacuum Evaporation

If a glass flask be partly filled with water and held over a spirit lamp until the water boils, and then be corked as it is removed from the flame, the boiling action will cease and a certain amount of steam will remain for a time in the upper part of the vessel. If cold water be now poured over the upper part of the flask the water inside the vessel will furiously boil. There is a simple explanation of

234 THE ROMANCE OF WASTE

this elementary experiment : the cold water condenses the steam and a vacuum is formed in the vessel, relieving the surface of the water of the atmospheric pressure, thus reducing the temperature at which boiling is possible. In a word, the boiling point varies with the pressure on the surface of the liquid ; and the practical applications of this important fact are of very great economic value in many of our industries. Thus, years ago in the manufacture of sugar it was found that in the evaporation of the syrupy liquid the long-continued heating seriously affected the crystallising properties of the syrup, thereby reducing the quality of the crystallised product. But when evaporating pans were afterwards fitted with closed covers, having an exit pipe to which was adjusted a vacuum pump and condensing apparatus, it was found that the liquid boiled freely at a temperature of 120° F. (instead of 212° F.), and the evaporation was effected in about one-fifth of the time required under the old system, besides giving a much larger yield of crystallised sugar.

Vacuum evaporation is now widely made use of, the finest distillates from petroleum being produced in vacuum stills, as with the low temperatures a purely fractional distillation is obtained without a decomposition and ultimate deterioration of the distillates. Again, we have seen with what economy the system is applied in the recovery of glycerine, etc. And in dealing with many delicate organic compounds the vacuum system is invaluable, as the dissociation or destruction of the chemical structures, which would occur due to high temperature and prolonged heating, is avoided. An additional economy is often effected in cases where large quantities of liquor are to be evaporated, by the use of continuous or multiple effect installations, a number of evaporators being so connected that the vapour produced in one is utilised in the next for the evaporation of another portion of liquid, which vapour is in turn used to do the work in the succeeding pan. Such arrangements are made in double, triple, and so on, the consumption of boiler-produced steam being proportionately reduced.

Utilisation of Waste Heat by Regeneration

The production of a temperature adequate to the fusion of steel and iron in large quantities has been much facilitated by the introduction of Siemens' regenerative furnace, in which the waste heat of the fire, instead of escaping up the chimney into the air, is accumulated in masses of fire-brick, and restored again to the furnace by the incoming air.

On this principle the hot gases escaping from blast furnaces, used for the production of pig-iron, are utilised to heat the incoming air blast, thus supplying the furnace with a hot blast, and in so doing conserving an immense amount of heat that would otherwise be wasted. This simple but ingenious invention has economised fuel to the value of many millions since its introduction by the late Sir Charles Siemens.

Sorting Iron and Brass Cuttings

In some machine-shop operations, mixed iron and brass turnings and borings, etc., fall into a tray in an oily mass. Years ago, after roughly draining the oil, this mass, containing valuable brass, was scrapped or dumped. The practice now is to first put the oily cuttings into a centrifugal extractor, in which the last drop of oil is recovered. The cuttings are then passed through a magnetic separator, a machine with powerful electro-magnets which draw away the iron chips as the cuttings pass through. The brass cuttings travel down a chute into a box, while the iron ones are held by the magnets until they reach a point where they are released and fall into a box.

Recovery of Metal from Lead Fume

The condensing flues of great length, sometimes more than a mile, forming a part of some lead-smelting furnaces, are examples of appliances used to condense lead fume or smoke, which was formerly allowed to escape, causing very considerable loss of lead. The fume contains 60 to 80 per cent. of sulphate of lead, small quantities of lead sulphide, lime, and zinc oxide, and it is deposited on the surfaces of the flues. These deposits are afterwards heated in the calcining furnace till they can be made to stick together, and are then smelted in another furnace called the slag-hearth, or they are worked up with another charge.

Gold, Silver, and Copper from Residues

In the production of sulphur from iron pyrites, the residues of oxide from the burners were formerly dumped, as they contained too much sulphur to be used as a source of iron ; but in 1865 Henderson introduced a method whereby the whole of the copper could be recovered by roasting the residues with common salt, lixiviating the mass with water, and precipitating the copper from the resultant solution by means of scrap-iron. And Claudet, in 1870, devised a method to recover the gold and iron remaining in the residues. Over 500,000 tons of pyrites are burned annually in England for the sake of the sulphur, the residues from which yield on extraction about 2,000 ounces of gold, 400,000 ounces of silver, and 15,000 tons of copper.

Recovery of Sulphur from Tank Waste

Practically the whole of the sulphur of the sulphuric acid used in the manufacture of sulphate of sodium (salt-cake) remains in the tank waste from the extraction of black ash. The dry waste thus produced was formerly a real nuisance, as it had to be either heaped up outside the works, or, if the annoyance due to the sulphuretted hydrogen evolved became intolerable, carted out to sea. The sulphur is extracted by the Chance-Claus recovery process (patented in 1888), and the remainder, containing chalk and gypsum, is employed as valuable material for agriculture.

Silver from Refuse

Some of the *refuse* from the old silver mines of Laurium years ago was bought up by capitalists, and put through the furnace to extract the metal left in it, with profitable results.

Recovery of Sulphur from Pyrites

Formerly, over a large district in the south of Spain, where cupreous iron pyrites occurs abundantly, the barbarous practice of burning this pyrites in the open air to get rid of its sulphur, and so lighten its weight, obtained, resulting in the loss of an enormous amount of sulphur sent into the air in the form of sulphurous acid, and in the destruction of vineyards and other vegetation. By modern methods of treatment it is claimed that some 96 per cent. of the sulphur is recovered.

Vanadium from Residue

Vanadium, used largely by the makers of special steels to impart the valuable power of resisting changes caused by vibration, is mainly used as an alloy, ferrovanadium, prepared by a variation of the thermite process, which is a remarkable instance of the utilisation of waste ; the mixture of metals obtained by reducing the rare earth oxides forming the *residue* of the monazite after the extraction of thoria is employed, *in place of aluminium*, to produce pure vanadiu .

Gas-Mantles from Thoria

Thorium, as a metal, has found no useful application, but its oxide, thoria, when heated directly in a flame, possesses the property of converting heat energy into light. Research was therefore directed to the utilisation of this remarkable property ; this led to the evolution of the modern incandescent mantle, a result of purely scientific investigations carried out with great patience and skill, and giving gas lighting a new lease of life. The world's production of mantles is estimated to be over 400,0 0,000 annually.

Utilisation of Waste Brewery Products

Dried yeast is used as a cattle food, and as a source of an excellent substitute for meat extract.

Carbonic acid gas is compressed for the aeration of beer and mineral waters, and is sometimes employed as a freezing agent.

Recovery of Tin from Old Tinware and Cuttings

Sardine and other tins, which are usually thrown into the dustbin, are to some extent collected in one way and another ; and much of these, with tin-plate cuttings and clippings, in pre-war days found their way to the London Electron Works (owned by Messrs. Goldschmidt), employing a large number of hands at Limehouse. This works operated one of the two electrolytic processes for detinning that were in existence—the alkaline process ; but as it was only suitable to certain classes of waste tin cans the bulk of the tinware collected here at a cost of some £30,000 a year was sent to Essen for treatment. The old tins were cut up into strips, and apparently without detinning were stamped into various petty articles which came back to the British market. From the remaining scraps the valuable tin was removed and the bare metal sent to the steel furnaces. Shortly after the outbreak of war the works were closed, but it is reported that they are soon to be re-opened as an all-British concern.

It is not a difficult matter to remove the valuable tin and solder from such tinware by heating : indeed, the borough engineer for Hornsey has installed a furnace into which he passes the tinware for the removal of the tin and solder, afterwards placing the remaining scrap in a hydraulic press to form it into rectangular bundles, for which there is a good market. The tin, of course, commands a high price (about £260 a ton in June, 1917). Such plants might well be installed by all municipalities. They would soon pay for themselves, as, apart from the solder, the tin on the plate represents about 2 per cent. of the weight of the plate.

A vast amount of waste is represented by the tinware to be seen all over the country lying upon the disfiguring rubbish heaps. By a little local organisation and the use of volunteer labour these pieces could well be deposited in the nearest railway-station yard for transit to Limehouse or elsewhere, and the proceeds could be given to some local hospital.

Fortunes from Sunken Ships

Many years ago £70,000 in Spanish gold coins was recovered by divers from the S.S. *Alphonso XII.*, 165 feet under the sea, off Point Gando, Grand Canary. A large quantity of silver bars was recovered from even the greater depth of 186 feet from S.S. *Skyro*, off Cape Finisterre. These remarkable operations show what will be possible after the War in recovering the fortunes lying at the bottom of the sea in the countless torpedoed ships. In recent years remarkable engineering feats in raising both ships and cargoes have been performed, and salvage companies are now busily engaged making plans for winning the hundreds of millions now awaiting recovery.

SECTION II

Miscellaneous Household Wastes and Economies

HOUSEHOLD wastes of a wide range are conveniently grouped in this section, and suggestions are made as to how many things that are usually regarded as wastes can be economically utilised.

Some paragraphs are devoted to the economies of cleaning, restoring, and mending ; and attention is called to the saving due to the preservation of certain foodstuffs that appear to be of importance, particularly to those living in the country.

Paragraphs are devoted to wastes and economies in lighting, and in the use of water ; and some important miscellaneous wastes that appear to demand attention are dealt with.

WASTE OF MORE OR LESS TRIFLING THINGS

Candles

In households using candles, the candle-ends are usually thrown into the dustbin. They can be utilised in lighting fires, thereby reducing the quantity of wood that is ordinarily used.

Matches

In recent years the cheapness of matches has led to a noticeable amount of waste, even on the part of the very poor. Indeed, the poorest of the poor may at times be seen sitting beside a fire and yet striking a match to light a candle, the gas, or a pipe, the economical use of a spill or twist of paper apparently being unknown. Our Continental friends, who have had for years to pay a tax on their matches, are becomingly careful in their use. The taxation of our own matches and the present shortage of supply will certainly make us more economical in their use. To economise in timber, each match should be made to strike at both ends. This is quite feasible, as very little wood is burnt away when a match is used. With this improvement, and a more frugal use of matches, we could easily save £500,000 a year.

All used matches and boxes, pieces of wax or tallow from candlesticks, etc., should be kept to help in the saving of wood in lighting fires. About two dozen match-boxes will save a bundle of wood.

Mustard

It is proverbial that more than half the mustard sold is wasted, as invariably much more than is likely to be required is mixed for use each day. The remedy in most cases seems to be in the use of smaller mustard-pots ; or, better still, in getting the manufacturers to supply it in the paste form, similar to the make-up of the French article. There seems to be a good opening in this connection for an enterprising firm.

Pins

Forty years ago we were producing daily in this country 50,000,000 pins, at an annual cost of about £220,000, an amount greatly exceeded at the present time. What becomes of them ? It is common knowledge that there is a shocking amount of wastage due to negligence in their use. The old phrase, " *Not worth a pin,*" is suggestive ! A careful mother teaches her children the use of a pin-cushion and the wickedness of wasting such trifles as pins. The number of *hairpins* daily lost must also be enormous.

R

Waste of Soap

An inexcusable form of household *waste* is the scrapping of soap remnants, particularly of those pieces which, through being negligently left in the water, are too soft for use, and are apt to be drawn into the waste pipe of the sink or lavatory basin. In all households where little economies receive attention such scraps should be utilised. They may be tied up like a blue-bag, kept at the sink, and used in place of a cake of soap ; or the scraps may be stored in an old jar to be rendered to the form of a solid block when a pound or more has been collected. The remnants should be sliced into thin shavings, placed in the jar, and have poured over them a cup of boiling water. The jar should then be set in a saucepan of boiling water, and its contents stirred until the soap is entirely dissolved and has about the thickness of golden syrup ; it may then be poured into an old tin biscuit-box, and when quite cold the sides of the box can be bent back and the solid block of soap removed. This should be cut into suitable pieces and kept in a drawer to dry and harden slowly without being exposed to the air.

This hardening is also applicable to all soap before it is used ; careful housewives, who buy their soap by the hundredweight for cheapness, cut it in pieces fit for use, and dry as explained. If exposed to the air during storage it is apt to dry too quickly and to break when used.

Formerly in laundries the soap-lees (sediment or dregs) was allowed to run to *waste*, but now in well-organised establishments it is stored for after treatment to obtain from it fatty acids.

Wherever practicable rain-water should be collected and used for washing purposes. This water is so soft that considerably less soap is required to produce a lather than with the hard waters of the public supply ; although it is true that some of these waters are remarkably soft and pure, notably those of Glasgow, Liverpool, Manchester, and some parts of Kent.

Odd Lengths of String

Careful people, and among these some of the most well-to-do, frugally put odd lengths of string from parcels, etc., into a string-bag or box, and not into the waste-paper basket. Sooner or later such pieces come in useful, and save expenditure on balls of string.

In the *Post Office Circular* attention is drawn by the authorities to the increasing cost of materials, and special reference is made to string, which is used largely in all departments. Post-masters are instructed to limit their use of string to the minimum quantity. Wherever possible, string should be re-used in the sorting office and no lengths should be discarded which can again be utilised.

The rag-pickers of Paris collect bits of string thrown into the rubbish-boxes that bring in £660 a year.

Brown Paper

If the brown paper from parcels, etc., be folded and put aside for further use, instead of being burnt or put in the dustbin, it is astonishing to find how useful the odd sheets sooner or later become, and how small the amount expended on new paper becomes.

Waste of Jars, Tins, and Glass Bottles

Day by day, in the aggregate, enormous numbers of jam, marmalade, and other jars, cream jugs, pickle, mango, and soup-bottles, and tins in which cigarettes, tobacco, and biscuits, etc., are sold, find their way to the dustbin, as in the majority of cases tradesmen refuse to take them back and allow some value in return. However small the cost of each of these articles, their manufacture in bulk involves a good deal of labour and raw materials, and their cost has been rising for some time, the glass articles in particular. There is bound to be a shortage of these receptacles sooner or later, and they should be saved now, so that they may be available when there is a call for them. This will also tend to reduce the cost of collecting from the dustbins.

The famine in glassware has brought about a great shortage of glass bottles used for wines, spirits, and medicines, and some spirit-merchants have paid as much as 3s. a dozen for black bottles. Many people return their wine and spirit bottles to the local wine-merchant, and throw their medicine phials and the like into the dustbin. This is a serious form of waste just now ; indeed, at least one society is collecting, cleaning, and selling such bottles in aid of a charitable fund. The Central Committee for National Patriotic Organisations has been in communication with the leading jam and pickle manufacturers in regard to the wastage of " empties," and this may inspire a hope that a scheme, having for its object the conservation of empty bottles, jars, jam-pots, and other articles at present wasted, could be made of universal application by means of municipal agencies.

As a rule, manufacturers would prefer to repurchase their own bottles and jars. In cases where " empties " bear the maker's name the process of sorting is simple enough, but in other cases it is necessary to sort into sizes, qualities, and grades. By general co-operation not only will waste be prevented, but a profit will be secured by those who assist the scheme, because good prices can be obtained.

Value of Used Tinfoil, etc.

The tinfoil used in packing tobacco, sweetmeats, etc., should not be thrown away by tobacconists and others, as if this valuable metal be saved until a pound or more has accumulated, it can be sent to Mr. L. Da Four, P.A., 1, Little Crown Court, Wardour Street, W., Honorary Secretary of the Ancient Order of Druids, who has been able to hand over to the Middlesex Hospital a total of £945 since 1913, by organising the collection of tinfoil wrappings from packets of cigarettes, tobacco, tangerines, sweetmeats, bottle capsules, solution and paint tubes, etc. An analysis of the mixed metals gave : lead, 87·71 per cent. ; tin, 11·30 per cent. : antimony, ·84 per cent. ; copper, ·15 per cent.

Cigar Ash

Tobacco ash is especially rich in potash, which is of value as a fertiliser. Save it for use in your garden.

Paying for Tea-Wrappings

Much money in the aggregate is wasted in buying tea put up in " inclusive-weight " packets, the leaded paper wrapper being paid for at the rate of some 2s. or more per lb., the packet being marked to the effect that it weighs a pound, or a half-pound, as the case may be. If a housekeeper took the trouble to keep the wrappers for a year, on weighing them she would be astonished at the number of shillings she had been paying out for nothing. Of course the remedy is to purchase the tea by weight and have it put up in ordinary paper. The present system, which has been allowed to grow without serious protest, is open to grave objection, and will shortly be made illegal.

A wrapper from half a pound of tea was found to weigh three-eighths of an ounce. At 2s. a pound this represents over a halfpenny, a serious overcharge for poor people to pay.

Writing Materials, etc.

There is a notorious amount of waste of stationery and writing materials occurring in our Government and Municipal offices, highly-finished, thick papers being often used when much less expensive ones would quite well serve, and double sheets are often used where a single one only is required. Money is too often lavished, not alone upon these primary things, but upon all the materials that are used, with little regard for economy. One is reminded of that prince of economists, Joseph Hume, who, noticing the gilt-edged paper of the Parliamentary notice, waited his opportunity, got up and bluntly declared : " I think that splendid gilt-edged paper unnecessary." And the gilt-edged paper vanished from the House. It is true that much has been done in recent years to cut down the amount of printed matter issued by many of the offices at great

246 HOUSEHOLD WASTES AND ECONOMIES

expense, matter that is very little read, as a rule ; but there appears to be still room for further economies in this direction. On the other hand, no one would suggest that we should go to the other extreme, and compete with Germany in the minute economies mentioned in the following Reuter's message, dated Amsterdam, April 29, 1915.

German Economy in Writing Materials

The following orders were issued on April 29, 1915, by the Berlin Municipality to its employees, calling upon them to avoid waste in the use of writing materials.

Beginning with WRITING PAPER, the order says :

" The instruction already given that in petty cash notes and such-like communications which can be put on a single page only half-sheets of paper are to be used is still often disregarded. The cases, however, in which a half-, or even a quarter-sheet of paper will suffice, can be considerably increased ; for example, notices of meetings. Of course, for taking notes, making calculations and so on, only scraps of paper are to be used."

Next come PENCILS, regarding which the order reads :

" In future, however, pencil-holders are to be given out for holding short stumps, in which way the life of pencils can be considerably prolonged."

Regarding ENVELOPES, the order says :

" Envelopes, if carefully opened, can be used again and again. In suitable cases also they can be turned inside out and the paper used again. SEALING-WAX is only to be used on communications for outside addresses."

Care is also enjoined with respect to INK, which is to be properly protected against dust and evaporation. Inkpots are always to be covered over after use, even if only with a sheet of thick paper.

Special attention is given to STEEL PENS, which the Municipality declares should be made to last at least a week.

Waste of Paper

We have called attention to the waste which occurs in using double sheets of writing paper where single sheets would serve quite well, but an enormous amount of paper and string are used by tradesmen to wrap up parcels. As a rule both are discarded as soon as the parcel is opened, and people are kept busy ministering to a wasteful habit. The thrifty Japanese expect the buyer to take away his purchase of any article, which does not soil his wrapper, in his own "fukusa," a square of soft closely-woven cotton of some dark colour, whose four corners are knotted over the article to form a convenient handle.

Value of Waste Paper

In many households waste paper finds its way to the dustbin, where, on the other hand, it might be used as dusters by crumpling a page of a newspaper to form a pad for cleaning windows, pictures, mirrors, etc., than as fuel in the kitchen range ; or it may be made into balls for lighting fires to replace or supplement firewood. All such paper left over should be put aside and allowed to accumulate until there is enough of it for disposal. There is a society, brought into being by the War, which collects waste paper, etc., from householders free of charge for the benefit of the War Funds. There are also several waste-paper merchants, and waste-paper works that purchase such paper, etc., direct. One of the former is Lendrum, Ltd., 3, Temple Avenue, London, E.C.4., and one of the best known of the latter is Messrs. Philips, Mills & Co., Ltd., Bridge Wharf, Battersea, and the following are the schedule prices from 1st November, 1917, delivered in quantities of 56 lbs. in bags, and properly separated :

		per cwt.	
		s.	d.
1.	Ledgers and account books, 1st quality (without covers) ..	20	0
2.	Newspapers tied in bundles, white or coloured	12	0
3.	Old letters, envelopes, invoices, circulars, old music, old printed books (without covers), old magazines	11	0
4.	Cardboard, brown paper, postcards, and coloured papers and covers	8	0

All parcels of one cwt. or over are fetched from within 12 miles of town FREE.

This paper is utilised in making low-grade papers, brown paper and cardboard, etc., and it can be used for making charge cases for shells,[1] etc. But in Germany the pulped waste paper, etc., also forms the basis of a *papier maché* kind of material which is pressed into shape to form such articles as washing-up bowls, babies' baths, and so on, and these are inexpensive, cleanly, strong, and light in weight.

The Royal Commission on Paper urges the public authorities to save waste of every kind. Schemes for the collection of paper are being organised by trade collectors, municipal bodies, and other agencies in many parts of the country. Business men in particular are asked to dispose of account books, vouchers, and similar goods which it may no longer be necessary to keep for the purpose of reference.

Provincial Enterprise in Collecting Paper

Between March, 1916, and the end of July, 1917, Preston Waste Paper Committee collected 551 tons, which were sold for £2,566. An official of the Paper Commission stated that on the basis of Preston's population it is estimated that the United Kingdom should produce 200,000 tons of waste paper a year, with a net clear saving of £450,000.

Munitions from Bus and Tram Tickets

Explosive tubes can be made from these tickets, and therefore there might well be a box on each vehicle for the reception of the used tickets—as there is on the vehicles

[1] The Royal Commission on Paper has drawn attention to the very serious shortage of paper, and to the fact that the amount of paper and paper-making material which can be brought to this country is now considerably reduced, whilst the demands, chiefly arising from the War, are more than double those prior to 1914.

It is understood that in the making and packing of munitions large quantities of paper-board are required, and that every shell and all the larger projectiles are fitted with an internal bedding of paper-board, the material of which is waste paper.

Half an envelope makes sufficient pulp for an explosive tube; a quarter of a pound of waste paper for a cartridge cylinder; a two-ounce sweet-box for a charge case.

of Glasgow. The used tickets fetch 4s. per cwt., according to Messrs. W. V. Bowater & Sons.

About 900 tickets weigh a pound, but as millions are used in London alone each week the saving would soon become appreciable. For example, the L.C.C. tramcars earned £13,000 on Whit Monday, 1917 ; assuming that the fares averaged 2d., this would mean that 1,560,000 tickets were issued. The number issued by the bus companies was probably not less, giving a total of 3,000,000, say. This number would weigh very nearly 30 cwt., which, at 4s., would fetch £6, a sum well worth saving, whilst supplying a much-needed raw material for munition work.

CLEANING, RESTORING, MENDING

Cleaning Steel Fenders, etc.

Much of the ornamental steel work about a house, such as fenders, fireirons, armour, etc., requires a good deal of labour to keep it clean. A coat of cold colourless lacquer on those pieces not exposed to heat, and on the fenders and fireirons in the summer (when fires are not used), will protect them from rust, and save the cleaning, whilst the kitchen steel can be cleaned with powdered ashes, and a sheet or two of emery cloth will be saved per week.

Cleaning with Petrol or Benzolene. A Warning

The cleaning of fabrics, etc., with these dangerous spirits should never be done in a room in which there is a fire or an exposed light, such as a gas-jet or candle, as the vapour given off, even at low temperatures, forms with the air a highly dangerous explosive mixture. In fact, such cleaning operations should always be done in the open air. Keep the bottles containing such spirits well corked to prevent waste by evaporation, and store in an outhouse, or in a room without a fire, to prevent an explosion in case the bottle should get broken.

Paraffin Oil for removing Dirt

This oil, known in America as kerosene, is much used for a variety of cleaning purposes, and also in some laundries for washing purposes, as, owing to its remarkable power of removing dirt, a great deal of the most laborious work is lightened ; but the articles after treatment require a thorough rinsing to remove every trace of the oil. If this is not properly done the linen has an unpleasant smell, which becomes more pronounced when the articles are under the iron or when worn. Only the best oil is suitable for this purpose, and although it is not so dangerous as petrol and benzolene, it should never be handled or stored near a fire or naked light.

Of course the clothes are not washed in neat paraffin oil ; only about 1½ to 2 tablespoonfuls are used in an ordinary-sized copper three-quarters full of water, into which about ½ lb. of yellow soap is shredded ; and when the water boils and the soap is melted, the oil is added before the clothes are put in.

Labour-Saving Devices in the Home

The servant problem of recent years has been accentuated by the shortage of labour due to the War. On the other hand, in many homes the economic effect of the War has been so much felt that the domestic staff has been reduced and perhaps a certain amount of the housework has been undertaken by the mistress and her daughters, with the result that many labour-saving appliances and devices that can be used to reduce or eliminate the drudgery and unpleasant work command attention. For many years in a large proportion of households such fatigue- and trouble-saving devices as knife-machines, which make the usually tiresome business of cleaning knives a quick and easy job ; and vacuum-sweepers and brushes, which do away with all sweeping on knees with dustpan and brush (the dust flying around), have been in use with the happiest results. But it should be more generally known that there are now available a number of other simple and inexpensive contrivances that should be more commonly used to economise labour and make it pleasant. Thus there are dustless dusters (chemically treated), which absorb the dust instead of flicking it temporarily away ; mops and polishers which do away with the old tiring method of polishing floors on hands and knees ; and floor-washers which do the same thing for washed floors without wetting the hands. There are chemically treated cloths which clean silver, brass, glass, etc., without any messy preparations in greasy and liquid forms ; and mops which save the hands from getting wet when washing up.

For the preparation of food there are a great many labour-saving devices to be had, such as bacon and bread cutting machines, lightning mincers, bean-cutters, rapid butter-shapers, marmalade machines, etc., all of which can be procured at most of the large stores.

Much labour can also be saved by fitting the bedrooms with suitable lavatory basins with hot and cold water, and by having drinking water laid on to each bedroom ; and the adoption of central heating, as explained elsewhere, means warm rooms, corridors, etc., night and day, with less labour.

Waste due to Laundry Methods

It is notorious that linen sent to laundries to be washed and ironed has a shorter life than when done at home, or by the old-fashioned methods. The waste due to the use of chemicals in rotting the fabrics, and the use of stiff, harsh, and metallic brushes in tearing away the surface fibres of fine linen, and to the straining effect due to the wringing and ironing machinery used, must be enormous in the aggregate, and it calls loudly for attention. Cotton and woollen articles also suffer, rapidly deteriorating. Then there is the annoyance and inconvenience due to articles being lost or misdirected by the laundry people. So no wonder people in increasing numbers are economising by eschewing starched linen, and by having as much washing done at home as possible ! Laundry prices up $33\frac{1}{3}\%$, March, 1918.

Restoration of Furniture, etc.

There are always plenty of things in every house too good to throw away and yet too shabby to be pleasant to look upon. Most of these things can be renovated, and their further deterioration arrested at an outlay representing some fourth or fifth of their cost ; and neglect in these matters implies waste. Such things as fenders, bedsteads, cornice-poles, lamps, electric light and gas brackets, chandeliers, fireirons, and door fittings, etc., sooner or later become tarnished and aged in appearance due to wear and atmospheric action. Such articles can be renovated by relacquering, and new effects can be arranged by choosing another colour, whatever the original finish may have been. Thus polished brass can be changed to dead gold, steel bronze, copper, or antique brass. Chairs, settees, and couches and other upholstered goods can be restored and chemically cleaned (without removing the coverings), and purified from moth ; and many a home has been beautified by covering such pieces of furniture with chintz, purchased perhaps during sale times at a fraction of the usual price. Mirrors, chimneys, and other glasses can be resilvered at the cost of a few shillings, and, if the regilding of them is too expensive, many a shabby-looking frame has been made pleasing to look upon by a coat of white enamel, particularly if the articles are for bedroom use. Where the spirit of economy rules, faded curtains, blinds, carpets, coverings, etc., will be cleaned and dyed, instead of being replaced by new ones ; and the bedding purified and remade, the outlay being a fraction of the original cost. In fact, not a little of the money ordinarily spent on household renewals, etc., particularly those due to alterations or change of residence, can be saved by a little intelligent management.

Invisible Mending of Clothes

Formerly, if the fabric of a garment got torn, burnt, worn in places, moth-eaten or cut, the suit or dress would be cast aside or disposed of in most cases ; but the invisible mending of the Artistes Stoppeurs de Paris, established in various places in this country, is so perfect, and the woven threads so beautifully matched, that the repaired part cannot be detected. The best known shops where this perfect work is done are in Oxford Street and Regent Street, London.

SAVINGS DUE TO PRESERVATION OF FOODSTUFFS, ETC.

Preservation of Eggs

Much waste occurs in normal times due to eggs deteriorating in cases where they cannot be marketed or used in a new condition, supplies being in excess of the demand for a few weeks in the spring. A very simple treatment preserves them for several months in a condition equal to well-kept eggs a few days old ; indeed, even after twelve months or more it is claimed the change in their condition is hardly noticeable. The methods in use [1] include (a) dipping in *waterglass* (or they may be kept in the liquid until sold or used), a solution of silicate of soda and water ; (b) pickling in *lime water ;* (c) cold storage ; (d) coating with butter or glycerine.

Preserved eggs should be sold under that name, and not as " new-laids," " breakfast," or " fresh " eggs.

Eggs should be kept in cool places, as when exposed in shop windows or other places where the temperature may be 70 degrees or upwards they may start incubating. Hundreds of thousands of eggs are annually lost through window displays. They should be kept in the cleanest, coolest, driest place, removed from mustiness, foul odours, or other sources of contamination.

Wicked Waste of Fruit

The way in which fruit in this country is allowed to rot on the trees and ground is notorious ; probably thousands of tons are wasted in this way every year. A contributor

[1] Refer to Leaflet No. 83, published free by the Board of Agriculture and Fisheries.

to the *Daily Mail*, September 15, 1915, throws some light on the matter. He said :

" I sent to Portsmouth Market recently 240 lbs. of sound Orleans plums and received back the enormous sum of 4s. 8d.

" Many jam factories have been buying plums in this district at one farthing a pound, which does not even pay the wages of the pickers."

There are countless gardens and small orchards up and down the country in which apple and pear trees are to be found, the fruit of which is not put to its most profitable use by the owners. Much is wasted altogether, and more suffers in quality through the neglect of certain simple precautions. There should be no excuse for ignorance in these matters, as most excellent leaflets are published by the Board of Agriculture and Fisheries, free, giving full instructions and hints on picking, grading, storage, and disposal, etc.

Special Leaflet No. 6. Waste of Apples and Pears.
Leaflet No. 250. Fruit Bottling for Small-holders.
Special Leaflet No. 5. Preserving Fruit without Sugar.

Preservation of Potatoes

The following is the method which hotel and restaurant-keepers practise in France to preserve their supplies for later use :

A large vessel of water being placed over the fire, and its contents raised to the boiling point, the potatoes, previously well washed, are placed a few at a time in nets or baskets, which are then thrust rapidly into the boiling water and retained there for about four seconds. Of course, as the introduction of so much cold matter lowers the temperature of the water, care must be taken to raise it to the boiling point again after each immersion before a fresh netful of potatoes is introduced. As each batch is withdrawn it should be shaken and spread out on the floor of some well-aired place. When all the stock has been dipped and is quite dry, it should be stowed away in some dark room free from damp. The potatoes will be found to have lost all tendency to germinate, and it is claimed will remain sound and well-flavoured till the next year's crop arrives.

In Germany, a considerable portion of the enormous annual crop of some 45 million tons of potatoes is dried in factories and used as food for both men and cattle ; such dried stock is being largely used in making bread during the War. The normal requirements are stated to be 13 to 14 million tons for human food, 20 millions for fodder, 6 to 7 millions for seed, and about 5 millions for spirits. The crop for 1915 was expected to amount to 52 to 60 millions of tons.

LIGHTING AND WATER

Value of Gas-Mantle Ash

In large establishments where incandescent lighting is extensively used, broken mantles and the ash from worn-out ones should be collected for sale. In this connection the London County Council has set an excellent example in municipal economy by having all such waste material collected from the schools and buildings under their control, and sold. The *L.C.C. Gazette* of May 25, 1914, gives the particulars of the sale of about 220 lbs. of gas-mantle ash to Messrs. Hopkins & Williams, Ltd., 16, Cross Street, E.C., whose tender of 10s. 1d. per lb. was the highest. Thus the ratepayers were saved the quite substantial sum of over £110, and, incidentally, all those engaged in the collecting of the ash were brought under the spell of the doctrine of " Let there be no waste."

Another indication of this praiseworthy spirit of economy which prevails in the administration of some of the departments of the London County Council is the following notice, published in the *L.C.C. Gazette* of March 29, 1915, when, owing to the lengthening days, artificial light would not be required during school hours :

" Incandescent Gas Lighting.—Schoolkeepers are to note that all by-passes fitted to gas-burners in rooms not used for evening occupations must now be turned off."

Waste of Gas in the Home

Incandescent lighting has become so general where gas is used, that it might appear unnecessary to call attention to the waste of gas due to the use of the old-fashioned flat flame-burners ; but as these are still too often seen in use it should be explained that the Welsbach incandescent burners give three and a half times as much light as the flat flame-burners for the same quantity of gas burnt. Although it is true that only an extremely small quantity of gas is burnt when the by-passes fitted to incandescent burners are in use, the gas should be turned off from the burner, to prevent waste, whenever the light is not required for a period of several days or longer. Further, the gas flare should be carefully regulated to save your mantles. Gas ovens and rings for cooking purposes require attention to prevent gas being wasted ; the taps regulating the flow of gas to the burners sooner or later work loose, allowing the gas to escape, so the gas-cock on the main supply pipe of the oven ring should always be closed when the jets are not in use. A more fruitful cause of waste is to put a kettle or saucepan on the gas and forget all about it, or the filling of a kettle when perhaps a quarter of its contents is only required for a small pot of tea. Gas is often wasted through leaving the lids off saucepans unnecessarily, as liquids come to the boil quicker when completely enclosed.

Worn-Out Electric Lamps Renewed

Electric lamps of any make when worn out or with filament broken should not be thrown away, as they can be repaired by the Allies Electric Lamp Repairing Co., Hammersmith, W., at a charge of about 1s. Or, in such a way that the repair cannot be detected, by the Renew

Electric Lamp Co., 83, New Street, Kennington, S.E., at about 1s. 3d. (since raised to 1s. 9d.—2s. 3d.), the latter company guaranteeing their efficiency, and a life of at least 1,000 hours.

High-Pressure Oil-Lighting

It may be explained that in recent years several processes have been introduced for using high-pressure oil-vapour and air in atmospheric burners, and using these for incandescing the mantle. The light is soft and less trying to the eyes than gas or electric lights, but it is doubtful whether oil lighting can compete with gas, although in the country and in isolated workshops where neither gas nor electricity is available it should be an ideal light.

Waste of Water is Waste of Fuel

Of the many so-called minor opportunities for effecting savings which reach large amounts in the aggregate, the question of water waste is not the least important. It should be remembered that although water wasted in the home does not involve any direct extra expenditure on the part of the householder,[1] it means waste of fuel, etc., at the waterworks, which in the aggregate is a serious loss to the country, particularly at a time when every pound of coal should be conserved.

Unfortunately, public opinion is not well formed on this or any other form of waste, and we often find that those we trust in a public capacity to look after our interests are often sadly at sea where municipal economies are concerned. Thus the Mayor of Chicago was reported to have said : " We are glad to have lots of water and waste it, for it makes Chicago a cleaner and healthier city."

The chief causes of *waste* are leaky fixtures,[2] badly adjusted floats in watertanks, running more water in the bath than is necessary, and the running-off of water to

---

[1] There are many large water undertakings in this country which are run at an annual loss. London is one of them. Why ? The loss has to be made good by the rate-payers through the ordinary council rates.

[2] The composition seating or washers often used are very much less durable than leather ones.

S

get it hot or cold as required, there only being a relatively small amount of leakage from the street mains. The Royal Commission on the Water Supply of London reported that 35 imperial gallons per head per day was ample supply for all purposes,[1] but it is well known that in some households this quantity is greatly exceeded, although in others very much less is used. It is true that the householder is not directly affected by the waste that occurs, but the recent decision of the Metropolitan Water Board to fine users who fail to keep their taps and valves from leaking is likely to have a desirable effect in preventing waste.

A similar notice was issued by the New York authorities,[2] followed in June, 1911, by a vigorous campaign against waste, a system of house-to-house inspection being instituted. A penalty of $2.00 was imposed for each leaky fixture. These measures had the desired effect. The estimated daily reduction in the consumption in Manhattan and the Bronx reached a maximum of 71,000,000 U.S. gallons in August, 1911, and averaged 50,000,000 gallons throughout 1912. The total saving to April 1st, 1913, was over 39,700,000,000 U.S. gallons.

Such savings can be well understood when it is realised that a half-inch tap left running will waste about 7,000 gallons in a single day, whilst a tap simply dripping wastes about 1,500 gallons a year.

A serious form of *waste* is the constant breaking up of streets in connection with the water supply to houses, and it is good news that the Metropolitan Water Board has adopted a scheme by which stopcocks will be provided to each house, if desired, at a fixed charge of 15s ; as, besides obviating the breaking up of the streets, these stopcocks will enable the supply to be conveniently cut off when repairs are necessary indoors.

[1] In March, 1917, 253,077,000 gallons were supplied by the Metropolitan Water Board on a daily average to 1,131,618 houses, and a population of 6,787,346, an average of 37·29 gallons per head per day, exceeding the estimated sufficient allowance by 2·29 gallons per head, necessitating the supply of an additional 15,543,000 gallons, in round numbers.
[2] *Proceedings of the American Waterworks Association.* Charleston, S.C., 1913.

Other forms of waste are frequently detected, or are created by new departures. Thus, the amateur photographer who puts his prints into a basin and lets the water run continuously over them for hours can soon waste a shilling's worth of water. Again, some time ago it was suggested that salted herrings before being cooked should be put in a vessel with running water for 48 hours. Just think of it! Suppose a half-inch tap was only half-open, then some 7,000 gallons would be run off in the 48 hours. This, at a shilling per 1,000 gallons, would mean a cost of 7s. to prepare perhaps a twopenny herring.

In 1916 the Metropolitan Water Board supplied 88,470,000,000 gallons of water. The fuel consumption for pumping, etc., was about 200,000 tons, costing about £300,000. This quantity of water would require a tank the size of Trafalgar Square and 29 miles high.

MISCELLANEOUS WASTES

Dustbins and Waste

The proper use of the dustbin is to receive the fine ashes and dust siftings from the sieve, after the used contents of the grates have been sifted, the cinders being put aside and utilised as fuel in the kitchen range. Rubbish, leaves, potato and apple parings, tea-leaves, orange peelings, paper, cardboard boxes, and vegetable and animal refuse of every kind and description should be burnt in the kitchen grate, and on no account be placed in the dustbin. Burning the rubbish at home will reduce the coal bill and relieve the Borough Council of a great deal of unnecessary expense, amounting to thousands a year, in collecting and destroying the refuse.[1] The sight of the insanitary

---

[1] The Borough Surveyor of Kensington reported in October, 1915, that over £300 a year might be saved in this way. Refer also to Art. on page 271. In Glasgow every householder, on application, is given a sack by the Corporation marked, " Glasgow Corporation," and numbered. It has an iron ring for hanging up. Into this every scrap of paper and cardboard is put, and once a week the Corporation van calls and collects and empties it. Also at each end of every tramcar a box with a slit is fitted, into which passengers drop their tickets as they pass out. All the waste paper and cardboard is reduced to pulp and used over again, saving thousands a year and preserving the amenities of the streets.

dustbins in really good neighbourhoods is too often disgraceful. As the *housefly* breeds prolifically in house refuse and decaying matter of all kinds, and produces disease by alighting upon food and tainting it, all food, especially meat, milk, and sugar, should be kept covered. It is an old saw, " If you kill one fly fifty will come to its funeral " ; the meaning of this is that it is worse than useless to try to deal with the effect while leaving the cause unattended to.

Extravagant Funerals

It is proverbial that the poor, and often the very poor, indulge in the most expensive mourning and funerals. The bread-winner passes away, and often almost every penny of the club or insurance money is spent on his burial. The psychology of this regrettable folly is not easily understood, the wicked extravagance in most cases being apparently due to some strange combination : of grief, vanity, and devotion. The widow too often fails to realise that no lack of respect would be shown by lessening the outlay and pomp on these last rites. Indeed, such costly displays are in striking contrast to the modest and inexpensive funerals the very rich often arrange by the special request of the deceased.

We have an example in the case heard before Judge Cluer at Shoreditch County Court, in October, 1916, in which it transpired that an order for an £18 funeral was given for a person who lived in a very poor district. Such extravagances in normal times are bad enough, but in these days, when we are all rightly called upon to practise the most rigid economy, attention should be called to a wicked form of waste that has too long been tolerated.

The learned judge remarked that " £5 was enough for any funeral, and he wished he could hope that no one would spend eighteenpence on his funeral."

The following still more wicked example of such waste was reported in the *Pall Mall Gazette* of February 21, 1918 :

"It is a lamentable waste of compensation money," said Judge Hill-Kelly at the Pontypool County Court, when an application was made for the payment of £130 in respect of the death of a collier. "I am almost afraid to tell your Honour the amount spent on mourning," said the solicitor. "I have one bill for £61 5s. 4d., another for £4 17s., and several smaller ones."

The amount of much-needed money wasted by the poor in this connection must amount in the aggregate to an enormous sum each year : but it is well known that the poor are very touchy on these matters. Even so, probably much could be done by the clergy and by district visitors to influence them in the right direction : but until the young are taught the true meaning of frugality and economy, and the folly of every kind of extravagance, there can be little hope for substantial improvement.

Waste due to Inadequate Fire-Protection

Many years ago it was estimated that the value of the insured property destroyed by fire all over the world amounted to from 30 to 40 millions of pounds sterling annually. It probably greatly exceeds a million a week now, and there can be little doubt that the greater part of this colossal loss is due to preventable causes, and inadequate fire-protection. It is true that in modern times great improvements have been made in the means employed for the prevention and extinction of fires, and for the salvage of valuable property. Broad thoroughfares have taken the place of narrow, crooked streets ; incombustible materials such as brick, stone, concrete, and iron are used in the construction of buildings, and in cities an abundant supply of water is available ; this, with powerful steam fire-engines, extension ladders, fire-escapes, the fire-alarm telegraph, and the telephone, secures the means for the more or less prompt extinction of fires when they occur. But the case is very different when we consider the requirements of country houses, particularly of those miles away from the nearest town. Such houses, the very old ones in particular, are largely built of combustible materials, and too often no well-thought-out system has been arranged for the prompt extinction of a fire before it gets a good hold of the building, or for the salvage of what may be its priceless contents. A well-filled water-tank on the highest part of the building or on a tower near it, with hydrants and hose on each floor, is of the first importance to secure an ample supply of water, but for the prompt extinction of a fire in its incipient stages there should also be an adequate supply of water-buckets, hand-pumps, and extinguishers distributed over the building ; and in the case of motor-garages, a supply of extinguishers and buckets of sand. Important mansions should also have a well-drilled estate or local fire brigade available, the question of water-supply, etc., having been carefully arranged by a competent engineer. Such precautions generally result in a great saving of property, but when a fire has obtained complete mastery of a building it is a recognised fact that the most powerful engines, even aided with unlimited supplies of water, are ineffectual ; then the efforts of the firemen are directed to confining the conflagration within the limits over which it has secured a hold.

Praiseworthy efforts have been made to bring the equipment of the London County Council Fire Brigade up to the latest date ; and its splendid staff responded to 5,820 calls during the year 1913, the number of fires being 3,877, of which 49 were classed as serious. It is interesting to note that this highly efficient service was maintained in 1914 at an expenditure on capital account of £51,463 and £309,431 on maintenance, including pensions.

In concerting preventive measures, a knowledge of the principal causes of fires is of the greatest importance, and the following abstract deduced from about 30,000 fires which occurred in London during the 33 years 1833-65 should be instructive :

" The percentages of different causes were : Candles 11·07, children playing 1·59, curtains 9·71, flues 17·8, gas 7·65, lucifers 1·41, smoking tobacco 1·4, sparks of fire 4·47, spontaneous ignition 0·95, stoves 1·67, other known causes 19·4, unknown causes 32·88. There is too much reason to suspect that a considerable proportion of fires attributed to no known cause are due to incendiarism ; and were an official investigation into the origin of fires instituted, it probably would result in a great saving of property."

Waste due to the Pollution of the Air

The annual loss due to smoke-begrimed curtains blinds, furniture, etc., and tarnished silver and picture-frames, it is well known amounts to hundreds of thousands a year. So it is good news that the Committee for the Investigation of Atmospheric Pollution has received a grant of £500 from the Department of Industrial and Scientific Research, which is intended to cover the cost of investigations made in the present year, 1917.

SECTION III

Trade, Industrial, and other Wastes

WASTE products and substances should be studied with the object of their utilisation, and in some cases also of the discovery of possible remedies for nuisances created by such products polluting our streams or creating encumbrances. This section is devoted to a fairly wide range of wastes that occur in our trades, industries, and activities other than purely domestic ones. In some cases attention is called to what has been done more or less efficiently here and there in eliminating or reducing waste that is worthy of further research or of general adoption.

In other cases attention is called to processes and possible economies that appear promising, and are cited in the hope that they may stimulate enterprise and research in the directions indicated.

Many important economies have been sadly neglected in the past ; so attention is called to a few of these in the hope that they may be heeded.

UTILISATION OF WASTE MATERIALS AND SUBSTANCES

Utilisation of Bones

Bones that find their way to the dustbin are often burnt in the destructor as fuel, or carried away with the refuse, a form of waste that should be severely condemned, as they can be profitably used

(a) for the production (by destructive distillation) of bone-black, with valuable oils and some ammonia as by-products. Bones, when treated with carbon bisulphide

264

at 104° F., yield about 12 per cent. of grease, and are still fit for making animal charcoal ;

   (b) for the production of glue ;

   (c) for the production of manures.

The manurial value of bones is very important, and it is due to some 33 per cent. of phosphates which they contain, in addition to about 3 per cent. of nitrogen. Fresh bones decompose very slowly when used as manure, but when they are previously fermented in heaps the nitrogenous matter becomes more readily assimilable ; but they have a higher value when crushed. In some parts of Germany [1] bones are sent to mills to be powdered, and the powder, when mixed with some nutritive stuff, makes an excellent manure much in demand by farmers. According to Liebig, the importation of bones for manure in 1827 amounted to 4,000 tons, and Huskinson estimated their value to be from £100,000 to £200,000.

But at the present time we are in urgent need of bones for the fat they contain, which is used in the production of glycerine for high explosives. Thirteen lbs. of marrow bones and 19 lbs. of other bones will provide about 2 lbs. of dripping, enough for the requirements of an 18-pounder shell. So every kitchen in the country should be raided for the contents of the swill-tub and bone-heap. Our workhouses, asylums, and other public institutions, also hotels and restaurants, could with a little co-ordination render material help in this direction.

Cattle Fodder from Coffee-Grounds

According to a Reuter's message from Amsterdam in December, 1916, all the administrations of military hospitals and prison kitchens in Germany have received orders to collect the grounds of coffee, which will be dried, and, after scientific treatment, will be used as fodder for cattle, etc.

[1] In January, 1917, the Municipality of Berlin, it was reported by Reuter, issued regulations according to which all bones, whether cooked or raw, will be purchased by the municipality at the rate of 5d. per lb. The fat will be extracted from the bones, and will be exclusively available for the population of Berlin.

Other extracts from dried coffee-grounds, it is added, can be used for human food.

Use of Diseased Potatoes

Diseased potatoes should not be regarded as useless. They are sometimes worked up for their starch by being subjected to a preliminary process of fermentation, and it is said that diseased wheat is treated in the same way, and yields a starch of good quality.

Use of Seaweed as a Manure

For a great many years seaweed has been most effectively used as manure, particularly in the northern coast districts, and now that town dung is becoming scarcer and dearer, more attention should be given to seaweed as a partial substitute.

" Analysis [1] shows that seaweed contains about as much nitrogen as farmyard manure, but as it is present as slow-acting nitrogen, it is scarcely so valuable as in average dung, in which a certain proportion is present in the active available form of valuable ammonia compounds. As the seaweed decays rapidly in the soil, however, some of the nitrogen soon becomes available. The amount of phosphate in seaweed is only about ½ to ⅓ that of dung ; on the other hand, seaweed is on the average considerably richer in potash. It will be seen, therefore, that it is desirable, as a rule, to supplement it with a phosphatic manure. Seaweed contains no fibre, and consequently does not produce the black structureless material characteristic of the dung-heap ; in decomposing it forms soluble substances which easily wash away. For the same reason it decomposes more completely than dung. It is even said to facilitate the decomposition of dung on light soils and in dry districts, but there is no definite proof of this. A ton of dung and seaweed would break down in the soil more quickly than a ton of dung alone, and would therefore have less of a drying effect if put on late.

[1] Leaflet 254, issued free by the Board of Agriculture and Fisheries. It contains valuable information relating to the use of seaweed as manure.

" The amount of seaweed obtainable must be enormous, and it is worthy of consideration whether it cannot be more widely utilised than it is at present, especially by farmers near the coast."

Many years ago M. de Molon produced a manure with seaweed or wrack (such as is found abundantly on the French coasts) and powdered phosphate of lime. He mixed these in successive layers in pits or sheds, in proportions best adapted for fermentation (proportions which vary with the nature of the phosphate used, the moisture, variety of the seaweed, etc.). This mixture is allowed to ferment six weeks to two months, according as the seaweed is hotter or colder; then, if the decomposition is not complete, the compost is mixed anew, for fresh fermentation till the wrack is entirely decomposed.

The manure thus produced contains, it is claimed, besides phosphate of lime, all the elements of fertilisation contained in vegetable matters ; namely, nitrogen, mineral salts, potash, and magnesia.

Formerly iodine was largely obtained from the ash of seaweed, but its production from this material has practically ceased, due to the competition caused by the preparation of iodine as a by-product in the manufacture of nitrate of soda.

The utilisation of seaweeds and their ashes (kelp) has received attention from time to time ; indeed, Mr. James Hendrick, B.Sc., discussed the subject before the Edinburgh Section of the Society of Chemical Industry in April, 1916. And it seems that further research might be profitably undertaken.

Oil from Seaweed

The researches of Mr. E. C. Stafford, made many years ago, showed that any kind of seaweed, when submitted to destructive distillation at a low red-heat, produced volumes of gas and oily tar, which on redistillation yielded paraffin oil (as he described it) in large quantities. It is said that from one ton of seaweed of the genus *fucus*, the most common of the marine growths, it is possible to obtain

6·7 gallons of oil. It would appear that further experiments might be well made with the object of increasing the yield of oil and utilising the by-products, and of seeing whether a commercial process of economic value is practicable.

Oil from Fruit-Stones

In June, 1916, the German papers appealed to the public to save fruit-stones, as valuable salad-oil can be extracted from them, which, though of little consequence in normal times, is now of great importance in view of the scarcity of oils. It is said that hundreds of thousands of tons were collected in one year.

Potash from Distillery Waste

A process of saving the valuable fertiliser potash in distillery waste has recently been made public by the United States Bureau of Foreign and Domestic Commerce. It is expected that it will be possible to extract potash from this otherwise worthless material at a price that will meet competition even after the War is over. It is estimated that 106 tons of potash are wasted each day by the 25 or more distilleries in the United States where the fermentation of molasses takes place.

Propellants and Pork from Chestnuts and Acorns

The Director of Propellant Supplies is most anxious that the public should appreciate the importance of harvesting the annual abundant crop of horse-chestnuts. From every ton of horse-chestnuts sent to the Director of Propellant Supplies half a ton of grain will be released and be available for human food, so that the collection effects a double purpose. The Director requests the collectors to unite their heaps, where feasible, so that one journey may be made instead of several. The work is being carried out chiefly through the education authorities, but there is a great insufficiency of collectors, and the suggestion has been made that the inmates of workhouses, both men and women, should be asked to assist.

The President of the Board of Agriculture urges upon stock-keepers the importance of making full use of the yearly abundant crop of acorns. In general composition acorns closely resemble the cereal grains, and require only the addition of green fodder and such foods as are rich in flesh-forming materials (oil-cakes and milling offals) to constitute a suitable diet for growing or fattening animals. Acorns are specially adapted for pig-feeding, and can often be used most effectively and economically when pigs are allowed to gather them where they fall. Owners and occupiers of land containing oak trees should, therefore, take all possible steps to see that the acorns are not wasted.

Utilisation of Sawdust

This waste material, which is a source of danger if allowed to remain on the premises in bulk, is employed in several ways. As a fuel in suitably arranged furnaces, with automatic feeding devices, it may be burnt to good advantage ; but, owing to its tendency to clog or " pack," and to the large amount of gases given off under heat, it is apt to prove a somewhat troublesome material to use as fuel. It may, however, be fed in with waste wood or chips, when it will burn well. Indeed, ordinary *saw-mill refuse*, consisting of sawdust and chips, gives good results. But a more efficient way of utilising this refuse is to use it as fuel in a gas-producer. In America, where there are 48,000 saw-mills, producing some 36,000,000 cords of wood refuse a year, an 840-H.P. plant [1] is worked satisfactorily by saw-mill refuse, consisting of 50 per cent. of sawdust and 50 per cent. of chips, and a gas of 130 to 135 BTU. per cubic foot is obtained, the engines giving a brake horse-power-hour on about $4\frac{1}{2}$ lbs. of this fuel, with very little ash, and there is little cleaning to be done. The changes necessary to burn this fuel consist in the removal of the coal-hoppers, which are replaced by a hollow tapered cylinder, fitted with slide gates top and bottom.

[1] *Journal of the Association of Engineering Societies*. Boston, Mass., 1912. Vol. xlix.

Sawdust is also somewhat extensively used in sweeping floors of schoolrooms and public buildings, and to spread on the floors of taverns, etc., in wet weather, the price usually paid for it for this purpose being 9d. to 1s. a sack. It is also to some extent used in the production of fire-lighters.

Sulphite Cellulose Waste Liquor. Need of Further Research

When wood is digested with a concentrated solution of bisulphite of lime, or bisulphite of soda, the matters of the wood other than cellulose are dissolved, leaving the cellulose or wood-pulp fibre, which is now so extensively used for making cheap qualities of paper. This is an important manufacture in Canada, the United States, Norway, Sweden, and Germany, but in Great Britain there are only some four sulphite cellulose mills. Many attempts have been made to convert the sulphite waste liquor from these mills into useful by-products, but apparently none of these has yet been successful on a practical scale.

" This waste product appears to have been studied more systematically (especially in Germany) than any other of the present day. Nevertheless, there are great possibilities for future investigation. A paper by Mr. Earle B. Phelps (Massachusetts Institute of Technology), entitled, ' The Pollution of Streams by Sulphite Waste : A Study of Possible Remedies,' is worthy of perusal in this connection." [1]

Waste of Valuable Tanning Material

Some of the waste liquors from tanneries, notably the lime waters, rank as amongst the most polluting of liquid trade wastes. The lime waters are usually saturated solutions of lime, with much lime and carbonate of lime in suspension ; they contain a very large quantity of dissolved nitrogenous and other organic matter, and they

[1] " Report of the Royal Commission on Sewage Disposal." Vol. i., 1915.

possess a most offensive smell. The Royal Commission on Sewage Disposal [1] reports that

" the tanner frequently sends to waste very large quantities of valuable tanning material. We feel sure that in this and other respects methods of working could be much improved, to the benefit of the trade itself, as well as of the rivers and streams into which the waste liquors are discharged."

Leather dust has been from time to time used as manure ; it contains about 3 to 4 per cent. of nitrogen, but the recorded experiments seem to show that it has little manurial value.

Waste of Surplus Naval Tobacco

It is common knowledge that tons of tobacco are burnt at the national dockyards every year. The explanation of this wicked waste apparently is that having contracted for a certain quantity of tobacco each year, the official way of dealing with the amount left over is to destroy it. To the man in the street, the obvious way of dealing with the surplus—after sorting out any part that may have got slightly mouldy—would be to carry it over to the next year and buy correspondingly less tobacco that year. Or in any case, rather than waste it, distribute it among the various naval and military convalescent homes, and among the service pensioners, and the like. Contraband tobacco, that has been confiscated, could well be utilised in the same way, instead of burning it.

Utilisation of Town Refuse

The refuse from dustbins or ashbins, [2] also trade refuse, amounting to from 1 to 4 tons per inhabitant per annum, has to be collected and got rid of by the town authorities. It is either dumped on waste land, taken out to sea and deposited, or burnt in destructors. When burnt the refuse is reduced to about one-fourth of its bulk and one-third of

[1] Vol. i., 1915.
[2] Refer to article on Dustbins, page 259.

its weight. The organic matters and cinders in the refuse form the fuel necessary for combustion. The residue, after combustion, consists of sharp ashes and clinkers, which have a small saleable value, the former being used for mortar and the latter in road-making. Usually the heat from the furnace of the destructor is used to generate steam for a variety of purposes, but as the destructor must be worked continuously night and day, in many cases, and steam is ordinarily required during the day only, or intermittently, it is not generally possible to instal an economical plant without expensive auxiliaries, such as thermal storage, etc., as the first and primary duty of a destructor is to destroy the town refuse. So although burning the refuse in destructors when the conditions are favourable is the cheapest way of disposing of it, it sometimes happens that it is less expensive to cart it away as explained.

If householders would only take the trouble to see that all combustible refuse was burned in their kitchen ranges, they would be buying less coal and paying less in rates, as the amount of refuse carted away would be considerably reduced.

The composition of the refuse burned in destructors varies greatly in different localities. The following is an analysis of London ashbin refuse [1] :

Breeze, cinders and ashes	64 per cent.
Fine dust	19 ,, ,,
Paper, straw and animal and vegetable matters	12 ,, ,,
Bottles, bones, tin, crockery, etc.	5 ,, ,,

The amount of heat generated varies somewhat. Mr. Keep [2] found at Birmingham that on an average 1 lb. of refuse will evaporate 1·79 lbs. of water ; and at Warrington that 1 lb. of refuse will evaporate 1·47 lbs. of water. Mr. Watson found at Oldham that about 40 lbs. of refuse was required to produce an effective horse-power hour. The refuse from the destructor when used on the land has a value as a fertiliser about equal to that of coal ashes of equal fineness.

There are good reasons for suggesting that not half the refuse collected by the municipalities up and down the

[1] " Report on Dust Destructors by the Medical Officer and Engineer of the London County Council," 1893.
[2] " Utilisation of Towns' Refuse." British Association, 1893.

country is put through destructors; in fact, much could be done to relieve the rates in most municipalities if the departments dealing with refuse were so organised that by a careful sorting of it the tinware, bones, glassware, etc., were put aside for the most economical handling, and if periodical collections of waste paper, rags, old metal, etc., were made and the articles marketed for the relief of the rates. The waste materials might be weighed on collecting and the householder credited with his contribution. Such a system would lead householders to put aside their materials, which are so badly needed as raw materials for manufacturing purposes, instead of burning them, as there are no means at present for their economical disposal. The importance of this problem is realised by the City Corporation, as £500 is being spent on improving methods of sorting refuse at their depôt. We are wasting millions a year through our folly in neglecting these matters. The failure of the borough and district councils to make full use of the refuse they collect was pertinently referred to by the *Weekly Despatch* of November 18, 1917, as follows :

" The lack of enterprise of many Borough and District Councils is resulting in the loss to the civil authorities of thousands of pounds annually.

" This they are losing through failing to make full use of the refuse they collect from their districts.

" At Camberwell, for instance, the refuse collected by the Borough Council carts is given to a contractor to be got rid of, and not only is he given the refuse, but is actually *paid for taking it away.* At Lambeth, again, a contractor, by paying a certain sum, is allowed to remove all the refuse and to make what he can out of it. Obviously he secures a large profit, or he would not remove the refuse.

" In this direction the civil authorities would do well to follow for once the example of the Army. Last year a Committee was formed with the object of disposing in the best way possible of camp refuse—bottles, tins, rags, fat, bones, etc.—the two last being of great value respectively in munition-making and agriculture. The sale of this refuse now realises close on £1,000,000 a year."

T

WASTE DUE TO FAULTY METHODS, IGNORANCE, AND WANT OF THOUGHT

Waste due to Transit of Cattle

One of the economic effects of the more general installation of public abattoirs to replace the numerous private slaughter-houses in the country would be to save the cost and inconvenience of driving cattle through the streets. Further, the loss of weight of meat under the existing system of sending live cattle to distant markets is something serious to contemplate. It has been proved that an animal slaughtered in Edinburgh, near where it was fed, and another taken from the same herd and sent to London as carefully as possible by railway and slaughtered there, will lose at least three stones in weight compared with the former; and three stones of meat represent over a sovereign. The same kind of wastage occurs whenever animals are driven any distance by road to and from the market, to say nothing of the cruelty which often takes place in driving the animals through traffic-crowded streets. They are often taken from peaceful fields, brought to London by train, reaching the market in a frightened and inflamed state, sometimes getting water, but more often none.

Loss due to Importing Flour instead of Wheat

In 1913 we imported flour, grain, and wheatmeal to the extent of nearly £92,000,000, and wheat to the extent of £43,849,173 ; whilst bacon is now almost at famine prices. There must surely be something wrong in this connection, as there is no substantial reason why we should not import wheat instead of flour and mill it all here. It is true that a certain amount of imported wheat is milled by us, but we should reap a rich reward if this amount was systematically increased until the whole of the flour consumed in this country was milled here, as it would (1) enable us by feeding hundreds of thousands of pigs on the bran and refuse to grow our own bacon instead of spending over £17,000,000 on the imported sides, as we did in 1913; (2) help in considerably developing our engineering industries in producing the prime movers and milling machinery required; and (3) greatly reduce the value of our imports.

Suitable sites for the mills could probably be found on or near the Manchester Ship Canal, within easy reach of important collieries.

Defective Leather

It is a common experience that the soles of boots and shoes of a given thickness have different degrees of durability. Doubtless not a little of the difference in the quality of the leather is due to the way in which the hide was tanned, or whether the hide was from a healthy animal; but there is a type of defect sometimes noticeable in the leather when it is cut with a sharp knife from the tanned hides of bulls, buffaloes, oxen, or cows, that the ordinary manufacturers of belting and of boots apparently know nothing about. The nature of the defect is that, instead of the leather appearing uniform in texture and quality throughout its thickness, it is streaky, one or more layers of fleshy or horny streaks being seen on the cut surface or section. The cause of this defect is that when the growing animal has an illness its coat is affected, it loses its usual lustre, and a layer of inferior hide is put on. Such leather must be regarded as wasteful, whether it be used for boots or for machinery belting, etc. When a good sole leather is gradually bent the grain should not break.

Leather is frequently adulterated with glucose, soluble salts, and barytes.

Common Delivery and Collection of Parcels, etc.

The number of men, women, and boys employed in distributing parcels and goods could be easily halved, by organising a common distributory and collecting system for each district.

Overlapping Bread and Milk Walks

In some scattered districts it looks as though it could be arranged for the baker and milkman to join forces for the distribution of their wares, with economic advantage.

Overlapping Tramway and Motor-Bus Services

The total annual loss due to the overlapping of these services must reach an enormous figure. If these services were properly organised we could probably reduce the importation of motor spirit by some 3,000,000 gallons a year.

Music-Printing from Type

German labour has been largely employed in cutting plates for music-printing, but apparently there is no valid reason why music should not be set up like type at a much less cost. The late firm of Mr. J. Figgins made some excellent music type, and supplied it to many publishers at home and abroad.

Waste due to the Pollution of Rivers

Rivers which are polluted by the flow of waste trade liquors and sewage into them are often made incapable of sustaining fish life ; and the riparian manufacturer is unable to obtain from them a supply of clean water for industrial purposes—necessitating the sinking of expensive wells, or the purchase of water from the public supply. This matter has received the most patient exhaustive attention on the part of the Royal Commission on Sewage Disposal, which issued its Final Report in 1915.

Waste of Sewage demands Attention

It is commonly known that in supplying sewage to the soil we return to it those constituents which the crops have removed from it, and that we renew its capability of nourishing new crops. China and Japan mainly owe their flourishing agriculture to the extensive use made of human

excrements, whilst we are spending many millions a year
by importing fertilisers such as guano and nitrate of soda,
and are wickedly wasting our valuable sewage and polluting
our water supplies by sending the solid and liquid parts
into the nearest rivers (and into the sea), and the gaseous
parts into the air. The importance of this colossal waste
can be best made clear by the following quotations from
Sir William Crookes' admirable address [1] on the wheat
problem :

"When we apply to the land nitrate of soda, sulphate
of ammonia or guano, we are drawing on the earth's
capital, and our drafts will not perpetually be honoured.
There is still another and invaluable source of fixed
nitrogen : I mean the treasure locked up in the sewage and
drainage of our towns. Individually the amount so lost is
trifling, but multiply the loss by the number of inhabitants, and we have the startling fact that in the United
Kingdom we are content to hurry down our drains and
watercourses into the sea fixed nitrogen to the value of no
less than £16,000,000 per annum. This unspeakable waste
continues, and no effective and universal method is yet
contrived of converting sewage into corn.

"Of this barbaric waste of manurial constituents
Liebig, nearly a quarter of a century ago, wrote in these
prophetic words : 'Nothing will more certainly consummate the ruin of England than a scarcity of fertilisers
—it means a scarcity of food. It is impossible that such a
sinful violation of the divine laws of nature should for ever
remain unpunished ; and the time will probably come for
England, sooner than for any other country, when, with all
her wealth in gold, iron, and coal, she will be unable to buy
one-thousandth part of the food which she has during
hundreds of years thrown recklessly away.'"

Having called attention to this immense waste which is
occurring, it is right to explain that engineers have wrestled
with the problem for many years past, but it is one that can
rarely be solved locally, for economic and other reasons ;

[1] British Association Presidential Address, 1898.

indeed, it should be regarded as one of those great national questions which will call for consideration after the War. A broad comprehensive national scheme would cost an enormous amount of money, and its economic practicability could only be decided after years of patient labour. Indeed, the last Royal Commission on Sewage Disposal, which published its Final Report in the year 1915, sat for seventeen years. But when it is realised that any scheme for the utilisation of human excreta is defective if it fails to collect the urine, which has the greatest manurial value, the difficulties to be overcome are apparent.

Sludges from the various town sewage systems, especially when they contain lime, are found to have some manurial value, but as their action is very slow they are regarded as only suitable for slow-growing crops and moist climates.

" The disposal of the sludge of London instituted by the Board of Works results in a national loss of over £1,000,000 per annum," said Mr. C. H. Cooper, C.E. " Two and a half million tons of sludge are dumped down at sea, and destroy fishing grounds which feed London, and the country is deprived of the manure necessary for food production."

It has been estimated that the total value of the constituents of sewage for manurial purposes is about 8s. 6d. per head per annum.

The Waste-Fish Question

Fish has always been eagerly sought after as an easily procurable article of food, and for many generations it has entered largely into the dietary of all classes in this country, particularly of the poor. With our unrivalled fisheries and the improved methods of fishing which we have used in recent years there should be, with reasonable railway freights, an entire absence of wastage ; and, with suitably situated curing works, a plentiful supply for the whole country at reasonable prices, prices appreciably below those which have obtained in recent years. But the somewhat alarming increase in the price of fish which has been noticeable for some years seems to call for attention. Doubtless with more economical methods of distribution the prices would come down, but there is reason to believe that there is far too much waste. Thus we hear of fish being used as manure rather than being sold below certain prices. Then from time to time hundreds of tons of *mackerel* caught in Loch Fyne are pitched overboard, as, strangely enough, Scotland will not eat mackerel, and at present great quantities cannot be got economically and expeditiously from Scotland to the markets. Of course they might and ought to be cured near where they are caught. Then again we daily waste myriads of tiny fish wrongfully called *whitebait* (young herrings), which are not whitebait at all, but immature fish of all varieties which should be protected by law. It should be explained that waste fish, consisting of sprats and " five-fingers," makes very good manure ; it is easily disposable in districts near the fishing areas, and East Kent farmers apparently favour it for use in growing mangolds and hops. It is also used in the manufacture of fish guano.

Salmon-Culture : a Promising Field for Enterprise

At a time when we are called upon to do all that is possible to increase the production of foodstuffs, we may well ask ourselves whether we are getting all out of our unrivalled rivers that is possible.

In a statement issued by the Fisheries Sub-Committee of the Empire Resources Development Committee, it is pointed out that the salmon offers so fine a field for scientific enterprise that it is possible once more to hope to see the fish retailed at 4d. per lb.

By the process of " stripping " salmon of their eggs— a process involving no injury to the fish—and protecting the eggs in hatching troughs, at least 95 per cent. come to the hatching stage, instead of, as in the case of wild spawning, some 5 per cent. at most ; and since a single hen salmon of 20 lb. weight deposits some 20,000 eggs, the possibilities are enormous.

A rough stocktaking by the late Duke of Richmond's

commissioner of the number of hen fish spawning in the Spey was attempted some years ago (points out the *Morning Post* of June, 1917), and the enumeration was about 6,000 pair of fish. Given an average product per fish of 15,000 ova, there would be for that river alone perhaps 90,000,000 eggs. If this mass can be fertilised and passed into hatcheries, and if five per thousand of the fry return as salmon the fifth year after, then the return to the Spey would be nearly half a million salmon—a larger number than are taken yearly in all British and Irish rivers.

In Canada the 56 Government hatcheries release yearly 100,000,000 salmon and trout, 493,000,000 whitefish, and 900,000,000 lobsters. In the United States similar enterprise has proved highly remunerative. For an aggregate Government outlay of under £1,000 fishermen of the Pacific Coast took in 8 years fish to the market value of over £38,000.

Wealth in Fish Offal

A company was formed in August, 1917, and a large plant erected for experimenting in the conversion of fish-skins and certain other kinds of offal into gelatine, glues, and animal foods.

A steam trawler working in Icelandic waters frequently takes on a three weeks' voyage from 70 to 90 tons of haddock, cod, plaice, coalfish, and the like. The offal taken therefrom would amount to from 40 to 50 barrels of livers alone, each barrel weighing from 5 cwt. to 6 cwt. Under present arrangement these are the property of the crew, and are known as stocker bait. The normal price fetched is 12s. per barrel ; now from 20s. to 25s. The latest developments include the splitting and curing of the fish at sea, during a voyage extending some-times to eight weeks. The livers are separated and melted to oil ; all heads, bones, and offal are made into manure ; even the skins have a commercial value, and not a particle of the catch is wasted. The amount of oil and manure landed from one trawler is from 500 to 1,000 gallons of the former, and from 10 to 20 tons of the latter, while the amount of salt fish landed is between 150 and 250 tons. The fish now fetches from £30 to £45 per ton, against £18 to £25 in normal times.

In July, 1917, 382 tons of fish were condemned at Billingsgate Market as unfit for human food. Of that quantity 339 tons were " wet " fish and the remainder shell-fish. The principal seizures were of herrings, plaice, and skate. It would be interesting to know what became of this valuable raw material.

The Empire Resources Development Committee, who are advocating State development of the fisheries of the Empire on terms that would bring to the National Exchequer a share of the proceeds, have prepared a memorandum showing the profits that may be made from a more careful conservation of fish offal.

Waste of Water in Industrial Works, etc.

Attention has been called elsewhere to the domestic waste of water, but there is reason to believe that a great deal of unnecessary waste occurs in many of our trades and industries. Thus in steam plants, in too many cases water is allowed to run from steam traps and separators into the drains, instead of being run into the hot-well, to save both water and heat. Not a little water is wasted by railway companies, one way and another ; indeed, such waste has received a good deal of attention in America, and a contributor to the *Railway Gazette* of New York calls attention to the good work which has been done by American railway companies in the direction of making savings by the reduction in water consumption. One investigation showed a possible annual saving of $10,000 (£2,083 6s. 8d.) at two terminals. On another road there was a reduction in the cost of its water supply of over $4,800 monthly, as compared with the previous year. In general it has been found possible to reduce the cost of water used 20 per cent. at terminals to which attention has been directed.

Leaking pipes and flush-boxes, and the careless use of hydrants, are common sources of waste. The importance of small leaks can be understood when it is realised that a three-quarter inch orifice will discharge 600 gallons per hour under ordinary city pressure. As an example of another type of waste : at one place it was found that city water purchased at a relatively high rate was being used for cooling an air compressor, and for other shop purposes, whereas the ordinary water pumped by the railway at its own plant and supplied to locomotives would have done equally well, and could have been supplied at less than half the cost.

Waste of Wood in Sawing, etc.

The thinner the saw used, the smaller the amount of timber converted into sawdust of little value. Sometimes, when timber is being sawn on the saw-bench, the saw used is thicker than it need be, owing to the machinist shirking the little trouble involved in changing the saw for a thinner one. This form of waste is bad enough when deal and other cheap timbers are concerned, but it becomes a serious matter when the expensive varieties are sawn.

Timber is increasing in price, as its supply is becoming more restricted, owing to the reckless way in which the world's store of timber is being used up. Therefore it is all the more gratifying to hear of cases where due regard to economy is exercised (even if the saving is not important), particularly if public money is concerned. Such a case is represented by the following extract from the *L.C.C. Gazette* of March 2, 1914 :

" Waste handicraft material.—Use in Infants' Department.—Certain exercises performed in the handicraft centres consist of cutting pieces of wood of various lengths from blocks 2 inches in width and 1 inch in thickness. These pieces would be of service as rough building blocks in infants' departments, and it is desirable that such pieces should be preserved for this purpose. Head masters should give the necessary directions to the manual-training instructor. The head mistresses of infants' departments who desire to have a supply of these blocks should apply to the head master."

Such an instruction as the above, coming from an educational authority, could not fail to help in keeping the question of economy alive in the schools.

Waste due to Wrongly Shaped Boxes and Bottles, etc.

Reference has been made to our shortage of timber, and to the necessity of using it with the greatest economy. Yet for years we have shaped boxes, packing-cases, etc., in the least economical manner, and shall probably continue to do so. Now the longer a box is in proportion to its girth the greater the quantity of wood required to hold a given amount of goods. For example, a cube-like box, with sides 1 foot across, would contain a cubic foot of goods ; a box 2 feet long, 1 foot in breadth, and 6 inches high, would hold the same amount, but the wood required for the former would be 6 square feet, while that for the latter would be 7 square feet, an additional sixth in the cost of wood, nails, and labour, reaching an enormous amount in the aggregate per annum. The ordinary square biscuit-box is correctly shaped, and the nearer any box or case approximates to it in form, the more perfect it is in point of economy. The same principle is applicable to bottles and other containers, as a tall, flat-sided bottle of the same capacity as a short, broad one will require more glass—and this at a time when there is a great scarcity of it.

These examples are typical of the economy that could be effected in scores of ways if we would only be guided by our intelligence, instead of blindly copying and following what was done with less discernment by former generations.

Loss due to Kemp in Wool

In South America, Australia, and New Zealand, where sheep are bred mainly for the revenue produced by the sale of the wool, more attention is perhaps paid to the quality of the wool, and to the presence of *kemp* in it, than appears to be paid in this country. Kemp is coarse, rough, whitish hair, and the objection to its presence in wool is that it

does not take the dye readily, and that it injures the
appearance and quality of even the commonest fabrics
made from the wool, giving them a harsh and inferior
appearance. Probably neglect on the part of our sheep-
breeders to give proper attention to this defect in the wool
produced is the cause of a large amount of loss. This
opinion is based on two incidents. An Australian sheep-
farmer, breeding yearly an immense number of sheep, had
never heard of kemp, and did not know that such a defect
existed in wool. A famous agricultural peer exhibiting a
fold of most beautiful sheep at a show, and hearing that an
expert in sheep and wool from South America (an English-
man) was present, invited him to have a look at his pen of
show sheep, seven in number, and tell him what he thought
of them. The peer was greatly shocked to hear from the
expert, after examination, that he would only pass three of
the sheep, as the others had too much kemp in their wool,
a defect the peer had not before heard of. When this
defect exists in the wool there are certain parts of the sheep
where it is most pronounced, and knowing where it is most
likely to be found the expert is able to make a rapid
examination. The study of kemp appears to be a subject
deserving the attention of our agricultural colleges.

Waste due to Rats

It has been estimated by Mr. Wallace, Edinburgh
Professor of Agriculture, that the rats destroy £15,000,000
worth of food in the United Kingdom every year, and that
if the injury done to woodwork and sacks be added, the
total is easily brought up to £20,000,000.

What is wanted is an organised campaign against these
pests. Probably it would be found impossible altogether to
exterminate them, but great areas could be certainly almost
entirely cleared and the total number enormously diminished.
Their bodies are needed for glycerine and fertilisers.

It is said that one of the rat-catcher's secrets of success
is never to touch a trap except with a glove scented with
aniseed, and to boil every trap which has had even the
slightest contact with human flesh.

The latest estimate places the loss to the nation caused by farm pests—the rat, the mouse, the house-sparrow, and the wood-pigeon—at £40,000,000 annually, or about £1 per head of the population. This figure includes a £15,000,000 debit to the account of the brown rat and £8,000,000 to that of the house-sparrow.

WASTE DUE TO NEGLIGENCE

Waste due to Negligent Use of Glassware

For many years foreign-made glassware has been dumped on our markets at prices below those which would enable our manufacturers to secure a profit, with the result that many British works have had to close, and also with the inevitable result that as soon as active competition ceased the foreign-made articles were raised in price. The war has cut off our supplies from abroad, which amounted to £4,546,267 in 1913, including earthenware, and we are confronted with a glass famine, particularly in chemical laboratory glassware used for educational and industrial purposes, and in articles made of jena, and similar metal. This has certainly brought home to us one of the disadvantages of our present fiscal system. It has also roused our attention to the immense amount of *wastage* due to breakages. Of course in handling such very brittle materials accidents will happen, but not a little of the wastage is due to negligence, and the want of intelligent care in handling glassware. A large percentage of breakages occurs in washing up, particularly in drinking vessels, the washed glasses being usually placed on a board to drain, which slopes towards an earthenware or lead sink and allows the articles to slide down and break. Of course a strip of wood fastened to the bottom edge of the board would prevent the glasses sliding off, but this is, strangely enough, rarely done. Another cause of breakages is placing such brittle things on marble and iron slabs without an intervening cover or mat. And still another cause is the pouring of hot water into cold, thick glassware, when,

owing to the want of uniformity in the expansion due to
the heat, the vessel often cracks. With thin glass the
expansion is more uniform, and even boiling water rarely
causes a fracture.

An immense fortune awaits the genius who succeeds
in producing toughened, unbreakable glassware, without
appreciably increasing the cost of production.

Waste due to Idle Running of Motor-Vehicle Engines

At a time when the precious motor spirit should be
conserved, taxis are commonly seen standing for long
periods with their engines running. If the drivers had to
pay for the petrol thus wasted whilst waiting for their
fares engaged in shopping, making calls, or being photo-
graphed, etc., it is safe to say that there would be little or
no such avoidable waste. Of course there is also a waste
of lubricating oil during these idle running periods, to say
nothing of the wear and tear of the engine itself.

Waste due to Inefficient Lubrication of Motor Vehicles

It is commonly known that there are in use in the
Services a very large number of the finest motor vehicles
turned out by British engineering firms, and it is notorious
that many of these magnificent machines have been treated
with the grossest neglect, vehicles being sent to the
repair works in such a condition as to clearly show that not
a drain of lubricant had ever been put into such a vital
part as the back axle [1] since the car had been taken over
by the Department. The wicked waste that has occurred
in this way must by now be represented by an enormous
figure.

Waste of Rubber Tyres due to Negligent Driving

As owners of motor-cars are well aware, the most
expensive item in the upkeep of these vehicles is the india-
rubber tyres. It is well known that a careful driver, one
who manipulates the brakes and clutch with intelligence

[1] *The Motor*, Feb. 22, 1916, p. 102.

and sympathy, will easily get twice the mileage out of a set of tyres that a careless driver can who is continually skidding his wheels in accelerating, stopping, and starting. Anyone living on or near the bottom of a hill constantly has his economic feelings hurt when he hears the grinding of motor tyres on the rough abrasive material of the road, as cars are allowed to rush down the slope unchecked till near the bottom, when a sudden application of the brakes causes erosion of the rubber treads, and perhaps tears out studs, and certainly strains the tyre fabric and shortens its life. Of course the machinery of the car also suffers when so unskilfully handled.

Rubber begins to deteriorate [1] if exposed to a strong light or to high temperature, or if brought into contact with rust, grease, or most of the acids ; further, the canvas fabric rapidly rots when exposed to damp, so spare tyres should be protected from the sun and light and stored in a dry place, the temperature of which does not exceed some 75° F.

Waste Utilisation Departments in Factories

Everyone with factory experience knows what a large amount of waste occurs due to things being thrown on the scrap-heap to rust and rot that could with proper organisation be economically utilised. In a large factory it would certainly pay to appoint a man solely for the purpose of taking care and making the most of all waste materials, whilst in a small factory a careful supervision by the manager or foreman will prevent much of the waste going on. An excellent article on this subject appeared in *The Motor* of July 31, 1917, in which Mr. Henry Sturmey said :

" I read a very interesting account in an American paper showing how this matter is dealt with in one of the large tyre factories in the United States. This concern, employing many thousands of hands, and using, of course, vast quantities of material in the course of its work, had

[1] Spooner's " Motors and Motoring," p. 175.

solved the problem of waste by the appointment of a special staff to deal with it; and the importance and magnitude of the matter may be gathered when I say that it was stated that a four-floor building was devoted entirely to this department. Every day almost, in all departments of the factory, scrap material was being thrown aside as being of no more service for the regular production of the business. Occasionally, by reason of a fault in material or design, considerable quantities of goods would have to be withdrawn from regular sale, and, so far as the factory proper is concerned, just scrapped.

" Department for dealing with Waste Material

" Well, it was the function of this department to deal with all this waste material. Not merely to find a scrap buyer who would purchase it, but to see if it could not be utilised in another form, and, if so, then it was the function of that department so to utilise it.

" It was the duty of the officials from this department to visit every day the different workshops of the main factory and to note and secure all scrap material, which was handed over to the ' Junk Department ' to deal with. Here it was examined and its possible usefulness investigated. Scrap tyres were stripped of their canvas, and both canvas and rubber made up into other constructions. Thus, for example, when a large quantity of non-skid covers which were defective had to be scrapped, they were cut up into shoe soles and made up in the ' Junk Department ' into tennis shoes and sold at an attractive price. Metal articles and vulcanite articles which, by a little work upon them, could be shaped for other purposes, were so dealt with, and buyers found for this newly-manufactured product.

" The ' Junk Department '

" The management of the ' Junk Department ' have, of course, not only to find a means of utilising the waste material but also to find a market for the transmogrified product when completed, and, according to the report, the department was run as a separate business organisation. The material was charged out from the factory to the department at clearance price and made up and utilised, or scrapped altogether and sold as junk where further utilisation of any portion was found impossible ; and it was stated that the annual profits shown by this department exceeded $1,000,000, so that it is seen that the organisation paid for itself to a very good tune."

MISCELLANEOUS

Daylight Saving

The Daylight Saving Scheme, first suggested by Benjamin Franklin in an article which appeared in the Paris *Journal* in 1784, but for many recent years strenuously advocated by the late Mr. William Willet, has been adopted by eleven European countries, including this country, to our great economic advantage.

Full statistics of the economies effected in lighting and fuel by this valuable scheme are not yet available, but it is generally known that the saving in artificial illuminants has been remarkable. In Edinburgh it amounted to more than £10,000, and in Manchester there was a saving of 134,000,000 cubic feet of gas, equal to about 11,000 tons of coal. It is estimated that throughout the country the saving in lighting and heating alone due to " summer time " for the year 1917 was £2,500,000.

Moonlight Saving

On moonlight nights all lamps in public places that are controlled from central positions could with considerable economic advantage be lowered or switched off.

Waste of Telegraph Forms

The Stores Department of the General Post Office estimates that every year there is a wastage of 70,000,000 telegraph forms. What becomes of them ? we may wonder.

U

Waste due to our Derelict Waterways

The 4,673 miles of canals and navigations in the British Isles cost tens of millions to construct and improve, and they are at present a striking evidence of our folly in neglecting to effectively and economically use them for the conveyance of bulky raw materials and manufactures, such as coal, cement, brick, stone, grain, fertilisers, and hardwares, etc. Unfortunately, we have allowed the railway companies to acquire some 1,144 miles of these valuable waterways, and to get control over a further 219 miles ; but as the sections in the hands of the railways are key sections, practically all competition on the part of the canals in cheap transport has been destroyed ; so nothing of importance is likely to be done in improving and developing our canal systems, and in more completely linking them up with our principal rivers, until they are nationalised. We have failed to grasp the true meaning of Brindley's famous dictum, that rivers exist to feed canals. The Germans do understand it, and have 8,629 miles of navigable canals, rivers, and lakes, representing a perfect network of arterial communications, splendidly organised. Vast sums have been expended in developing their canal systems under the State, and in 1911 a total of 76,632,000 tons of goods were carried on the national waterways, against 400,879,000 tons carried by the railways. The cost of conveyance by water is always a great deal less than by rail. For instance, the freight rate for corn from Hamburg to Berlin by water in 1910 was 2s. 6d., against 13s. 9½d. by rail ; and for coal 2s. 1d. by water and 7s. 4¾d. by rail. An objection to water transport often raised is the slow speed ; but when the time lost in shunting and delays on railways is taken into account, there is often little difference in the time required for delivery by the two systems.

The working of the Government scheme for the decentralisation of our canal system will be watched with interest. Three sub-committees have been appointed to control the waterways. The London Committee has control of the Grand Junction, Regent's Canal, Oxford

Canal, and the Birmingham and Warwick and Napton Navigations. The Midland Committee has taken over the Trent and Weaver Navigations, the Birmingham Canals, the Shropshire Union, Severn Navigation, Gloucester and Berkeley Ship Canal, and other connecting or subsidiary navigations. The most important waterways of which control has been assumed by the Leeds committee are the Aire and Calder, the Rochdale Canal, and the Sheffield and South Yorkshire Navigation.

Doubtless these committees will be able to organise a more efficient and economical working of our waterways. But if we are to have a canal system comparable with the best of the Continental ones, a carefully considered scheme of reconstruction must be worked out ; and if this is done on a comprehensive scale it could mean an immense amount of work for our soldiers and sailors on their disbandment after the War. New main routes, and branch and connecting routes, would be constructed, with lifts where the conditions were favourable ; and of a breadth and depth suitable for heavier and speedier mechanically propelled barges, the existing canals being broadened and deepened to the section decided upon.

The subject cannot be further dealt with in these pages, but it is one that calls for earnest and early official attention. The pity of it is that there are no people more capable of dealing with such a problem than ourselves if we could only get urged into action.

Savings due to the Use of Incubators

If we are ever to produce enough poultry and eggs to supply our requirements, we must make more extended use of incubators, nursing mothers, and feeding apparatus, etc., than we are doing at present. It should be more generally understood that a hen can be more profitably employed in egg-laying than in sitting on a nest for three weeks, and spending succeeding weeks scratching and fussing in caring for her brood.

Strangely enough, the hatching of poultry by artificial heat was practised by the ancients centuries before the

Christian era, Diodorus Siculus, the Greek historian, describing it as an ancient practice.

The ancients obtained the heat by the fermentation of manure, but the modern Egyptians have for many years conducted the business of egg-hatching on a large scale by using the regulated heat of ovens, paying a license to the Government. A typical building, called a "maamal," contains from twelve to twenty-four ovens, and its charge may be 150,000 eggs. An official report for 1831 gives for Lower Egypt 105 of these establishments, using 19,000,000 eggs, of which about 13,000,000 produce chickens, and in so doing save the valuable time of some 1,500,000 hens. There are many inexpensive and efficient incubators to be had, but for hatching on a large scale something more permanent and extensive, which could easily be constructed, would doubtless be required. On the other hand, in the past many enterprising farm-workers have done well in their spare time by installing a modest incubator, and getting ducks' eggs from Ireland for hatching, and by rearing and fattening the young birds for the market.

The rearing of geese should be even more profitable, and should be encouraged, as if the birds have the run of a stretch of waste land, or common land, they forage for themselves, and do not require grain or other bought foodstuffs. They can stand all but the severest weather, and only need shelter at night from foxes and other vermin. They inexpensively provide a succulent meat rich in fat, of which there is at present such a shortage.

The following are the periods of incubation; temperature 140° Fahr. :

Goose, 35 days. Turkey and duck, 28 days. Hen, 21 days.

Waste due to Emigration

It is well known that during several past decades many of the ablest and most highly skilled of our industrial workers have emigrated to the United States of America and to our Dominions beyond the seas. In these countries they have been not a little instrumental in developing indu ries that are in competition with those of the country of their birth. That the economic loss to our country due to this emigration is serious cannot be denied, as it tends to reduce the amount our production exceeds our consumption, which is a measure of our prosperity and represents the increase in our wealth. It is true that those who settle in our Dominions remain citizens of the Empire, and happily help to people those vast countries with our own stock : but, on the other hand, the emigrants who become citizens of the United States are for economic purposes lost to us for ever. Indeed, Sir Alfred F. Yarrow, in a letter to the *Times*, May, 1916, truly said :

" The effect of emigration from a country is to cause a constant drain of wealth. Thus, if an average man of productive age cost to feed, clothe, and educate, say, £400, the country which he leaves and in which he has been brought up loses equivalent to £400, because the emigrant is not an article of commerce, and nothing is received in exchange. Thus, if 100,000 people leave a country per annum, assuming the cost of producing an emigrant is £400, it represents a loss to the country of £40,000,000 sterling per annum. Such a loss, if productive employment were obtained for the emigrants in their own land, would not only be avoided, but the wealth of the country would be increased to the extent of what they produce."

Now, as a matter of fact, in the year before the War (1913), the British Isles lost by emigration as many as 469,640 persons, the destination of the emigrants being : to British North America, 196,278 ; to the United States, 129,169 ; to Australia and New Zealand, 77,933 ; to South Africa, 25,955. Assuming that of these 200,000 were men, the loss to the country, on the fair estimate of £400 per man, was about £80,000,000. Referring to the wonderful industrial progress in Germany, Sir A. F. Yarrow said that " in spite of an annual increase in population of three quarters of a million, emigration has nearly ceased, because ample employment is found for all in their own country, and thus loss of wealth due to emigration is avoided."

The Child: What will he Become? Worker or Waster? Citizen or Criminal?

We have in our adorable children the finest raw material in the world for the production of the perfect citizen and the ideal worker. Are we making the best use of this bounteous supply of miraculous plastic organisms? Are we successful in producing a high percentage of healthy, wholesome, well-informed, efficient, contented, and prosperous citizens from the divine little humans that come to our hands to be trained and moulded into the finished products?

Well may we pause for an answer!

Let us think of the millions we are spending on asylums, workhouses, hospitals, penitentiaries; on the maintenance of criminal police, and on all the other machinery for the detection and punishment of crime!

Let us think of the countless thousands who pass away before their fiftieth year is reached, instead of living a hundred years or more, in accordance with the physiological law of longevity; and surely we can only conclude that there must be something radically wrong in the methods and systems we employ in rearing, educating, and training our young people.

One is reminded of the posters that were to be seen on our hoardings many years ago, advertising the "Popular Educator." It was entitled, "The Child: What will he Become?" and the picture depicted, on one hand, his development under the most favourable conditions, with progressive culture and prosperity, and with perfect physique; culminating in the highest form of intellect and character in old age. On the other hand, the deteriorating effects of neglect and of evil and unhygienic surroundings were shown by a descent in degradation, ending in the drunken sot and wastrel of the criminal type. There can be no reasonable doubt that this picture truthfully illustrates the evolution of the extreme types we see around us day by day, and the wonder is that we have tolerated for so many years the colossal wastage due to our neglect in organising a real and effective system of education and physical and vocational training.

Now, although a discussion of this great problem is beyond the scope of this work, a remark or two on it may not be out of place.

Unfortunately, we can only produce permanent changes slowly and gradually, but the Education Bill of January, 1918, which provides thirteen years of compulsory education for children from five to eighteen years of age— parents or employers who fail to send them to day-schools or continuation-schools being liable to legal penalties— will carry us a long way in the right direction, if we see to it that no mere system of teaching, as contradistinguished from education, prevails. It is not enough to lengthen the period of school years ; the curricula of our schools needs revising from bottom to top, if every child born in the kingdom is to be well educated. For such an education, it may well be suggested, should embrace a competent knowledge of all the laws of health, the necessity of proper attention to diet, cleanliness, exercise, ventilation, and moderation in all enjoyments ; and if the education also embraced, as it should do, a sound moral training of the feelings and sentiments, as well as an inculcation of just moral principles, founded on the precepts of the Gospel of Truth, and a practical habituation to the meek, gentle, self-denying, and benevolent interchange of acts of kindness which that gospel enjoins, then we could well believe that three-fourths of the disease and debility which now afflict the working classes would disappear, and nearly all the crime that defaces the community would vanish. We should then have a system that would not only train the memory and enlarge the intellect, but develop into a harmonious whole the physical and mental man, with all his perceptions, faculties, sympathies in due course brought to maturity, and his passions brought under control.

As things are at present, we spend more time, effort, and money to put down crime than to prevent it.

Such reforms in our educational system, with the help of a Ministry of Health and a solution of the housing problem, would bring into being a more enlightened people, and such an era of industrial harmony and prosperity, that Britain, we may hope, would become the country envisaged by Confucius, the ancient Chinese sage :

"Where spades grow bright, and idle words grow dull :
Where jails are empty, and where barns are full."

Waste of Good Human Material

A certain proportion of boys leave our elementary schools as soon as by age they are allowed to do so, boys who are ranked as incorrigible dunces and failures by their teachers, and who from the moment they leave school begin to deteriorate, and, alas, in too many cases to become potential criminals ; whereas, if they were weeded out in time and put into special schools of the type represented by our splendid industrial schools, the majority would become excellent recruits for our industries and for the Army and Navy, as the fine records of such schools abundantly show. The Navy in particular would appeal to most of these boys, and we should have in them fine raw material for the senior service. Mr. Blatchford, in the *Weekly Dispatch*, happily dealt with the important question in the following words :

"RECRUITING FOR THE NAVY

"We have always been a great naval power, with a fine naval tradition ; yet our method of recruiting our Navy has never been placed upon a really sound and systematic basis. There are in this country always tens of thousands of boys who could be trained for the Navy, and should be trained for the Navy, but are left to drift about in our big towns until they become wrecks, or casual labourers. These boys are wasted. They are no use in civil life and they would be valuable in the Navy. They would be happier and healthier in the Navy ; no one can doubt that who has seen the splendid boys of the *Mercury*. After the War many things will be changed, and the Method of recruiting for the Navy will be one of them.

Waste due to Inattention (Psychology of Attention)

There is much educational waste in our schools owing to the small amount of consideration given to the psychology of attention and to the cultivation of the powers of observation. Neglect in these directions means slow and unsatisfactory progress, and often want of success in after life, no matter what calling may be followed ; certainly all kinds of workshop operations and processes necessitate close observation.

Dr. Johnson [1] understood the psychology of the learner and the importance of attention, for writing on Milton as a teacher, he remarked that—

" Nobody can be taught faster than he can learn. The speed of the horseman is limited by the power of the steed. Every man that has undertaken to instruct others can tell what slow advances he has been able to make, and how much patience it requires to recall vagrant inattention, to stimulate sluggish indifference, and to rectify absurd misapprehension."

In this connection teachers might well endeavour to learn some of the secrets of the animal trainer's art. One of these was explained by Darwin [2] as follows :

" A man who trains monkeys to act in plays used to purchase common kinds from the Zoological Gardens, at the price of £5 for each ; but he offered double the price if he might keep three or four of them for a few days in order to select one. When asked how he could possibly learn so soon whether a particular monkey would turn out a good actor, he answered that it all depended on their power of attention. If, when he was talking and explaining anything, its attention was easily distracted, as by a fly on the wall, or other trifling object, the case was hopeless. If he tried by punishment to make an inattentive monkey act, it turned sulky. On the other hand, a monkey which carefully attended to him could always be trained."

[1] " Lives of the English Poets."
[2] " Descent of Man," vol. i.

In the training of policemen and of men employed on
public service vehicles the cultivation of the powers of
observation should receive a good deal of attention : for
so far as the latter class is concerned, it is safe to say that
almost everyone has experienced the annoyance and
inconvenience of failing to arrest the attention of the driver
or conductor of a passing vehicle or of one that has stopped
at a taking-up place, where perhaps people from different
directions have been hurrying to catch the bus or tram,
only to see it move on without the slightest attempt on the
part of the conductor to look around and see whether
passengers were approaching. This lamentable want of
attention means vexation and waste of time for the public,
and loss of revenue for the bus and tram companies.

Waste due to Superfluous " Marshals." The Cost of the Law

We are a strange people and tolerate many official
unjustifiable extravagances, an example of which attention
was called to in the *Evening Standard's* admirable columns,
" A Londoner's Diary," August 24, 1917 :

" Another substantial sum might be saved if the
judges' marshals were abolished. These officials, whose
services cost the country about £2,000 a year, are usually
young members of the Bar, whom the judges select for their
companionable qualities. The Hon. Frank Russell, K.C.,
for instance, once accompanied the late Mr. Justice Day on
circuit, and found that the chief duty required of him was
the singing of songs in the judge's lodgings. The office is,
in truth, entirely a sinecure, and might be abolished without
the slightest loss to the State, and with very little inconvenience to the judges. Its continuance is another
striking proof of the strange disinclination of the judges
voluntarily to set their house in order."

" Londoner's " views on the circuit system are also
well worth quoting :

" The wasteful circuit system adds largely to the
expense. The ' circuit expenses of the judges and their

suites,' which are entirely personal in their character, amounted to nearly £10,000. If the smaller assize towns, at which there is little or no business for the judges to do, were struck off the judges' visiting list, half this amount might easily be saved."

"*This field is so spacious, that it were easy for a man to lose himself in it; and if I should spend all my pilgrimage in this walk, my time would sooner end than my way.*"—BISHOP HALL.

INDEX

Waste due to inattention, 297
,, ,, inefficient lubrication of motor vehicles, 286
Waste due to injurious fatigue, 83
,, ,, laundry methods, 251
,, ,, negligent use of glassware, 285
Waste due to our derelict waterways, 290
Waste due to our faulty education system, 293
Waste due to pollution of rivers, 276
,, ,, ,, ,, the air, 263
Waste due to rats, 284
,, ,, red tape, 26
,, ,, smoke nuisance, 135, 138, 262
Waste due to superfluous marshals : the cost of the law, 298
Waste due to traditional methods in management, 34
Waste due to transit of cattle, 274
,, ,, wrongly shaped boxes and bottles, etc., 283
Waste-fish question, 278
Waste handicraft material, 282
Waste heat, utilisation of by regeneration, 235
Waste, household, 4
,, justifiable, 5
,, land, 14, 167, 178
,, ,, cultivation of, 173
,, ,, estimated income due to its cultivation, 178
Waste land, reclamation of, 179
,, ,, utilisation of in Surrey, 173
Waste land, value of produce from, 171
Waste lands an economic factor, 177
Waste liquors from woollen mills, use of, 218
Waste liquors, illuminating gas from, 221
Waste liquors,india-rubber from,221
Waste material, collection of, 19
,, new, 6
,, of animal, mechanical, and manual power on farms, 152
Waste of brown paper, 243
,, ,, candles, 240
,, ,, child-life, 73
,, ,, food in camps, 98
,, ,, fruit, 253
,, ,, gas in the home, 256
,, ,, good human material, 294
,, ,, jars, tins and glass bottles, 243

Waste of life due to contamination of milk, 75
Waste of life in factories and workshops, 78
Waste of matches, 240
,, ,, mustard, 241
,, ,, odd lengths of string, 243
,, ,, paper, 247
,, ,, pins, 241
,, ,, public time, 25
,, ,, rubber tyres due to negligent driving, 286
Waste of sewage demands attention, 276
Waste of soap, 242
,, ,, stationery, 26
,, ,, surplus naval tobacco, 271
,, ,, time at Assizes, 28
,, ,, ,, in Parliament, 29
,, ,, valuable tanning material, 270
Waste of water, chief causes, 257
,, ,, ,, in industrial works, etc., 281
Waste of water is waste of fuel, 257
,, ,, wood in sawing, etc., 282
,, ,, writing materials, 245
,, paper and cardboard, etc., 19
Waste paper, Edinburgh, Birmingham, and Preston collecting it, 20
Waste paper, value of, 247
,, prevention, doctrine of, 5
,, romance of, 198
Waste telegraph-forms, 289
,, things from the battlefields : millions to be saved, 200
Waste utilisation departments in factories, 287
Wasteful movements, 38
Wastefulness, crime of, 96
Wastes, elimination of, 4
,, trifling, 4
Water-drinking, its effects on longevity, 64
Water, fuel consumption in supplying London, 259
Water, hot, the only true stimulant, 63
Water, house-to-house inspection of fittings, 258
Water, number of houses supplied daily by Water Board, 258
Water of life, 62
,, quantity flowing through half-inch tap, 258
Water, quantity supplied by Water Board, 259
Water, same effects in human engine and gas engines, 63